# HOW JANE WON

# HOW JANE WON

### 55 Successful Women Share How They Grew from Ordinary Girls to *Extraordinary* Women

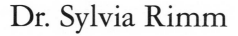

## Dr. Sylvia Rimm

### WITH DR. SARA RIMM-KAUFMAN

CROWN PUBLISHERS
New York

Published by Crown Publishers, New York, New York.
Member of the Crown Publishing Group.

Random House, Inc. New York, Toronto, London, Sydney, Auckland
www.randomhouse.com

CROWN is a trademark and the Crown colophon is a
registered trademark of Random House, Inc.

Printed in the United States of America

Design by Susan Hood

Library of Congress Cataloging-in-Publication Data
Rimm, Sylvia B.
How Jane won : 55 successful women share how they
grew from ordinary girls to extraordinary women /
Sylvia Rimm with Sara Rimm-Kaufman.
Includes index.
1. Girls—United States.    2. Women—United States.
3. Success—Psychological aspects.    4. Achievement
motivation in women.    I. Rimm-Kaufman, Sara.
II. Title.
HQ777.R56    2001
646.7′0083—dc21    00-058929

ISBN 0-609-60758-8

10   9   8   7   6   5   4   3   2   1

*First Edition*

To the successful women
who gave of their valuable time to share
their stories to inspire girls and women

# Acknowledgments

Our thanks go first and foremost to the successful women who shared their inspiring life stories with us. We dedicate our book to them. Although my daughter Sara and I did brand-new interviews for this book, we've also included a few interviews that were done for *See Jane Win.* For those we'd like to thank interviewers Meredith Gunlicks, Kathy Baldwin, Beth Farrell, and Marian Carlson.

We have many people to thank for helping us to attract people to our book, beginning with our family members Dr. Alfred Rimm, Janet Rimm, Dr. David Rimm, Allison Rimm, Dr. Eric Rimm, Dr. Joseph Madsen, Dr. Ilonna Rimm, Dr. Alan Rimm-Kaufman, Vivian Lopatin, and Carol and Sigmund Rimm. Others we wish to thank who assisted in recruiting outstanding women for the book are Pierre Lehu, Maria Balise, Joseph Hahn, Steve Ross, Betsy Rapoport, Dr. Mary Walborn, Marian Deegan, Ellen Bartel, and Cathie Black.

My special thanks go to Joanne Riedl for her editorial and organizational assistance. Her thoroughness and dedication are consistently *extraordinary.* I also greatly appreciate the further assistance of Marilyn Knackert, Marian Carlson, Alice Poduska, and Kathy Whitney in gathering information, contacting woman for interviews, and transcribing tapes. I especially value their commitment in the face of extreme time pressures. Additional research support from graduate student assistants R. Diane Moyer and Kim Lannoch was also very helpful, and I thank them.

Additionally, we would like to thank our editor, Betsy Rapoport, for her many creative ideas and her skill in assisting us in getting to the heart of these inspiring stories. Thanks also to Steve Ross, vice president of the Crown Publishing Group, for his continued support, and Pierre Lehu for his enthusiasm and guidance in arranging for the publication of this book, and his continued and unflagging encouragement.

# Contents

# HOW JANE WON

# Introduction

In *See Jane Win,* we compiled data from questionnaires completed by over a thousand successful women to determine what factors lead to a young girl's ability to fulfill her potential as an adult. Mainly a research-based book, *See Jane Win* offered parents practical advice on how to raise their daughters. This companion, *How Jane Won,* is a how-to book for girls and young women. Here, successful women tell in their own words how their apparently ordinary girlhoods sowed the seeds for their prominence. Stories of triumph despite discouragement can help women, young and old, understand and develop resilience. Stories of how successful women were inspired can encourage a new generation to search for role models and be open to opportunities.

In the *See Jane Win* report, we emphasized the similarities among women in various careers that our research underscored. *How Jane Won* literally gives these findings a voice and helps readers to understand and celebrate the many individual differences among successful women. Because our women shared their very private stories, their uniqueness becomes much more apparent. These successful women not only differed in age, race, geographic location, and religious background, but they varied in lifestyles, temperament, and even narrative style. Some women spoke in passionate voices, leaping from turning point to turning point, while others described their lives in very linear, matter-of-fact ways. While CEO Marilyn Carlson Nelson recalled falling in love with William Shakespeare, engineer Teresa Culver proclaimed that poetry never made any sense to her at all. Some women were brought up in poverty, while others were reared in protected middle-class environments. *Brady Bunch* mother Florence Henderson was the youngest of ten in a very poor family, while senior vice president Charlotte Otto was an only child who owned the spotlight at the center of her parents' lives.

Our successful women ranged in age from thirty to eighty. The women in their thirties, forties, and fifties often discussed how they managed to balance work and home life in an era that puts the "supermom" on a pedestal; others made choices not to have children or marry at all; while still others considered their families as the center of their fulfillment. Women in their sixties and seventies were able to offer a perspective on a whole life span of accomplishments, including the joy of discovering new talents and forging new relationships as they matured. The older women's stories come with the deeper perspectives and wisdom that are often provided by our grandmothers. I firmly believe that girls and young women can learn from women of all ages.

Younger women looking for good counsel and inspiration for whatever positive and challenging lifestyle they prefer will find it here. More experienced women can identify with the challenges these successful women have faced and overcome. Words of wisdom from our successful women will be emphasized by bold print.

Unlike many other books about girls, our emphasis is not on psychopathology such as eating disorders but on how successful women coped as girls with society's prejudices against them as well as with the ordinary problems facing most girls and women.

The seeds for this book were sown on July 12, 1999, when *See Jane Win* was featured on the Oprah Winfrey show. Oprah introduced our research by pointing out that, indeed, the extraordinary women in our findings began as apparently ordinary girls. Cathleen Black, president of Hearst Magazines, and plant physiologist Dr. Camellia Okpodu shared their stories on that program (they are also included in this book). Cathleen Black invited me to speak that summer at Body, Mind and Soul, a women's retreat. After listening to other speakers, I found myself asking these fascinating, intelligent women about their childhoods. What made them succeed? The concept for this book was thus incubated among the magnificent mountains of Colorado, the location of this wonderful retreat.

Although the successful women in our study appeared to be ordinary girls in many ways, many might not have described themselves that way. Some of them talked about "making their mark," feeling compelled to do their best, setting goals, feeling different or special, challenging themselves to live up to the successful women they observed in their lives or read about in biographies. Many described role models they admired and wanted to emulate. Parents, grandparents, aunts, uncles, coaches, Girl Scout leaders, and teachers often inspired these girls to be what they could be.

During the course of the interviews for *See Jane Win* and *How Jane Won,* many of these women recalled a specific set of experiences that influenced their decisions, changed their behavior, or affected their trajectory. Sometimes a single great disappointment redirected them from their original goal but in a serendipitous way paved the way for better opportunities. Some women described the challenges of gender, racial, or religious prejudices. You will never forget Dr. Camellia Okpodu's renewed commitment to her studies after Booker T. Washington's autobiography literally hit her on the head while she huddled in her college library, on the brink of dropping out. These women's stories bring their hurdles to life.

Our interviews with the women in this book were uplifting, inspiring, and extraordinary. My daughter Sara and I came away from each interview feeling exhilarated and awed. We would often call each other in excitement after an interview to share a special story. We felt fortunate that such successful, wonderful people were willing to share their lives with us and our readers. Even as Sara and I shared conversations during Sara's recent job search, we reminded each other of the words of wisdom from Dr. Alexa Canady, not to expect to be patted on the back for everything accomplished; from marketing director Tamara Minick-Scokalo, reminding us that there are always trade-offs; and from attorney Martha Lindner, about how what you think is the worst thing that could ever happen can turn out to be the best thing. We learned together from these women, and our lives will forever be richer and more meaningful. We hope we've conveyed this to you in their stories.

Although this book is primarily intended for girls and young women, we hope that parents will also read it, because the stories can be the basis for better communication between parents and their daughters. Chapter 1 includes the findings from the *See Jane Win* research and general advice for girls and young women. Chapters 2 through 7 include stories and words of wisdom of successful women in many careers, including the categories of Lawmakers and Adjudicators, Shatterers of Glass Ceilings, Healers and Discoverers, Nurturers, Artists and Musicians, and Communicators. The careers of some women sometimes fell into more than one category. We have placed them in their current chief career area.

There are more opportunities opening up for women now than ever before. As these continue to unfold, women who want to fulfill themselves and make contributions to our society will have more opportunities to live their dreams. We hope these stories will inspire those who want to develop the drive to make important contributions to our country's future.

# 1

# Searching for New Identities

WOMEN of my generation discovered that we were oppressed, and we vowed to change that for ourselves, for our daughters, and for the generations of women who would follow. Most of the world had assumed for too many years that women couldn't be doctors or scientists, attorneys or elected officials, executives, presidents of universities, or highly ranked artists or musicians; and we surely couldn't be news anchors or television producers or editors (of anything other than women's magazines). Although there were a great many other "couldn't bes," at least we could be excellent teachers, nurses, social workers, mothers, and wives. As a matter of fact, it was assumed that we could cook and clean and shop and diaper a lot better than men could.

We had studied history, and it had indeed been *his* story—the story of men, with only a few contributions from women like Betsy Ross, Florence Nightingale, and Marie Curie. We had studied the psychology of motivation and achievement and barely noticed the footnotes that indicated the subjects were always boys or men. We learned about Erik Erikson's theories of adult development and were told that we would find our identity through the men we married. We lived the various lives that permitted us to be good helpers but provided few avenues for self-fulfillment. Most of us were even contented with our lot. Fortunately, some of us were not, and we changed the world forever.

Now women have entered almost every career field closed to them earlier. We continue to struggle with glass ceilings and sticky floors, and with balancing careers, relationships, and families. We are still pioneering the paths that will permit us to fulfill ourselves or combine careers with family and relationships, depending on our choices.

Although each generation will create its own and somewhat different path, the survey for *See Jane Win* and the stories of *How Jane Won* were created with the assumption that the research and stories behind successful women's lives can provide road maps for the future. For girls and women who wish to be successful, there's a wealth of wisdom in these pages. This chapter summarizes our results from *See Jane Win* and extends our findings to provide some helpful advice for girls and young women. It also provides the organization for the stories that follow.

## *Defining Success: Are You Fulfilled?*

Success isn't a title or a paycheck. As we defined it for our *See Jane Win* study, it's personal fulfillment. Simply put, to be happy and fulfilled is to be successful. Although we selected some broad, high-status nontraditional and traditional careers that we assumed parents might like to direct their daughters toward, there were no arbitrary measures within those careers for determining whether women were successful. Instead, we asked the women in our survey to rate themselves on a five-point scale from very unsuccessful to highly successful. Those who rated themselves as three, four, or five were included provided they also rated themselves as reasonably happy in their family and relationships. In other words, success is happiness at work *and* at home.

Advertisements brought the volunteers to our *See Jane Win* study. For *How Jane Won,* we sent out letters to celebrities, award winners, and well-established successful women in the same career fields that we researched in *See Jane Win.* The women in this book met the same criteria for success in their careers and at home. However, while many women included in *See Jane Win* chose to remain anonymous, all the women in this book have identified themselves and tell their stories in their own words.

## *Findings and Advice for Girls and Women from* See Jane Win

I'd like to summarize the findings of *See Jane Win* briefly here.

### RESEARCH FINDING NO. 1:
### GIRLS GROW THROUGH HEALTHY COMPETITION

Many of the successful women from our study listed "winning in competition" as an important positive experience for them. In their interviews they frequently described the exhilaration and motivation that's derived from winning. However, it's important to note that these successful women didn't always win. They had to cope with a continuum of personal and professional losses and the emotional fallout, which varied from feelings of disaster to beating themselves up to rationally recognizing how to learn from those losses. Also, some successful women specifically indicated that winning had never seemed important to them; they didn't need to compete with others. Their motivation seemed to come from within themselves; they competed only with their own past accomplishments.

### GUIDELINE FOR GIRLS AND WOMEN NO. 1:
### DARE TO COMPETE

Take the risk of entering competitions in either your school or your work world. Enter some competitions where you feel confident so you can experience the exhilaration of winning. Of course, awards look good on your applications and résumés and are personal affirmations. But also enter some competitions in which you feel less skilled. Not expecting to win helps you learn not to be too hard on yourself, and even small improvements can help you build confidence.

Personal best competition, which measures your improvement against no one's standard but your own, is less risky than competing against others at first. Competing as part of a team will keep you from feeling totally responsible for wins or losses and builds the joy of collaboration. When you're not feeling like you're doing as well as others around you, it helps to compare yourself to those who are doing less well. Also, admiring, praising, or learning from those who are doing better than you gives you a sense of personal control, and your competitors are more likely to give you boosts when you need them. There will always be those who do better than you and those who do less well. Furthermore, your place in competition or steps up the career ladder are temporary. Your position may be changed by hard work and perseverance, but even when it changes or you're promoted, you will always find yourself among those who do better or worse. Assessing your personal progress, or what you've already accomplished, is often reassuring. You need to teach yourself to feel good about your progress without expecting perfection.

Competition and collaboration are not opposites. Selecting the appropriate occasions for cooperation and competition is part of learning to function successfully in a competitive society.

If indeed you hate competition and don't wish to learn the skills of competing, you might be happier investigating the more traditional career paths for women. They tend to be less competitive than the career fields that have been led by men.

If you find yourself steering toward a highly competitive career, you might want to balance it with one of the many recreational activities that are rewarding in themselves, such as gardening, hiking, yoga, or keeping a journal. A balanced lifestyle, which includes intrinsically rewarding interests and relationships, may give you some relief from your competitive career and will add to your sense of personal fulfillment.

### RESEARCH FINDING NO. 2: GIRLS WHO SEE THEMSELVES AS SMART ARE POISED TO SUCCEED

We asked the successful women in our survey to choose from a long list of characteristics those words that best described themselves in childhood. The words they selected most frequently were "smart," "hardworking," and "independent." Also very popular were "adultlike," "happy," "mature," "creative," "tomboy," "bookworm," "brainy," and "good little girl." They often chose "sensitive," "kind," "shy," "emotional," "perfectionistic," and "self-critical." They rarely selected "troublemaker," "rebellious," or "fashion leader."

### GUIDELINE FOR GIRLS AND WOMEN NO. 2: IT'S COOL TO BE SMART AND WORK HARD

If you're not a hard worker, you probably won't accomplish much, but it's never too late to become involved. You may wish to direct your energies to your areas of greatest strength and interest first, so you can reap the rewards of hard work most immediately.

Feeling smart doesn't mean you have to be the smartest, nor does it mean you have to feel capable in every area. Finding your strengths and interests will help you feel good about yourself. However, don't totally avoid or write off subjects or fields that seem difficult to you. Sometimes getting the right tutor or finding the appropriate mentor is all you'll require to get over your fears, anxieties, or feelings of helplessness. For example, quite a few women in our survey had assumed they couldn't do math, until they received appropriate help. There were women in business, media, and science who deemed themselves failures before they received guidance from mentors. Your learning style may be different, and once you've overcome a difficult hurdle, concepts may become clearer. Your values may not fit with a particular job, and you may need to search for your own niche. Neither situation means you're a failure, only that you must search creatively for your right place.

It can be quite difficult to be independent from your peers in school because there are so many pressures to conform. Being independent doesn't mean you have to live a life of isolation without friends, only that you should select friends that fit with your values and that you should think carefully about those values.

Developing independence from your parents is a gradual process that accelerates from early childhood to adolescence and adulthood. Becoming independent is a more difficult problem when you are theoretically an adult but are still financially dependent, such as during college or your early career. Independence from a romantic partner is another developmental leap you'll need to make in balancing both career and relationships. Perhaps the best way to look at independence is on a continuum, because no woman is a woman unto herself alone (nor is a man). Determining how much independence you need so you can have both close relationships and the ability to separate yourself out to search for your own goals is a continual struggle for adults of all ages. Knowing that there is a continuum can help you determine how much independence is enough to give you reasonable freedom and how much will keep you from having friends and relationships. It's also important to acknowledge and appreciate how much you rely on your family, partner, and friends, and they on you.

Some of the other descriptors chosen by women in our study will help you realize that you can be successful even if you view yourself as sensitive, shy, too emotional, perfectionistic, or self-critical. If you describe yourself as a troublemaker, you could simply have a healthy sense of rebellion, but if others view you that way, whether you're a teen or an adult, you may indeed require help from a psychologist or psychiatrist. Is your rebellion helping you or hurting you? If you're open to outside assistance, it is more likely to be helpful to you.

### RESEARCH FINDING NO. 3: ALL-GIRL INDEPENDENT OR PAROCHIAL SCHOOLS CAN BE GOOD CHOICES

Although most of the successful women in our study attended public schools (79 percent), twice as many attended parochial or independent schools as did children in the overall population. Attendance at all-girl middle schools, high schools, and colleges was considerably higher than in the overall population. Twenty percent of the women acknowledged that boys and social life adversely affected their seriousness about school and learning in high school. The survey didn't include that question about college, but some of the women interviewed commented on the distraction of men during college as well. The women who attended girls' and women's schools tended to be positive about their experiences, but so were the women who attended public schools. Whether these women attended public, parochial, or independent schools, they often described specific teachers as having great positive, even life-changing, influences on them.

### GUIDELINE FOR GIRLS AND WOMEN NO. 3: CHOOSE THE SCHOOL THAT FITS YOU

Family economics and your own personality should be important factors to consider in making decisions about schools and colleges. Your parents have made your earlier decisions, but your input will be an important consideration in further decisions. You need to consider your personality honestly to determine whether you need to build assertiveness. If you are particularly shy or quiet, an all-girl or all-woman environment may encourage you to speak out. It may also provide you with more opportunity and more courage to accept leadership. Also, be honest with yourself about the effect of boys or men in your environment. They may or may not be a distraction, and only you can make that determination.

You must surely consider economic factors and your parents' willingness and ability to pay for the cost of an all-female environment. If you are making a decision for high school, you may wish to discuss the financial trade-offs that may need to be made for college. Sometimes public schools will consider girl-centered classes in math and science. Your parents and your school principal may be able to make that happen for you and others.

If you don't have a choice about your school, you can always search for good teachers as mentors in whatever school you attend. You'll have to do your share. Teachers are more likely to direct their energies toward students who are engaged and interested.

Understanding your personality will also help you make a choice about mostly single-gender environments in adulthood. Some careers are dominated by either men or women. In your career world, you may be functioning in an environment that favors one gender. If you are in a male-dominated environment, as you rise in your career, reach out a helping hand to women who may still be struggling.

## RESEARCH FINDING NO. 4:
### PEERS MATTER, FOR BETTER OR WORSE

The successful women we surveyed were not always comfortable socializing with their peers. Although approximately 25 percent were more social than typical, 40 percent assessed themselves as less social than typical, and 15 percent actually recall feeling isolated during elementary, middle, or high school. Most of the women in our survey tended to befriend like-minded peers who valued learning and achievement, and although some had experimented with alcohol, tobacco, or drugs, few were regular users. More women in highly social careers, such as government, business, education, and the media, tended to be highly social in childhood.

## GUIDELINE FOR GIRLS AND WOMEN NO. 4: CHOOSE FRIENDS
### WHO SHARE THE VALUES THAT MATTER MOST TO YOU

Being social is neither bad nor good as long as your social life doesn't interfere with your learning during your crucial school years. If you select friends who value learning, you're likely to support each other in the process and still find time for fun. Extracurricular interests like music, sports, government, debate, drama, science, and math teams all combine learning and fun. Religious groups and special-interest groups in high school, college, and adulthood often provide comfortable neighborhoods for friends, discussion, support, and leadership. Even if you pride yourself on your independence, research shows that teens and adults alike are affected by peer pressure. Thus, if you select or fall into a negative or boring peer group, with time you'll find your behavior and values becoming more negative or boring, despite your assumptions to the contrary.

If you're going through some lonely times, at least you'll know you're not alone. Don't be too hard on yourself. Hopefully, family members can be supportive during this time; if not, you'll need to be strong and independent. If you can find interests to become involved in, with time you will surely find a few friends who share those interests. Specialized summer programs (e.g., chess, music, soccer, art, computer, or filmmaking) also provide new opportunities for friendship. If you find yourself struggling too much with loneliness, seek out a counselor who can give you insights about your own personality and needs and help you learn some social skills.

There may be lonely times among your colleagues at work as well. It takes time to make friends and to network. This time and effort are worth it to help you build social confidence and advance your career. Good people skills have a big payoff.

### RESEARCH FINDING NO. 5:
### TRAVEL HAS A BROADENING INFLUENCE

Our successful women selected travel second most frequently, after "winning in competition," as a positive experience. They often described travel with their families as adventurous or providing family bonding. Independent travel or travel with school groups during high school and college had dramatic effects on their independence and broadened their perspectives. Sometimes travel influenced their future career choices or helped them advance in their careers.

Traveling because the family had to move was viewed either positively or negatively, depending on whether the women perceived their school or social life as better or worse compared to where they had moved from.

## GUIDELINE FOR GIRLS AND WOMEN NO. 5:
## GET OUT AND SEE THE WORLD

Enjoy travel with your family if you have the opportunity. In order for you to benefit from your experiences, you'll need to be open to them. There may be times when you'd rather stay home to be with high school friends, but for the most part, those experiences will simply blur in your memory. Your travel is more likely to stand out as unique and help you grow as a creative person.

Try to encourage your school to organize a travel group to better understand a culture related to a foreign language, art, or science you're studying. Participating in a student exchange program will give you a unique and unforgettable opportunity. If you're a college student, consider spending a semester or summer abroad or in a different area of this country.

Adult travel can be an interesting way to extend your horizons and relationships. Single adults often make lasting friends through group travel. Meeting colleagues from other environments may even expand your career opportunities. Travel for adult couples, with or without children, can provide needed times away from daily stresses and cement relationships.

Family moves may seem traumatic, but be open to the experience, even if you're in high school. Although that's probably the most difficult time to move, it has the advantage of broadening your world and helping you think of your future in a different way. The kinds of adjustments you'll need to make can be important learning experiences for your future. You'll find lots of stories here from women who explain how they and their parents accommodated those moves.

You may not have a choice about where you go to college, but it'll probably be a better growth experience if you can move away from home to a different community. Living on a college campus will stretch your thinking and increase your independence.

As an adult, moving may seem challenging, especially if you have a family. Consider it a temporary discomfort, and don't let your fear of a new environment close off your career opportunities. Moves that involve spouses often take special planning, but we are beyond the days when women were the only "trailing" spouses.

## RESEARCH FINDING NO. 6:
## SUCCESSFUL WOMEN HAD SUPPORTIVE PARENTS

Most of the successful women we surveyed had very good relationships with their parents. When asked to rate their relationships with their parents during the teen years, the women most often described them as good or excellent; a small percentage characterized them as fair or poor. In general, they found their parents supportive and valued their advice and guidance. Approximately half of the women identified with their mothers, one-quarter with their fathers, and the other quarter with teachers, other relatives, or friends. The women also mentioned multiple role models they looked up to while traveling their paths to success, including some from books and biographies.

## GUIDELINE FOR GIRLS AND WOMEN NO. 6:
## LET YOUR PARENTS BE A RESOURCE

Although adolescence and young adulthood is surely the time to establish yourself as more independent, don't rule out parents' recommendations that are based on their love for you and their experiences in the world. Although you should have many choices by this time in your life, during your high school years, your parents have the moral and legal responsibility for setting limits. Assume they are doing this in your best interests, even when you disagree with them. As you move into more independence in college and adult life, stay in touch with them. They're unlikely to expect you to consult with them on your day-to-day decisions, but many of our successful women did turn to their parents for advice on careers, education, family, and relationships during their adult years. The final decisions are yours, but families have much to offer. Furthermore, during the ups and downs of establishing your career, it's good to have a dependable support system. Your family members may become your lifelong friends.

There may, of course, be times when you'll make a decision that's not the one your parents would want for you. They may or may not appreciate that, but as an adult, you'll have to live with the consequences of your own decision making, and you'll need to be courageous enough to assert yourself with confidence after you've explored all the alternatives.

Good role models abound, and you'll need to search out those from whom you can learn. Fortunately, many women understand the important role of mentors and may be willing to give of their time if you ask for their guidance. When you're selecting a position, consider whether the people you'll be working with are likely to be good mentors.

### RESEARCH FINDING NO. 7:
### BIRTH ORDER MAY NOT MATTER, BUT SIBLINGS DO

All the career groups in our survey had women of all the possible birth orders; thus we can't assume that birth order is a limitation for any career. Being firstborn proved an advantage for almost all careers other than mental health, nursing, and homemaking. There were more youngest children in mental health, an equal percentage of oldest and middle children in allied health (nursing, physical therapy, occupational therapy, and the like), and mostly middle children among the homemakers. There was approximately the same percentage of only children in each profession, except for orchestral music, where there was a slightly higher percentage of only children.

Many women described rivalry with a sister or brother who was highly talented in one area as the reason they stayed away from that subject or interest. They felt that area "belonged" to the sibling and believed they wouldn't be able to distinguish themselves. Others talked about extreme differences between themselves and their sisters or brothers. Competition between siblings can set very different directions for children, even though parents may teach their kids similar values. There seem to be gender differences in family competition; the successful women tended to "lose" to brothers and "win" over their sisters. On the other hand, the girls in all-girl families seemed to fare well and often all were successful.

### GUIDELINE FOR GIRLS AND WOMEN NO. 7:
### DON'T LET YOUR SIBLINGS HOLD YOU BACK

Don't let your birth order prevent you from taking the risk of leadership. Leadership may not feel as comfortable to you if you are the middle or youngest child, but do make deliberate attempts to take charge of committees or organizations so that you can learn to lead. If you're the oldest in the family, don't always insist on control. Stepping back and letting others take the lead from time to time may free up some creative energy and give you the freedom to make occasional mistakes. A balance of control and creativity is important for most careers.

When it comes to exploring your own talents, don't avoid areas just because a talented family member seems to have claimed the spot. You may find you are equally talented, or at least more talented than you'd believed. You can have less talent than a brother, sister, mother, or father and still be very capable compared to the rest of the world. But talent isn't the only issue. If you can stop yourself from feeling too competitive with your sibling or parent, you may actually find you enjoy and can share many of the same talents. If you do feel competitive, you don't have to disguise your feelings. It's better to talk them through and even learn to praise and admire your sibling or other relative. Of course, it's possible that you may have other and different talents as well, but you don't need to feel that you must have your own area of expertise in the family. Families thrive when all members become lifelong cheerleaders for one another because it broadens everyone's possibilities for learning.

## RESEARCH FINDING NO. 8:
## OPPORTUNITIES SPRING FROM OBSTACLES

The successful women in our survey overcame many obstacles. They struggled with poverty, health problems, social problems, learning difficulties, or racial, religious, or economic prejudice. Many hit walls at various times in their lives and needed to change directions or take time out. Some were plagued by depression and anxiety, and many lost confidence in their abilities from time to time. They usually responded to these barriers by persevering through them or by changing direction in their personal lives or careers. Overcoming unanticipated obstacles was an essential part of their success.

## GUIDELINE FOR GIRLS AND WOMEN NO. 8: PREPARE TO BE
## CHALLENGED AND GET SUPPORT TO DEFEAT OBSTACLES

Your pathway to success is likely to be indirect. At some point, you'll face lessons that will seem impossible to learn, challenges that will feel insurmountable, closed doors that you will be unable to open. Determining whether you should persevere, get help, or change directions will be the test of your resilience. You don't need to face those obstacles alone. Try to get siblings or other family members and friends to support you, or seek out professional help to guide you. You may feel lonely and alone, and in the long run, it is you who must make the final decisions. Make your decisions based on what they may mean in six months, a year, and five years. Think about short-term and long-term goals. It helps to realize that overcoming obstacles is part of success. You may have to change your goals, and those new goals may fit better than the ones you originally targeted. Sometimes, you may even have to come to terms with real limitations in your abilities, but determination and effort can help you achieve much more than you first believed.

### RESEARCH FINDING NO. 9:
### SUCCESSFUL WOMEN HAVE A PASSION FOR THEIR WORK

"Challenge," "contribution," and "creativity" were the three words most frequently used to describe why our successful women chose their careers. Most indicated a passion about what they were doing and truly loved their work. A criterion for being included in our study was job satisfaction, so by definition these women were, on the whole, satisfied with their work. Of course, there were women in all careers who voiced some dissatisfactions: for example, not enough money, too much competition, too much time commitment to their careers, and not enough time for family. Although some women were motivated to pursue a certain career from childhood, most identified their career direction in high school or college. Many changed majors while they were in college, and quite a few changed careers during their adult lives.

### GUIDELINE FOR GIRLS AND WOMEN NO. 9:
### BALANCE PASSION WITH REASON

Consider the values you want to derive from your career. Be realistic in balancing your love of the work with the availability of jobs, financial remuneration, time commitment, and its fit with your family and relationship goals. Don't feel committed to one career direction too early. College and life will give you opportunities for exploration and change. Although change may be appropriate, don't be too quick to leave something you really love. Most people don't love their work all the time and don't love every aspect of that work.

There is wisdom in passionately loving your work, but despite your passion, you may not be able to achieve success, because some careers are simply too competitive. You may have to discover a passion for a new career and cope with leaving your first passion to others.

### RESEARCH FINDING NO. 10: BALANCING WORK AND FAMILY LIFE IS AN ONGOING CHALLENGE

Our successful women struggled and sacrificed to balance the roles of mother, wife, and professional. They sometimes experienced fertility problems caused by delayed childbearing. Their husbands sometimes changed their own careers to share parenting or even take on the major parenting role. Some women redirected their careers or took time off to spend more time with their family. As a result, they sometimes felt penalized in their careers. Women in some careers commented on "glass ceilings" and "sticky floors"; promotion opportunities sometimes seemed unfair. There were times when they sensed that being a woman offered either a distinct advantage or a clear disadvantage, but only rarely could they be certain that opportunities or the lack thereof was gender-based. In our study, women in traditional careers rated their family lives as excellent slightly more frequently.

### GUIDELINE FOR GIRLS AND WOMEN NO. 10: EXPECT THE BALANCING ACT TO BE A STRUGGLE

You may have many choices about the timing of your career and whether or not you want to combine your career with marriage or family life. You can expect to struggle psychologically with those issues, and a race against the calendar for family planning is not unusual. You may choose not to marry; you may choose to marry but not have children. Be prepared to struggle with some career choices in which you may never be certain if your success or lack thereof is tied to your abilities or to your gender. Expect to pioneer in devising ways to balance your career and family life, and if you should decide to marry and have a family, it is important that you and your partner discuss your desire to balance family and career before you get married, to be sure you both have the same expectations. Although you may change those plans after marriage, depending on the direction your lives take, it's important to establish some ground rules of agreement prior to commitment. Balance is a dynamic process. It means that sometimes things may get off-center in one direction or another. There's not one perfect, ideal way to perform life's balancing act.

# 2

# The Lawmakers and Adjudicators

$O$NLY a generation ago, there were almost no women in government and very few in the legal profession. The TV shows might have us believe that women are equally represented in law and half of law school graduates are women, but only a quarter of our present attorneys are women, and as of 1994, only 6 percent had achieved partnership status. As for achievements in government, percentages of women vary between 10 and 20 percent at local, state, and national levels. We do have a distance to go.

Our survey for *See Jane Win* showed how women in law and government were prepared by their childhoods for leadership, litigation, and assertiveness. Although many of the women in elected government offices earned law degrees as part of their preparation for office, there were also some significant differences between those who chose to stay in law and those who ran for office.

## *Results from the* See Jane Win *Study*

The women in government were more social as girls than were the women who chose to practice law. They described themselves as leaders in their childhood more often and were most frequently involved in school politics and student government. As early as elementary school, many of the women in government developed an interest in politics. Both the attorneys and the politicians were frequently involved in drama, debate, and forensics.

When asked to describe themselves during their childhood, more of the attorneys picked "brainy" than did the women in government, although both also frequently used words like "smart," "hardworking," and "independent." More attorneys than any other career group were very early talkers and readers, and they tended to rank higher academically in their graduating classes than the women in government.

The subjects most favored by the women in these career categories were history and social studies. Higher percentages of these women attended women's colleges and held leadership positions during college, and many of them credited their colleges for providing important formative and confidence-building experiences.

The lawmakers and adjudicators in our survey expressed quite a few concerns about their jobs taking too much time from their families, and the women in politics frequently mentioned their low remuneration but emphasized that the contribution they believed they were making helped offset the smaller paychecks.

## *How Jane Won*

Governor Christine Whitman of New Jersey and Congresswoman Shelley Berkley were both involved in politics early; while still in high school, Governor Whitman planned a mock political convention, and Congresswoman Berkley actually distributed campaign literature for Democratic candidates who, many years later, would in turn support her. Both of them continued their political activities in college as well.

District Attorney Martha Coakley was elected governor of Girls State, a state organization specifically intended to train girls for leadership in government. She was also active in speech and debate from elementary school forward and honed her litigation skills on her winning debate team.

Almost all the litigators and adjudicators were excellent students throughout school. The exceptions were attorney Martha Lindner, who struggled with dyslexia during her elementary and middle school years but nevertheless became an outstanding college and law school student, and Governor Whitman, who didn't apply herself when she didn't like the subject or felt threatened by the challenge. In college, where she found classwork to be more creative, she, too, became a high achiever.

Many of the women in these careers described themselves as very independent girls. Justice Sandra Day O'Connor's description of her independence was perhaps the most marked. She spent the school year away from her parents from kindergarten on and, when home, was expected to do her share in rounding up cattle on her family ranch, starting at a very early age. Imprisonment by the Japanese in a camp in China, away from her family, was a unique and unpleasant form of independence training for New Jersey Representative Mary Previte. Congresswoman Nydia Velázquez's independence became evident when she immigrated to New York, first as a student, then as an adult, determined to make a difference for the Puerto Rican community. Governor Whitman considers her independence during her middle school years to have prepared her for the lonely and challenging job of governing a state.

Notice the arrangements that lawmakers and adjudicators made for balancing busy careers and family lives. Attorney Lindner pointed out the advantages of directing her own practice because it gave her the freedom to attend her children's school functions. Congresswomen Barbara Cubin and Shelley Berkley and Governor Whitman all talked about important assistance from their husbands. Several of the women in government had no children, and District Attorney Coakley pointed to the difficulty of raising children while pursuing a time-consuming career as part of her decision not to have children. Representative Previte delayed much of her career until after her children were grown. Congresswoman Cubin described her real job as being a wife and mother, not a politician, and worked hard to maintain her family's closeness despite her political commitments.

# Strong Enough to Stand Alone

## Christine Whitman

### GOVERNOR OF NEW JERSEY

*Governor Christine Whitman, at age forty-seven, was elected the first female governor of New Jersey and was also the first person to defeat an incumbent governor in a general election in modern state history. In 1995, she was the first governor to give the formal response to a president's State of the Union Address. Being first began in her childhood, where Christine honed her independence and leadership skills.*

**My parents made the biggest difference in my life. They placed no gender barriers before me. My father promoted my mother, and she promoted him.** They were both involved in politics in New Jersey, and my dad encouraged my mother to run for office because she was so involved in the political process. **I grew up thinking women can do anything.**

I'm probably more like my mother, who raised me. That was apparently the deal they made. My dad said, "Okay, I give up, you take her." My mother was the Republican National Committee chairwoman for the state for ten years, not a paid job, but she definitely worked outside the home. My dad was Republican state chairman and worked with a major construction company.

I was the youngest of four and eight years younger than my nearest sibling, so I had the enviable position of being treated like an only child, yet my older sister and two older brothers toughened me up early in life. They were in boarding school and college during my most formative years, **so I soon learned to depend on myself.**

We lived in Paris for a year when I was about eight, and I went to the American School. Mom was summoned to the headmistress's office and asked how she and my father got along. When she said everything was fine, the headmistress said to her, "I have to tell you that when he chases you around the house with an ax, it really upsets your daughter." I'd been really bored by show-and-tell, and I'd made up stories. I was creative that way.

**I'm not sure anyone would have predicted my future leadership based on how I behaved as a girl.** Once I organized a revolt at camp when we didn't like our counselor. I convinced my friends to take their favorite stuffed animal and climb a tree. We climbed just out of reach of the camp counselors and told them we wouldn't come down unless they changed our counselor. It worked. Not exactly democracy in action.

My father set very high standards—perhaps too high. He insisted, "Anything worth doing is worth doing well," so when I wasn't good at things, I would retreat. I did well with the subjects that interested me, like English, history, and creative writing, but in Latin, math, and grammar, I did miserably. I think part of it was being spoiled. I developed a defense mechanism, which was "If I don't try, it's not that I'm dumb, it's that I didn't try." **I didn't give myself a chance to prove myself.** It's not something I'm dearly proud of and I certainly never mentioned it to my children when they were growing up.

I never pictured a career in politics when I was a little girl. I figured I'd be a surgeon, since I liked to pick up frogs, but my parents' experiences rubbed off on me. When I was in high school in New York, I organized my first political convention and **got the school interested in current affairs. We learned a lot about the political process.**

I confess I was still more of a problem than a leader. **I had a few good friends but was mainly a loner.** I was sure it was all my fault that I didn't have more friends. I was a prickly kid and not easy to get along with. **I learned to enjoy being alone and depending on myself. I grew up on a farm, loved being with the animals and taking walks in the woods. I still do. Getting away from people is perhaps the best way to get perspective on the day again.** Taking the dogs for a nice long walk, being outdoors, is as relaxing a thing as I can imagine doing; that's always been part of my makeup.

**I was a late bloomer and hit my stride at Wheaton College in Massachusetts. I was vice president of the class and head of the Republican Club. My international government professor challenged me** and encouraged me to analyze situations and solve problems outside the norm. I also enjoyed the independence of college. I had the freedom to think and approach subjects from different angles, and it helped me graduate with honors. **College got me excited about government,** and after college, I became involved.

I wanted to help the Republican Party reach out to minorities. They weren't considered to be on the Republican screen. At the time, kids were burning down college campuses to protest the war in Vietnam. The Republican Party had to learn how to communicate with dissident groups. I met the chairman of the Republican Party at a luncheon and pitched my idea to him. I was fortunate. He believed in young people and wanted to build the party, so he took a flyer and said, "Fine, go ahead, put your idea together and do it." I was off and running.

**The first full-time job I ever had was running a program I designed in Washington.** I called it the "Listening Program." At twenty-two, I was traveling around the country, talking to groups of blacks, college students, and senior citizens to analyze their involvement with the political system. If they weren't involved, I tried to figure out why they weren't. If they were, I determined whether they were Republicans, and if they weren't, I asked what our party could do to attract them.

I was naive and didn't believe there were barriers. One time, a director of youth for the Republican National Committee asked to come along to see my meetings with college students. We were supposed to meet with members of the Black Disciples Gang in the East Ward in Chicago at about 10:30 at night. The director was scared to death. In retrospect, late-night meetings with gangs might not have been my smartest move, but things worked out fine.

I had a number of other political jobs around Washington and Colorado, then ended up with the Peace Corps at a desk job working for Ghana and Nigeria. I had written my college thesis on Nigerian constitutional development and really wanted to be in the field. I didn't like the idea of a desk job, so I didn't stay there long.

I then moved to New York as a freelance consultant, and got married in 1974. After two and a half years in England, we moved to New Jersey, where I was appointed by the local party organization to be a trustee at the county college. Then I ran for the local governing body, which is called the Board of Freeholders. I was a freeholder for six years and chairman of the board for two. **I was also the only woman on that board.** Then the governor appointed me president of the state's Board of Public Utilities. I later resigned to run against Bill Bradley for the United States Senate. After I lost that election, I put together a political action committee that did a lot of issue research for the local candidates, and then I ran successfully for governor.

**As governor, at the end of the day, you're the one who makes the decisions, and you have to stand alone,** particularly if the decision goes south. It's amazing how quickly the people who encouraged you will jump overboard if it doesn't turn out the way it was supposed to. You have to have the ability to analyze and believe in your decision, and then stand by it. **You can't define yourself in terms of others if you are in a leadership position.**

We now live on the farm where I grew up. Our children are twenty-one and twenty-two. I couldn't have done all this without my husband's support because he was wonderful with the kids and totally supportive, but **I was fortunate because my first job as a freeholder was part-time, and I was able to take the kids to school in the morning and pick them up in the afternoon.**

**I hit many walls as a woman.** The biggest and most obvious was when I ran for the Senate, because I had absolutely no support in the party. They didn't believe a woman could defeat Bill Bradley. I actually had a news reporter say, "How dare you run against him?" The Republican Senatorial Campaign Committee redirected significant dollars they had promised us away from our campaign in the last weeks. We weren't even on the air for two and a half weeks because they knocked our budget out from under us. **We were able to persevere, and with less than a million dollars we took on Bradley within two percentage points.** A lot of people had to eat crow.

**It was lonely being the only woman, but the challenges were such that I didn't have time to think about that. I found that once I was in a position, the men became supportive.** The first job I was given as freeholder was overseeing the construction of a county courthouse. At the first meeting with the construction people, they looked really askance when a woman came in, but once they figured out that I signed the checks, they fell right into line. We brought the building in on time and under budget.

When I first ran for governor and put forward the income-tax-cut proposal, the stories were brutal, and the undercurrent was, "She can't have thought of this herself because she's a woman; she must go to her husband for help." **I finally stopped worrying about that. I just got done what I had to do and decided they would eventually figure out that it wasn't my husband or any other man behind me.** I do know what I'm talking about and what I want to accomplish. **As with every woman who charts new grounds, I ran into obstacles because people were very suspicious of women.** Those kinds of things take time, **but I can't spend my time focusing on the negative.** I need to get on to the next task.

I wasn't an exceptional child. I didn't know I wanted to be in government all my life. Things have a way of coming together over time, and **because I received such strong support from my family, it gave me the self-confidence to succeed, in spite of the fact that I wasn't a good student.**

# $J$HELPING THE POOR AND DISENFRANCHISED IS HER MISSION

## Nydia M. Velázquez

U.S. CONGRESSWOMAN FROM NEW YORK

*When Congresswoman Nydia Velázquez, at age sixteen, entered the University of Puerto Rico and then graduated magna cum laude in 1974, she was the first person in her family to receive a college diploma. That was only the first of many firsts.*

*Nydia became the first Hispanic to serve on the New York City Council. In 1992, she was the first Puerto Rican woman to be elected to the U.S. House of Representatives from the Twelfth District in New York. In February 1998, Nydia was named ranking Democrat on the House Small Business Committee, the first Hispanic woman to serve as chair or ranking member of a full committee in the history of the House of Representatives. Nydia's family struggled out of poverty, and her story should inspire us to know that firsts are possible for all.*

I grew up very poor in a rural town in Puerto Rico. My father was a sugarcane corder. Neither of my parents had a formal education, but **both instilled in me the value of education.** Every time my father left our home in the morning, **he reminded us that education would be the only way out of the cycle of poverty.** While he worked in the sugarcane fields, my mother worked at home, not only raising us, but preparing meals to sell in the sugarcane fields. **My mother's hard work encouraged me to immerse myself in study.** I wanted to help her with the farmwork, but she always said, "No, you have to go home and get to your books." **I worked hard, got straight A's, and it was such a celebration that I knew that this was the way for me to say thank you to her for working so hard.**

I'm a middle child of nine and have a twin sister. My brothers all did well in school, got good grades, but didn't pursue college, even though they were smart. Because of our economic conditions, they needed to get jobs and help my parents. One of my sisters became an anesthesiologist; another continued in cosmetology, opened a school, and became a businesswoman; and my third sister is a successful businesswoman. All the women in my family are very strong.

**My father was always active in politics in Puerto Rico.** Our very small, three-bedroom house was always filled with neighbors because my father was an organizer. **My father, who only had a third-grade education, was an impassioned speaker. When I was only five, I knew I wanted to be like him.**

In first grade, I was the first to get a book because I was the first to learn to read. I told my father I wanted a set of encyclopedias. Even though we didn't have much money, he bought them for me. My brothers and sisters would be playing games, and I'd stay in the room surrounded by books. **I thought if I read the entire encyclopedia, I'd become an intellectual.**

Because I always got straight A's, I skipped second grade. My two older sisters did most of my work around the house so I could focus on my studies. **I had a teacher I adored because she devoted so much time to me;** she even visited me at home on weekends. **I wanted to be a teacher like her. She was my role model.**

**I had boyfriends, but education was my number one priority.** Kids called me "Socrates." **They'd pick on me because they weren't doing as well as I was.** I invited some of them to come to my home, and I became the teacher. I spent a lot of time explaining things to them and sharing with them, and I took a leadership role at a very early age. I made the choice not to do any extracurricular activities. **I wanted to get great grades so I could go to college. I knew if I didn't have a good average in school, I wouldn't be able to get a scholarship.**

At sixteen, I went to the University of Puerto Rico. I never took a summer off, so I graduated magna cum laude when I was nineteen. **A very assertive, analytical, knowledgeable woman who was a professor at the University of Puerto Rico inspired me, and I kept saying to myself, "One day I want to be like her."** I wanted to become a college professor, so I pursued graduate studies, got a full scholarship, and came to New York University and majored in political science. I earned my master's degree but didn't finish my Ph.D. because my mother became ill, and my father asked me to come back to Puerto Rico. I became a professor at the University of

Puerto Rico. **It was the most rewarding experience to be able to teach at the university from which I'd graduated.**

I taught for a year, then became a chair of a department there. It was an amazing experience because not only was I the youngest and a female, but I had so quickly reversed my role from student to teacher. I became the boss of those who had been my teachers. That role at so early an age prepared me for the role I'm playing now.

Then I decided I needed to take a break because of the difficult political climate of Puerto Rico. The governor of Puerto Rico and his administration were very conservative, and I couldn't make the changes we were advocating for the university. Some young Puerto Ricans had been killed by the police, and there was a big scandal. We didn't have freedom of expression, and to me, that was a fundamental principle. I took a leave of absence and came to New York.

In New York, I became an adjunct professor at Hunter College. A year later, I was invited to an interview on a radio program to discuss Ronald Reagan's policies toward the Caribbean. A former student of mine who was listening to the program contacted me, and that was my first encounter with the Puerto Rican community in Brooklyn. When I went to visit him, I saw how neglected the community was and asked him why. He told me, "We don't have political power," and introduced me to a Puerto Rican city councilman, Luis Olmedo. I said, **"I would like to see how we can get some attention and how we can get delivery of services to this community." He told me we didn't have the power because the community doesn't vote. I was determined to change that.** We put together a committee, and two weeks later, I purchased a folding table and some folding chairs, and started registering Puerto Ricans. It was my initiation into New York City politics. I became involved in a congressional election and became special assistant to Congressman Edolphus Towns. A year later Councilman Luis Olmedo was indicted and convicted, which was a very painful experience for me because I hadn't known he was doing anything wrong.

I didn't give up. I was appointed for nine months to the City Council, filling the vacant seat of the convicted councilman, and became the first Hispanic woman to serve. After those nine months, the governor of Puerto Rico, who was a friend of mine, asked me to become the head of the government of Puerto Rico offices in the

United States. I told him I'd accept it only if he would support an agenda to empower Puerto Ricans. I initiated the most comprehensive voter registration campaign in the history of the Puerto Rican community. Over five years, we registered more than 250,000 Puerto Ricans.

The political landscape in New York changed. David Dinkins became the first African-American mayor, and I can tell you that my voter registration had a lot to do with that because, for the first time, Puerto Ricans were coming out to vote in large numbers. **My position was that the best help the government of Puerto Rico could provide to the Puerto Rican community was not services but helping them to empower themselves politically.** I believe today that that has to be the focus of the work we do, to empower the community through educational, political, and economic opportunities. If we do what is right, there will be a day when there will no longer be a role for the office of the government of Puerto Rico in the United States.

**Coming to the United States took a personal toll on me.** I was totally immersed in trying to help my community here and my family in Puerto Rico. I was working for the governor of Puerto Rico, trying to create an organization to help Puerto Ricans who were suffering from AIDS and HIV, working with the voter registration campaign, and dealing with my youngest brother, who was suffering from drug addiction in Puerto Rico. When I couldn't achieve those goals with the speed I wanted, it became too much for me to handle. **I became very depressed. I sought help and learned that I needed to take a step back, relax, and assess where I was. I realized I was human, like any other person, and I couldn't resolve everything, and that part of human nature is not to succeed in everything I set myself to achieve or accomplish. I was in therapy for a year and learned a lot about myself. I felt stronger than ever.**

A year later, I ran for office for the United States Congress and won. I've been in Congress eight years. When I became the first Puerto Rican woman to serve in Congress, I knew I had a responsibility to the people of my district to represent Puerto Ricans in the nation. I also knew I needed to hit the ground running because of the issues facing my community. **Because I had worked for a** congressman for so many years, I knew the dynamics in Washington. I am the ranking Democrat on the Small Business Committee, which is historic; it usually takes at least twenty years for any congressperson to become ranking member or chair of a committee. I am the only female and the only Hispanic, Republican or Democrat, to be in a ranking position of a full committee. I sit at the table with twelve other chairmen to discuss the budget. **A seat at the table is important.** The president came to our district for the inauguration of a small-business-development center and a lending co-op that will allow Hispanic businesses to access business capital. That was something I put together, and I'm proud of that.

**The driving forces behind my success were my parents. I never used the fact that we were poor as an excuse.** Poverty challenged me to excel, to go to college, to become a professional, and to be able to provide for my family. Everything I wanted to do was for my parents to be proud of me. **I cherished how hard they worked and knew they worked so hard because they loved us.**

I talk to my parents every week. I go back to Puerto Rico and spend holidays with them. When I was elected, my campaign people were trying to decide who would introduce me. Fifteen hundred people would be there to watch me be sworn in to become the first Puerto Rican woman in the U.S. Congress. Politically, we were very cautious. People said, "If you choose the mayor, then the governor is going to be upset that he wasn't chosen, and if you choose the governor, the mayor will resent the fact that he was not the person introducing you." I decided my father should introduce me. He offered the most moving words that morning. He spoke from his heart and brought tears to the eyes of everyone in that room. He said, "I'm here representing my family, and I want to thank you all for supporting Nydia, but more importantly for having faith in her. **I can guarantee you that she will always be there for the poor and the disenfranchised.**"

# $\mathcal{A}$ Taylor Never Says "I Can't"

## Mary Previte

NEW JERSEY STATE ASSEMBLYWOMAN AND
ADMINISTRATOR OF CAMDEN COUNTY YOUTH CENTER

*From her teachers in a Japanese prison camp in China, Assembly-*
*woman Mary Previte learned the principles that guided her to in-*
*spire students first at Camden High School, New Jersey, then as the*
*administrator of the Camden County Youth Center. As a Democra-*
*tic assemblywoman in New Jersey, she's determined to make policy*
*differences that will affect troubled youths in her state. Her evolving*
*career provides a role model for women of all ages and stages. She en-*
*tered her new career in the New Jersey General Assembly at the en-*
*ergetic age of sixty-six.*

I was born Mary Taylor in China and grew up in a family where my
father was the third generation of missionaries serving in China.
"You're a Taylor" **meant you were going to achieve, go to college,**
**and be a role model for others, and that was what God ex-**
**pected.**

At age six, we went to the Chefoo School for children of missionaries. It was especially important to have God in our lives because
World War II was exploding around us. Our parents never imagined
that America would get sucked into it. They prepared us by having
us memorize portions of the Bible. At our house, confidence in God
was a way of life. My mother said, "I will put the wonderful
promises of the Bible to music, and we will sing them every day at
our family worship." While Mother played the pump organ, our
Taylor family choir gathered around to sing verses from the Bible
every single day after breakfast. Some of our favorite verses were "A
thousand shall fall at your side and ten thousand at your right hand,
but it shall not come nigh thee" and "He shall give his angels charge
over thee."

My parents left us at an English-speaking boarding school while
they returned to their missionary work in the heartland of China. A
year later, the day after the attack on Pearl Harbor, we awoke to find

Japanese soldiers on the doorstep of our school. Those words "He shall give his angels charge over thee, He shall give his angels charge over thee" were deep inside us like the old-fashioned gramophone records with the needle stuck right in the groove. The soldiers said, "The school belongs to the Great Emperor of Japan," and everything in it was marked "Property of Japan," with seals on desks, pianos, equipment, and even on us. We wore armbands to indicate our nationality, with "A" for American or "B" for British. The Japanese decided that our beautiful school on the ocean, which had been built and dedicated by my great-grandfather in the 1850s, would be a wonderful military base. They marched us into concentration camps. I can remember distinctly walking in a long snaking line of teachers, children, and retired missionaries, and singing from Psalm 46: "God is our refuge and strength; therefore, we will not be afraid."

That was the beginning of three years in a Japanese concentration camp. Our missionary teachers insisted school would go on even with war, Japanese guard dogs, bayonet drills, prisoner numbers, horrible food, and twice-daily roll calls. It didn't matter that we were eating pet food out of a tin can or a soap dish. The teachers would come up behind me and say, "Put your back up straight, Mary Taylor, and don't eat and talk at the same time," or "There is not one set of manners for children in concentration camp and a different set for the princesses in Buckingham Palace." We were in the most calamitous circumstances, yet the teachers expected us to have nice manners.

We'd line up for inspection and the teachers asked, "Are you clean? Are you neat? Do you have your mending done?" They checked to see if we had holes in our socks or dresses. We could not be raggedy or patched. Everything had to be as normal as possible. We could not give up.

We didn't have desks, and there wasn't one chair in the entire concentration camp of fourteen hundred prisoners, but school went on. We sat on steamer trunks, on the floor, or under the trees. Teachers told us, "We will get out of this place, and when we do, you will have to compete with other children." The grown-ups in our camp were cheerleaders of hope. One of them was Eric Liddell, about whom the Academy Award–winning movie *Chariots of Fire* was written. He was the Olympic athlete who would not run on Sunday because it was against his religious principles, and who won a gold medal in the 1924 Olympics. "Uncle" Eric created games and activities for us so we would not give up hope.

The Salvation Army Band was another group that built our spirits up. They said, "We're going to win the war, and when we're rescued, we're going to play a victory medley. Americans or British or Chinese or Russians—one of these will rescue us." They blended together a medley including "Happy Days Are Here Again" and the national anthems of the four countries. Every Tuesday night outside the Japanese commandant's office, ten or twelve scrawny musicians practiced for the day of liberation.

Our teachers reminded us not to give up hope in the midst of all the things that would normally terrify us. It didn't matter that there were guard dogs, electrified wires, bayonet drills, and all those horrendous things, or that we were far away from our parents. We would get up every day at the same time, and someone was in charge of the little potbelly stove in the middle of winter, and we all had to scrub our patch of floor around our steamer trunk so it was spotless and shiny. **Every day it was the same way; nothing could interrupt our predictable world or our learning how to be good people, to be successful in school, and to be successful as friends.**

My first taste of success came in that concentration camp. I'd always felt like such a dunce. All the other girls at the school seemed so bright and engaging and popular. I never did. For grades, the teachers gave us percentages instead of A's or B's because it was a British school. When we were handed our percentage scores for all of our classes, to my astonishment I found my percentage was the highest in the entire school. It was so delicious, and I was so excited inside. We weren't allowed to boast, but inside my soul, I was exploding. **That feeling of success was an extraordinary thing. We have to find ways to give success to all of our children because each success inspires another success.** It was a landmark experience that I wanted to feel over and over again.

On August 17, 1945, I was lying on our steamer trunk feeling puny. My stomach had been upset with dysentery and diarrhea. Sanitation was horrible in the camp, and there were flies and rats. I heard the sound of an airplane, rushed to the window of the barracks, and saw an American B-24 bomber flying low over the treetops of the camp, so low I could almost see the pilot's face. The belly of the plane opened and these six American "gods" parachuted out of the sky into the field beyond the camp. Unbelievably, the plane was called the *Armored Angel.* I recalled the Bible verse my mother had made us learn, "And He shall give His angels charge over thee." It was an instant cure for my diarrhea.

I began running for the field, thinking I'd be the first one there, but out of 1,400 prisoners, 1,399 got there before me. We burst out of the gates of the camp. We poured into the field and went berserk, pounding the ground, weeping, dancing, and waving our hands at these "gods." The men of the camp boosted the Americans up onto their shoulders. These gorgeous American men, sun-bronzed, with meat on their bones, were being carried by these pale, emaciated prisoners on their bony shoulders to the gates of the camp. Up on a mound by the gate, the Salvation Army Band started playing the victory medley. When they got to "Oh, say, does that star-spangled banner yet wave / O'er the land of the free and the home of the brave?" the young American major slithered down to a standing salute. One of the youngsters in the Salvation Army Band crumpled to the ground and wept. We were free.

My family came to America after the war was over. We settled down in a tiny little dot on the map in Michigan and my siblings and I went to a small Christian high school that was a slow-paced adjustment into the helter-skelter American way of life.

A year after we came back from China, when I was fourteen years old, I lost my left hand in an accident. I was with friends on a farm and caught my hand in a revolving saw. I can remember watching my father tiptoe through his grief. One day, he was braiding my hair, getting me ready for school because I didn't yet know how to braid my hair with one hand. He was about to wrap a rubber band around the end of my braid when he said, "Mary, Sweetheart, can I tell you a story?" (**I loved it that my daddy called me his Mary, Sweetheart, and I loved my daddy's stories.**) He said, "Do you know what your little brother, Bertie, said when he heard that you lost your hand? Bertie said, 'Now Mary can't ride her bicycle.' Mary, Sweetheart, do you know what I said to Bertie? I told him, 'Well, I don't know why not.' " My daddy's words have been like a banner written across my sky for more than forty years. **My daddy believed in me. He said, "Handicaps have nothing to do with the outside of a person. Handicaps are only on the inside of a person." He said his Mary, Sweetheart, has no handicaps on the inside.**

That year, when it came time for me to write my English term paper, my daddy suggested, "How about a topic called 'Handicaps' with a question mark?" He helped me find the story of Franklin Roosevelt, a president who didn't have the strength to lift his own body out of a wheelchair because he was paralyzed with polio, but lifted the spirit of the whole world during a bloody war, and the story of Helen Keller, who had lost the ability to hear and see, but grew up to inspire the world. That was how my daddy jump-started me. I was worrying about how boys weren't going to like me and how I was going to tie my shoes or play the piano. **My daddy refused to let me sink into the world of "I can't." He pulled me into the world of "I can."** Today, I tie my shoes, make quilts, hang wallpaper, drive a car, type, and work on the computer. **My daddy's believing in me was a defining moment in my life.**

**My mother didn't let me play "pity me" when I lost my hand.** When I said, "Well, I can't do the dishes," she made me march to the sink and take my turn with everyone else. I had been taking piano lessons. After I lost my hand, my mother switched me to organ lessons so I could play with one hand on the keyboard and my feet on the pedals below. In my head, I was living in a world where boys weren't going to like me anymore, I wasn't going to play volleyball, and my mother refused to let me live in that world. Lots of people thought my mother was harsh, but she was absolutely right. **The saying in our family was "A Taylor never says 'I can't.' "**

I graduated as salutatorian of my class and went on to college and graduated magna cum laude. I majored in speech and starred in intercollegiate debating.

I started teaching and was married in a couple of years to a college classmate. I taught at Camden High (a very poor, inner-city high school) for five years. I stopped when my daughter, who is now an attorney, was born. **I went on to get my master's while she was growing up.** When I taught at Camden High, I was the newest, greenest teacher there. I tell students, **"You have nine seconds to**

**make a first impression.**" I was so young, and most of the teachers had blue hair, and a lot of the students thought I was one of them. Did I think that anyone was watching me? I didn't think so, but clearly one was, one of the boys in my homeroom in the twelfth grade, Lewis Katz, a youngster that could've gone one way or another. I began seeing his name a few years later in the newspaper. He had gone on to college and was becoming rich and famous. One day we bumped into each other. He'd been elected to office, become a freeholder, and been put in charge of an overcrowded juvenile lockup. Three months later a fourteen-year-old youngster had hanged himself to death at that youth center. Lewis said, "Why would a fourteen-year-old boy want to kill himself in a place that is supposed to be helping boys and girls?" He called it something out of *Oliver Twist.* He declared he would change the place from top to bottom and started from the top. He remembered me from Camden High. I was the one who'd be at the ball games throwing my coat up in the air, screaming and shouting when Camden was winning, or who would have a tumble of students in my living room at home pasting up the student newspaper, eating pizza and drinking soda. This man appointed me to take over this juvenile lockup in 1974 until he could find someone suitable. That was twenty-six years ago, and I've been the administrator of the Camden County Youth Center ever since.

**I was wobble-kneed when I was asked to take this job. I had never done anything like it before, but it seemed like everything I was doing in my life was something I had never done before. On the outside, I said, "Yes, I can," and was the picture of confidence. Inside, I felt very, very wobbly.**

I was flabbergasted a couple of years ago when a young man I didn't know who is a state assemblyman called me up and said, "Mary, what would you think about running for the New Jersey General Assembly?" I had never been politically active. I was unaccustomed to the rough-and-tumble world of campaigning and going door-to-door. I'm just starting my second term of two years, and last week I gave an impassioned speech on juvenile justice. I told the story of what the impact of this legislation will be, and I felt highly respected for what I was doing.

I continue to run the youth center because my assembly job isn't

full-time. **I wrote *Hungry Ghosts,* the only book ever written
about a juvenile detention center. The themes and messages that
those missionary teachers poured into us—structure, a predictable world—are the themes I pour into the boys and girls I
work with today.** These teenagers are boys who kill, girls who sell
their bodies, gang members. I don't deal with cream puffs. It is a secure facility. **The first gift we give to children is, "You are safe
here. We will not let anyone hurt you, and we will not let you
hurt anyone else while you're here."** We see the "fists up" attitude of the children melt immediately. That was a lesson I learned in
the concentration camp from those wonderful missionary teachers.

A little over two years ago, when I was running for office, I was
asked to speak at a reunion of a veterans' group called the "China-
Burma-India Veterans Association." A lightbulb went on in my
head. I thought, "Could one of my heroes who rescued me be there?"
I was so excited that I looked up the records and found the names of
those men who liberated our camp. At the reunion, I read a proc-
lamation to 150 men and women in their seventies and eighties
who had served as veterans. I honored them for what they had done.
Then I said, "I know it was not an accident that I was invited here
tonight." I told them the story of the Americans dropping out of the
sky to liberate fourteen hundred prisoners, then read off the names
of our liberators. I asked, "Are any of my heroes in this room?" None
was, but these veterans wept and wrapped me in their arms. They
persuaded me to write my story in their national magazine. I found
every one of my heroes as a result and created a fuss all across the
country to honor them. I visited each one.

**Incidents like this shape our lives. They are part of the fabric
of who we are.** I shout it from the housetops: These are the stars in
a hug-the-world event in my life. Triumphs like these make us who
we are.

# *H*ER FAMILY'S RANCH TAUGHT HER
## INDEPENDENCE

~

## Sandra Day O'Connor

ASSOCIATE JUSTICE OF THE UNITED STATES SUPREME COURT

*Justice Sandra Day O'Connor's brief story showcases the beginning of her independence and excellence. She is a true pioneer in law and justice. She's had a private law practice, was assistant attorney general in Arizona, and served three terms in the Arizona state senate, where she was the first woman senate majority leader. Sandra was also elected judge of the Maricopa County Superior Court and appointed to the Arizona Court of Appeals. Every woman in the country cheered when, in 1981, President Reagan nominated her to be the first female associate justice of the Supreme Court. With all these accomplishments, she somehow also managed to raise three sons.*

I grew up on a remote cattle ranch in the Southwest, where I learned to be independent. We had to do everything ourselves. If something was broken, we couldn't call a repairman; we had to fix it. If we wanted something built, we had to build it. If we wanted something done, we had to do it. **I was expected to do many things and do them well without complaint. That was probably a good thing for me to learn. Other people depended on me doing a good job.** For instance, going out on a roundup of cattle, we would start out on horseback very early in the morning before daylight. Each person on the roundup would be assigned a certain territory to cover, and we had to gather all the cattle within that territory no matter how obstreperous they might be or how much they didn't want to go. We would have to get them and move them along to join the larger herd being gathered for the roundup. Every member of the roundup crew depended on every other member to do a good job, or it couldn't be done. I learned early to be part of a team and to carry my share of the load. I did all this when I was a very young child. **Those were experiences that taught me early independence and a sense of responsibility.**

I had to go away to school from kindergarten through high school and live with my grandmother in El Paso, Texas. I was homesick most of those years for the ranch and felt sad that I wasn't there. We didn't have a telephone, so we wrote letters occasionally. I developed my study habits and my activities at school without having any parent available to talk to or to encourage me in any particular direction. **I was pretty much self-directed.** My grandmother really loved me, and she would constantly tell me that I could do anything I wanted to do, and that I was an important person. That probably was a good thing in the long run, but at the time I thought it was ridiculous and didn't believe her. She was an adoring grandmother, and I was lucky to have her when I was so far away from my parents. I went home to the ranch at Christmas, spring break, and summer.

I had some very good teachers in the private grade school I attended. I took dramatic arts classes with a teacher named Miss Fireovid, who was a very demanding, marvelous teacher. **I was shy, and it was hard for me to get up in front of people and say things. Under her direction I learned to do that, and it is something that probably helped me the rest of my life.**

In school I always earned good grades, but once I got to the public high school, I didn't want people to know that I did, because those who got good grades were considered nerds. It was better to be quiet about it. I had some close friends in high school in El Paso, and some are my friends to this day.

I didn't decide to go into law until I was an undergraduate at Stanford University. I took an undergraduate class from a law professor who was very inspiring. There weren't many women who went to law school, and when I entered I didn't know if I would enjoy it, but law school turned out to be a great experience. I was discouraged at first when I couldn't get a job after law school. Law firms would not hire women lawyers in those days, and I think I was naive in not realizing that it would be hard to get a job. I finally persuaded the district attorney of San Mateo County in California to give me a job as an intern. I loved my internship, and I was then given a job as a deputy district attorney, and gained some excellent experience in that position—experience that helped me from that time forward.

# She Grew Up with Las Vegas

## Shelley Berkley

U.S. CONGRESSWOMAN FROM NEVADA

*The decision of Congresswoman Shelley Berkley's family to explore possibilities for work in Las Vegas changed the direction of her life forever. Shelley found Las Vegas to be a city to grow in and grow with. As early as high school, she was driven toward politics in the Democratic Party. Shelley wanted to make a difference in her community, which she's done as a citizen, a parent, a professional, and an elected official. She had the joy of serving on the Nevada Board of Regents, which governed the University of Nevada, from which she had graduated. First elected to the state assembly in 1982, and then to the U.S. House of Representatives in 1998, Shelley serves her state and nation and manages to balance that with staying close with her family and parenting her two sons.*

My grandparents literally walked across Europe to come to this country. My father's side of the family comes from the Russia-Poland border; if they hadn't gotten out when they did, they would never have made it out. My mother's side comes from Salonika, Greece. At the beginning of World War II, the vibrant Jewish population of seventy thousand made up half the population in the city where she grew up. After the war, there were fewer than one thousand Jews left. If they hadn't escaped when they did, neither side of my family would have survived the Second World War. They came to America with absolutely no money or possessions. They couldn't speak English and had limited skills. My grandmothers told me about how they expected the streets to be paved with gold and that there would be an abundance of food on every street corner. The reality was not quite what they had envisioned, but it was far better than what they had before.

My parents were raised on the Lower East Side of New York. My father had a ninth-grade education because he had to quit work during the Depression to help support his family. Though my parents were not well educated, education was stressed in my home. It didn't matter whether we were popular or pretty. It only mattered that we did well in school, because that was the way to live the American Dream. If we got all A's, they put the report card up on the refrigerator. If we got a B in a subject, they made an appointment with the teacher to find out why we were doing so poorly. **There was tremendous incentive in the house to do well, and we did.** I have one sister, five years younger. We're close sisters and close friends. Even now we have a twice-a-day-telephone-call relationship.

When I was eleven, we left upstate New York and decided to seek our fortune out west. We were traveling to southern California and had packed everything we owned in a U-Haul. When we got to the Hoover Dam, there were wooden signs inviting us to come to Las Vegas, only thirty miles away. Since it was the middle of the summer and we didn't have to be in school, my parents decided to stop in Las Vegas for the night. We never left. The next day, my dad got a job as a waiter, and we rented a little apartment. A month later, my sister and I enrolled in school. The best thing my parents ever did for me was to move to Las Vegas. It opened up opportunities that I couldn't have had anywhere else. It's not so much that I grew up *in* Las Vegas as I grew up *with* Las Vegas. When we moved here, there were about 150,000 people in this city. Now there are 1.2 million. My dad was a waiter all the years I was growing up, but because the economy was so strong and the gaming industry provided so many opportunities, he was able to put a roof over our heads, food on the table, clothes on our backs, and his daughters through college and law school. Not a bad accomplishment.

Both my grandmothers were widows, and they raised their children without husbands. Both went to work in the sweatshops. They were seamstresses, tailors, and they brought that skill with them to America, and that's how they raised their families. They were strong women. They were uneducated, they didn't speak English, they never had money, but **they were role models for survival and family values.**

My mother wanted something different for her kids, and she struggled for everything that we needed. I wore new dresses at bar mitzvahs, but she didn't. My parents poured every penny and every ounce of hope into their children, and we are the result of it. They have two happy, well-adjusted, good kids.

**My sister and I never doubted our parents' love.** Despite their rocky marriage, there was never a question in our minds that we were the glue that kept our family together. We were the reason they stayed married, and **that made me want to succeed even more** because I knew it was a difficult relationship for them. We've given them nothing but *naches* (pride). **Their expectations were high and we met their expectations.**

I wasn't the prettiest or the most popular. I was very gawky with curly dark hair that I went out of my way to Dippity-Do and iron and straighten at a time when having straight blond hair was in. **I was very active in student government and Jewish youth groups. I was president of everything. I was always very involved in my faith. It was important to me because it gave me a sense of identity.** We had a very small Jewish community, but it was a very cohesive one. My social life revolved around temple activities and Jewish youth groups. I was president of Las Vegas B'nai Brith Girls. **I was committed to standing up for what I believed in.**

**I was politically active in high school.** In 1968, as a high school senior, I walked precincts for two young assembly candidates, Richard Bryan and Harry Reid, who many years later became our two U.S. senators. When I ran for Congress in 1999, they walked precincts for me.

I was the first person in my family to go to college. I was part of the tenth graduating class of the University of Nevada, Las Vegas. Most of us in the class were first-generation college-goers. There were waiters, waitresses, bellhops, and valets all sending their kids to school for the first time. In my freshman year, there were about four thousand students at UNLV; now there are over twenty thousand.

I loved college, and I blossomed there. **My family and college convinced me that there wasn't anything I couldn't do.** My mother was a stay-at-home mom, but **because of her belief that we could make something of ourselves, we did.** In the middle of the women's movement, **I was very lucky to be there when women were beginning to appreciate that they could be some-body on their own.** When I was in high school, I was student body secretary, but by the time I was in college, I was the first woman stu-dent body president. **Somewhere between those four years, it oc-curred to me that I didn't have to be a follower; I could be the one in charge.**

I became very involved in Democratic politics during college. **An-other benchmark in my life was when I was selected for a college program to go to Washington, D.C., to work for U.S. Senator Howard Cannon. After my Washington experience, I knew that I was going to be in public service.**

I applied to law school to get the background to run for office and was accepted at the University of San Diego. In my year, 1974, there was a push to enroll more women, so I was in a class of 20 percent women, which in those days was phenomenal.

After I completed law school, I had a very strong sense of destiny. I knew what I was going to do and how I was going to do it, and I've been relentless in pursuing my goals and dreams. I met a fellow stu-dent in law school, and we were married, moved to Las Vegas, and started our life together.

I was appointed deputy director of the State Commerce Depart-ment by then-governor Mike O'Callaghan, who was a very early friend and mentor. After that, I became in-house counsel for South-west Gas Corporation, so I gained a background in commerce and utility law. I ran for the Nevada state assembly in 1982 and won my race. That same year I had my first son, Max. I served in the Nevada state assembly, so he's known no other mother but a political mother, because he was born to it.

I lost one election for the Nevada state senate, and I was heart-broken and thought my political career was prematurely over. **I've always believed things happen for the best, because ten months after I lost that election, I gave birth to my second son,** Sam. If I had won that election, there might not have been a Sam. If you ask me if I would trade one day of Sam for twelve years in the Nevada state senate, my answer would be categorically "Not a chance." I didn't run for office for a number of years, but those years were probably my most productive in my community. I became president of the Women's Democratic Club; I was national committeewoman for the Democratic Party; and I became involved in a myriad of community endeavors, including the UNLV Alumni Association, where I served as secretary. I was president of the public broadcasting station in Las Vegas. **It was a time of tremendous personal growth.** My husband and I divorced, but he continued to be a deeply committed father to our boys.

During all this time, I also practiced law on the side. In 1990, I was hired by one of the hotels as their director of government and legal affairs. That was the beginning of eight years of an incredible work experience in the gaming industry, the lifeblood of my community.

I could do all this only because my first husband is the best father I have ever met. He was more than a partner in raising our children. Furthermore, our children's grandparents live in Las Vegas, and they were very hands-on. My political career has been a family endeavor, and I think it would have been extraordinarily difficult otherwise.

I was appointed to the University and Community College Board of Regents to fill an unexpired term. I stood for election twice, so I served eight years. Talk about going full circle: I was part of the governing body of the university system, and one of the schools, of course, was UNLV. So here I was governing the same institution of higher learning that I had attended as a first-time college-goer in 1968. From there I ran for Congress in a very difficult election, and now I'm serving in Congress.

**I always had my priorities set. The most important were my kids and my family. They were my source of strength when I was growing up and are my source of strength now. From that, everything else flows.**

My life pretty much mirrors modern American life. I've been a student on her own, I've been a married woman, I've been a young mother, I've been a divorced mother, I've been a single parent, I've won elections, I've lost elections, and we've had health problems in our family. **Life is based on faith, but if you believe in yourself, and you know what is important to you, you're going to be okay.**

I believe one person can make a difference, and **public service gives me the opportunity to give back something to this country that has given my family so much.** That is the very essence and core of what I do and why I do it. **I'm extraordinarily patriotic because I know what this country has done for my family,** and I know we are just one of millions of people that would agree.

# SHE LEARNED AS MUCH FROM HER FAILURES AS HER SUCCESSES

## Kay Bailey Hutchison

U.S. SENATOR FROM TEXAS

*Kay Bailey Hutchison, Republican senator from Texas, is the first woman to represent her state in the U.S. Senate. She graduated from the University of Texas and U.T. Law School and fully expected to become an attorney. When the major Texas law firms refused to hire women, she backed into a career that became her springboard to political success. She was elected twice to the Texas House of Representatives. Senator Hutchison's great-great-grandfather signed the Texas Declaration of Independence.*

I grew up in the small town of La Marque, Texas. My father was a small businessman, my mother a homemaker. My dad worked very hard and was principled and honest. Mother was smart, creative, loving, and committed to family. **I identified with both my parents equally. I was the middle child, between two brothers, and my parents treated us equally.**

I took ballet lessons almost every day from kindergarten through high school, **learning discipline and practicing incessantly. Ballet kept me attuned to fitness and helped me develop my appreciation for the arts, which certainly has helped me throughout life. I̦ learned to perform before audiences in school events and civic programs. Ballet also taught me how to get along with others.** We didn't have girls' team sports, **but ballet was the closest I could get to teamwork and sports performance.**

**Brownies, Girl Scouts, and church activities taught me values, and I was active in student government.** I read so much that when I was in the sixth grade I couldn't fulfill the biography reading requirement because I had already read every biography in the library. **Those biographies were so inspirational. They encouraged me to think I could do what I wanted to do and break the mold, that I could contribute to my town, my state,**

or my country. I had a special confidence that I could do whatever I wanted to do even though I didn't have women role models. I never thought it was remarkable that I would want to go to law school or be someone in my own right.

My parents were very encouraging. Every time I wanted to do something out of the ordinary, they were slightly surprised but never negative. My public school teachers were wonderful. I'm still the office proofreader in my Senate office because I learned to speak and write English properly. **We respected our teachers and our elders; it was the kind of childhood that every American child should have.**

**I was always among the top students.** My mother told me I had a very high I.Q. but never told me what it was. **I also had setbacks.** I was neither the prettiest girl nor the best dancer. **If I didn't get the part that I wanted or wasn't the lead in a ballet performance, I worked harder until I could get ahead. I tried out for cheerleader in my sophomore year at the University of Texas and didn't win, but worked and worked at it, so when I tried out again in my junior year, I won. Those minor setbacks helped me prepare for later, bigger setbacks.**

I didn't study in college and made only average grades. I belonged to a sorority, and was involved in student activities. In law school, I really enjoyed studying and was in the top half of my class. **I realized in law school how much I had missed in college by not studying.**

When I graduated from law school, I couldn't get a job because law firms didn't hire women. I'd looked for about three months and kept hitting a brick wall. Then I got a job in TV that was better than what I had originally wanted. I actually backed into it. I was driving by the NBC affiliate in Houston on my way home from another interview. I turned in on a lark, walked in the door, and said to the receptionist, "I'd like to interview for a job." She asked, "What kind of job?" and I answered, "Well, a news reporter job." The news director actually came out to see me, and I told him I didn't have any experience in news, but I had a law degree and would be interested in becoming a news reporter. He kept a straight face and said, "I don't have anything, but don't take another job until you hear from me again." Two weeks later, I was offered a job in the legal department for the city of Houston. I called the news director of the television station to tell him I was going to take the city job. He shocked me by saying, "I was just about to call you, because I have a job for you." He wanted to assign me coverage of the legislature and politics and thought I'd be the "perfect person" because I had a law degree. That position started a whole new movement in television in Texas, because until then, local television stations did not cover the legislature full-time.

I was then asked to consider running for the state legislature by the Harris County Republican Party chairman. I was twenty-nine years old. When I told my parents, they were concerned because they thought politics would be a very tough life, but they totally supported me. Dad walked door-to-door with me when I was campaigning. I was the first Republican woman elected to the Texas House of Representatives in 1972, and was reelected in 1974. I left the legislature to take an appointment from President Gerald Ford, where I stayed until I got married and moved to Dallas, Texas.

I lost a race for Congress in 1982. I was very disappointed and thought my political career was over. I bought a business, invested in a new bank, was civically active, and became president of a chamber of commerce. It wasn't until eight years later that the tide of Texas turned. I thought Republicans could be elected statewide and ran for state treasurer on the Republican ticket, worked hard, and won. When Senator Lloyd Bentsen vacated his seat in 1993, I was in a very good position to run in the special election to succeed him. If I had won that original seat in Congress, I'm convinced I wouldn't have had the same opportunity. **I've learned as much from my failures as I have from my successes, and I've had a lot of both in my life. Learning that you can pick yourself up, dust yourself off, and keep on going paved the way for me to do something better than I had originally sought to do.**

**Anne Armstrong,** whom I interviewed for my television station when she became the co-chairman of the Republican National Committee, **was an important mentor.** She gave me my first real experience in national politics. I had been thinking of running for the legislature at the time I interviewed her in 1971. She asked if I would be interested in being her press secretary in Washington. I offered to do that for six months, but told her I wanted to come home and run for the legislature. Anne has shown me much about how hard women have to work to succeed. **Ours became a lifelong friendship. She's the mentor in my life, my parents have been the anchors, and my husband has been my partner.**

I've been married since 1978 and have two stepdaughters and five grandchildren. My husband was a state representative from Dallas. We met in the legislature and have been great friends and partners ever since. He's the most loyal friend and supporter I have. **My very first absolute is to keep our family intact. Everyone has set-backs in life. It's having a supportive family no matter what happens that keeps me on an even keel. I believe we must nurture those relationships and make them our first priority in order to stay level with the ups and downs of life.**

**My advice to girls is to work hard and not expect anyone to give them what they haven't earned.** Some young women graduate from business or law school and expect to become vice presidents or partners in two years without earning it. But **experience determines success. If you get a break, that's great, but if you don't, you can make your own breaks. In life, perseverance is more important than luck.**

**My present goal is to be the best United States senator that I can be.**

# DRIVEN BY THE NEEDS OF HER PEOPLE

## Wilma P. Mankiller

### PRINCIPAL CHIEF OF THE CHEROKEE NATION (1985–1995)

*Wilma Mankiller was the first woman ever to hold the office of Chief of the Cherokee Nation. She led the second-largest tribe in the United States, with 140,000 people over 7,000 square miles. People did not take easily to the idea of a woman as chief, but Wilma brought about major economic, social, and educational improvements for Native American people while overcoming incredible difficulties. Wilma's name, "Mankiller," is a historical term of respect for Indian warriors who protected villages.*

I'm a middle child of eleven children. My parents had an enormous influence on me. I identified primarily with my father, who introduced us to reading. There were always books around our house, which transported us into another world, and **we read anything we could get our hands on,** from Nancy Drew mysteries to *One Flew Over the Cuckoo's Nest.* My father sometimes acted as an interpreter in our isolated rural community for Cherokee people who received legal documents or other papers they didn't understand. **Our home was a gathering place for people in our community.**

Even compared to other children in our community, we were very poor. We had no television, no indoor plumbing, no electricity, and very little contact with the world outside our community, but **we did all kinds of things as a family.** We played board games, Chinese checkers, cards, and dominoes. We also went visiting, to tribal ceremonies, or to church. My father and brothers fished, and we cooked the fish right on the banks of the creek.

**There was always a backdrop of music, people playing guitar or fiddle. We considered the entire natural world as art. We had all of nature to learn from and appreciate.** There was an ever-changing landscape right outside and lots of living plants and animals to be fascinated by. We gathered water for our household from a natural spring on our land, and we shared that spring with bobcats, mountain lions, wild pigs, and other animals.

As long as I can remember, people have said I always tried to find a way to put things in a positive light. I learned by watching how important community was and how important it was for people to be interdependent. For example, if someone had eggs and someone else had crops or milk, they would trade with one another. They were forward-thinking, trying to find something good about the most terrible circumstances. As a result of that, I have had a lifelong commitment to helping to support and build communities.

Our one-room country schoolhouse that my father had helped build was predominantly Cherokee. We really did walk three miles to school. There were fewer than one hundred children in our first through eighth grades. School was a mixed experience, and I was an average student. We were sometimes teased because we were poor, but school was also an exciting place where I could learn new things, have new experiences, and make friends.

Adolescence was very devastating. When I was ten, we moved from a rural Oklahoma setting to the San Francisco Bay area as part of a Bureau of Indian Affairs relocation program. The federal government told my father that we would have a better life there. We got on a train in our little town in Stillwell, Oklahoma, and a few days later we were in downtown San Francisco at a rugged hotel, followed by a very rough housing project. That became the "better life" that the government had promised us. We stayed in San Francisco for almost twenty years before I returned home in the mid-seventies.

Public schools in San Francisco were like another planet. Going from a small, predominantly Cherokee country school to a large urban school was completely disorienting. In Oklahoma, people knew us; they knew "Mankiller" was a name of respect. In San Francisco, the fact that we spoke with a different accent and dressed differently, like country kids, immediately labeled us as different. We were teased about our name. It was a stressful experience.

The San Francisco Indian Center, a community center that helped families who had moved from various tribal communities around the United States, became our social center and oasis. There we could talk with other families who had been through similar experiences, which helped a lot. I was influenced by the many strong and interesting Native American women involved in the Indian

Center. They faced daunting problems but still managed to contribute to the community and do volunteer work.

By high school, I had made more of an adjustment and spent a considerable amount of time at the Indian Center, where there were a television, a billiards table, snack bar, jukebox, and other kids. The Indian Center was the place I felt most comfortable.

Education was definitely not the biggest influence in my life. **I never fit in in high school.** I was a great student in English literature and social studies, but not in math and the sciences. After high school, I attended Skyline College and then transferred to San Francisco State. My overall major was social sciences because I did well in them. I both worked and received some scholarships and eventually went to graduate school at the University of Arkansas at Fayetteville. While I was in graduate school, I was seriously injured in a head-on collision on my way back to the Cherokee Nation to see if I could do contract work. It took me about a year to recover from it. My friend was killed in the accident. The accident changed my life. **I had experienced death, felt its presence, touched it, and then let it go. It was a very spiritual thing, a rare natural gift. From that point on, I've always thought of myself as the woman who lived before and the woman who lived afterward.**

**The greatest influences for me were the women's, Civil Rights, and free speech movements, and the conflict over the Vietnam War.** I was riding on a bus in San Francisco by the armory at 14th Street and Mission and saw antiwar demonstrators being attacked simply for expressing their opinions. **Seeing women stand up and assume leadership positions and talk about issues that were important to all Americans had a great impact on me. I watched Native Americans speaking out. We were looking for a different way of life.**

In 1969, my whole family got involved by helping to support the occupation of Alcatraz Island, which is off San Francisco Bay. It was a Native American statement about federal lands being returned to native people. I volunteered for the Pitt River Tribe of Northern California for four years and for the local Native American adult education programs.

**As with many women, I became involved in politics by volunteering.** I moved from being the woman who made copies, wrote speeches, and arranged meetings to someone who had definite, strong opinions and spoke up at meetings. **I crossed a line during that period of incredible activity, and once I crossed it, I never went back to being a support person only. Instead, I initiated activities.** I became director of a Native American youth center in Oakland, even though I didn't know anything about running a youth center or developing a curriculum. I managed to put all that together.

**I had to overcome being different from other women in my generation.** I'm fifty-four, and most women of my generation seemed content being mothers and wives. I felt many internal struggles. I was married and had two children, but I wanted more than that. **I wanted to be engaged in the world around me.** I asked myself, "Why can't I be like everybody else? Why am I different?" I had to make a conscious choice during that time about whether or not I wanted society to define what it meant to be a woman. I decided that even with sacrifices to be made, I was going to define womanhood for myself. **I accept being different as part of what I am. I'm motivated more by issues, by passion, and by things external to myself than I am by individual personal achievement or by what society tells me I should be doing.**

**Everything I've done that led me on the path to being Chief was motivated by passion and by the issues.** For example, I learned to type very fast because the tribe I volunteered for needed help typing their legal briefs. I learned to write grants because I wanted to develop programs for the San Francisco Bay area Indian community. When I ran for office of Deputy Chief, I ran because I had skills. I became director of the Cherokee Nation's Community Development Department because I had skills in housing. There were some of our people who really needed housing, so I felt I could do something about that. **Even if I lacked self-confidence to run for office, my feelings about the issues at hand would overcome that because I felt so strongly about them. I haven't followed a linear path or thought of my work in terms of a career but rather as a way of life. I saw needs and felt moved to try to do something about them.**

I left Oakland and returned to Oklahoma, divorced, with my two children, and I had no idea what I was going to do. I just knew it was time to go home. I had no money or car. We rented a U-Haul with all of our belongings, came home, and I got a low-level management job with the Cherokee Nation.

Six years later, our Chief asked me to run for office, and I declined. **Then I went with my present husband to a rural community and saw people living in very terrible conditions. I decided I had to run for office. There was every imaginable kind of opposition to my running.** I was a newcomer, and I'd been involved in Alcatraz Island and other Native rights issues that some people considered radical. **The biggest issue was my being a woman, which had never occurred to me initially.** I had expected to have a lot of support from women in my initial election. Surprisingly, my biggest support base was the older people. I served as Chief of the Cherokee Nation for ten years.

**The most important thing that anybody can bring to leadership is a positive attitude.** People don't want to follow leaders who are whiny or negative, or who give up. When we meet people, we have choices about how we deal with them. We can focus on either the negative or the positive attributes of their personality. **It's very critical to focus on the positive. If you're forward-thinking and have a positive attitude, you see barriers as challenges.** We need to look for ways around or over or under the barriers, but we can't see them as reasons to give up.

Native American people and Native American girls have been quick to recognize the importance of women stepping up to leadership. **Our world can't be balanced unless we hear the voices of both men and women, and have equity. Native American girls must step up to lead in good and positive ways.**

# $\mathcal{A}$ Wife, Mother, and Congresswoman

## Barbara Cubin

U.S. CONGRESSWOMAN FROM WYOMING

*Some women lose their sense of identity when they struggle to balance many roles. Many outwardly champion career first, perhaps worrying that others will take them less seriously if they identify themselves first and foremost as wives or mothers. Congresswoman Barbara Cubin represents herself as mainly a wife and mother, but in that role she represents Wyoming well. Her strong identity makes her a more impassioned and effective champion of family-centered political causes. In her 1994 election to the U.S. House of Representatives, she carried all but five of Wyoming's twenty-three counties. Her sons are happily off to college at the University of Wyoming. Barbara's husband, Dr. Frederick Cubin, and their boys have always been her steadfast support system.*

My mother, a divorcée with four children, married my father when I was about four. There were seven children, and we lived in a twenty-room home with nine bedrooms. My father had three children from his first marriage, and there were six of us between the ages of three and six when they married. This was in the fifties, when blended families weren't common, and I remember people saying to my mother, "Now which are yours and which are Russ's?" and she would say, "They're all mine, they're all ours." That's the way we all feel about one another today too.

My father was the organized, practical one, and was also extraordinarily honest. He would say, "Don't do anything when you're by yourself that you wouldn't do if someone was there."

My mother tackled every adversity and taught me compassion and empathy. If there was a stray kid or a family in the neighborhood that needed help, my mother would take them in. My brother had a friend who had a drug problem, and one night we invited her out to dinner. She agreed but wanted to take her clothes to the Laundromat before she came. While we were out, everything she had was stolen from the dryers. The next morning my mother woke me to go downtown to buy linens, clothes, towels, pajamas, and everything we could to set this woman up again. Anyone else wouldn't have given this woman the time of day.

I went to public schools in Wyoming. **I was in student government all through junior high school and was the class president in seventh grade and student body president in ninth grade. I lost the election in eighth grade. The only other election I ever lost was for prom queen.**

Despite all those honors, I was most insecure in junior high. I was the oldest girl and very small, and both my sisters had started their periods before I did. I thought I was ugly and felt like a creep. **I appeared to be successful, but in reality I suffered in silence. I felt envious of others who were invited to parties and wished I were prettier.**

Fortunately, in ninth grade I met my friends for life. We called ourselves the Swift Six, and they did wonders for my self-confidence. We were actually so close that if one of us didn't have a date, the rest of us would cancel our dates because we weren't going to leave one out. The six of us still get together every year and float down the Platte River on a rubber raft, one raft for us, and one with food, beer, and wine. **The values I see in myself today come from my friends of the same sex.**

I remember two teachers in high school who gave me the benefit of the doubt when I didn't deserve it, and **their confidence and trust in me is what kept me worthy of confidence and trust.**

I remember once there was cheating going on in calculus class. I wasn't one of the people doing the cheating, but **I was letting others crib off my paper. I went to the teacher afterward and said that I felt bad to have been involved in this.** He said, "Barbara, you said your responsibility is not to let other people look at your paper, but your **true responsibility is to learn calculus.**" I realized that showing the other students my paper wasn't worthy. I wanted to be good because it was the right thing to do.

**I was an excellent student in high school and was very active in sports. I set records in track and field.** At one track meet I got four first-place ribbons and one second. I went home sobbing my eyes out because of the second-place ribbon. **My mother was so mad at me because I didn't appreciate what I had won, only what I had lost.** That was a valuable lesson in perspective.

I went to Creighton University. Neither of my parents had been to college, and I had no clue what it was about. I always had an interest in and an aptitude for science and math and started premed, but **I got preoccupied with partying and having fun, and my grades went continually downward.** Chemistry was the only thing I could major in and still graduate at the same time as my class.

As the only girl in the chemistry department, I was discriminated against. At first I'd been rejected by the department, although my grades qualified me. I went to the chair and said, "What's the deal?" He said, "Women don't belong in chemistry." After I complained to the dean, they were forced to take me, but from then on, my life in the department was hell.

I had to give a senior thesis in front of the whole department and was terrified they were going to tear me apart. The night before, I was sitting in the science library reviewing my notes when I broke down crying. Two graduate students asked me what was wrong, and I told them. They looked at my paper, told me how to improve it, and coached me on the questions that would be asked. The next day at my orals, I gave my paper in front of those same graduate students and their friends. They asked me the very questions they had prepared me for. The chairman of the department was happy; he thought the graduate students were really grilling me. **I was happy because they'd known how bad it was for me and prepared me. I passed with flying colors.**

After college, my oldest brother was killed in an industrial accident on a drilling rig, and my mother had a nervous breakdown. I went home to take care of the family. I married my high school sweetheart, who was also my brother's best friend, probably to preserve my brother's relationship for me. The marriage didn't last.

A few years later, I married my present husband, who is a physician. We had two sons. For the next eleven years, I was a stay-at-home mom.

My life in the legislature started when I went with two busloads of people from Casper to the state legislature to lobby for medical malpractice tort reform. My husband's medical practice had attracted my interest in the topic. When we arrived, the legislators were patronizing and rude to us. The speaker of the house at the time had been my junior high school social studies teacher. We told him how disgusted we were, and he suggested I come and help him do something about it. I responded, "I have a seven- and an eleven-year-old. How can I do that?" **He told me simply, "You can," and that's how it all started. I was the reluctant dragon.**

I completed the filing form to run on the Republican ballot for the state legislature, but at the moment I couldn't imagine leaving my children for two days, let alone for the time the job would require. I put the form in an envelope, drove up to the mailbox, and paused before dropping it in the box. The envelope had languished in the car for three weeks and was decorated with muddy dog paw prints, french fry grease, and peanut butter. **I prayed about it, took one last look at the horrible envelope, stuck it in the mailbox, and that was it.** I ran, and I won.

Wyoming has a citizens' legislature, so I only had to go for a month at a time. **All of the legislators stay at the same hotel, and our families are like one big family.** My sons would come and spend a week with me, or I'd go back to Casper on the weekends. It was actually good that I got away from the kids a little because **they learned how to cook and do dishes and lots of things they wouldn't have learned if I'd been there waiting on them.**

I decided I could do more in Congress, so I ran for higher office. There were eight other people in the primary, and **I was the only woman.** The other seven people in the race needed a job. **I was the only one who didn't.** This was what set me apart; I positioned myself as someone who could make the kind of a vote that she, in her heart and conscience, thought was the right vote and not worry about being reelected. I won the election.

**Now I'm a member of Congress, but being a wife and mother is my real job. That's a big difference between men and women in Congress.** I've seen many men become senators or congressmen, then go through mourning and grieving when they leave. I did just the opposite; I did my mourning when I came to Congress because I'd left my support systems—my friends, my family, my husband, my dog—to come to Washington, where I didn't know who the bad guys or good guys were. **I've already had my identity crisis, so when I leave, I will go back to who I am.**

This is my third term in Congress, and I'm running for my fourth. **I ran in the first place because I wanted my children to have a future,** and I thought we were stealing their futures away from them by building a national debt. Young families pay 40 percent of their income in taxes, and that means one of them works to feed the family, and the other works to feed the government, and I think that's so wrong. My goal is to change that.

# SHE WANTED TO BE ANOTHER PERRY MASON

## Martha Coakley

DISTRICT ATTORNEY OF MIDDLESEX COUNTY, MASSACHUSETTS

*Martha Coakley's prosecution of the Louise Woodward "nanny" case, in which a caretaker was charged in the death of an infant, stirred every career woman's fear about child care and also propelled Martha into the public eye. Martha graduated cum laude with a bachelor's degree from Williams College in 1975 and from Boston University School of Law in 1979 with a J.D. degree. She was elected district attorney of Middlesex in November 1998. Her wish to become involved in litigation stemmed from her school debate team experience.*

I grew up the middle child of five, four girls and a boy. **My parents were** Irish-Catholic, firm disciplinarians, and **committed to education as a way to get ahead in life.** My dad served in the navy during World War II, left, then went back during the Korean War. Jokingly, I say I'm a Korean War baby because I was born in 1953. My dad graduated from Brown University in 1942 with a degree in English and had applied to Harvard Law School. He'd been accepted but couldn't afford to go because he was already married with two kids. He went into the insurance industry instead. My mother, a bright woman, was a stay-at-home mom. I'm more like my mother in personality and emotions, but professionally, I'm more like my dad.

**The nuns in our Catholic schools provided us with role models of single career women. We realized that getting married and having children was only one of many options.** My older sister married and had children but also went to college and worked as a teacher, then a banker. Another sister earned graduate degrees in banking and is a career professional. I went to law school, and my younger sister earned a Ph.D. in neuropsychology. **Education, doing our best, independence, and excelling at what we could do well were themes in our childhood.**

The Catholic schools were very big on oratory, and even in the fifth, sixth, and seventh grades, **we were involved in speech and oratory contests.** In fifth grade, I competed in a contest to write an essay and speech on President Kennedy's words, "Ask not what your country can do for you; ask what you can do for your country." I delivered the speech in front of the whole school and wasn't nervous. Later, I was in the Catholic Diocese League for girls' extemporaneous speaking. I won first place in the state, which, as a freshman, I thought was cool. **I had the ability to take in a lot of material on short notice, process it, and then speak about it and be fairly articulate. I did well in competition.**

I also traveled a lot. I'd visit my sister in Washington, D.C., when she was going to school, and would occasionally skip school with my parents' consent to see a play in New York. **I was responsible and never pushed limits or got into trouble. My parents weren't overly restrictive. I never gave them any problems, so I probably got away with more than anyone, and they never worried about me because they trusted me.**

**There were childhood precursors to my political career.** I was secretary of our student council, the typical female role. In the fifth and sixth grades, I was vice president of the Dominic Savio Club (a Catholic youth club named for the patron saint of youth). I participated in something called Girls State as a junior in high school, a weeklong process of exercising democracy. We set up a legislature, mayors, and towns, and elected constitutional officers. **I was governor of Girls State** in Massachusetts. It was the first time anyone from Berkshire County, where I had grown up, had been elected to that position.

**I knew I would have a career very early.** I started college in 1971, on the verge of women's consciousness-raising groups. **It seemed like anything was possible. I could do what I wanted as long as I worked hard. The American Dream was going to be available to women!**

I went to Williams College, **was involved in the newspaper, the radio, and student government there. I liked history and current events. Law school made the most sense for me because it would give me both the academic ticket I needed and the skills to maybe be another Perry Mason. Law was a career in which you could win or lose in the courtroom based on your** merit, not your gender. I thought of it as an end run around what I still saw as the sexist ways the world worked.

I went to law school at Boston University, and one-third of the class members were women. I participated in moot court, which is researching and writing briefs and oral argument for cases. **I was named the best speaker, and our team won the regional championship in the national moot court competition in 1978. It made sense for me to go into litigation.**

**Women are still underrepresented in litigation.** In the '70s, women tended to go into family law or corporate or financial work. They were being hired by firms in representative numbers from their law school classes, but **the real differential came at the fourth-, fifth-, or sixth-year level, a time when many women were having children but also when there were the biggest demands on their time and energy if they were going to become a partner. The firms then and now require total commitment to the billable hour. Women often felt like they had fewer options then, that to have a family meant they had to take jobs with fewer hours. Therefore, some women decided to take jobs with smaller firms, with part-time schedules, or with the government.**

I worked at an insurance defense firm doing litigation. I was in court three out of five days a week, and it was exactly what I wanted. I did my own motions and watched other trial lawyers. After about a year, I realized I preferred broader subjects, so I went to work for a corporate law firm with a litigation department. **I worked with some of the best litigators in Boston.** I thought, "What really happens is that civil cases by and large settle, they don't go to trial; and **if you really want to practice, you want to be in the courtroom; a criminal practice is where it's at.**"

After five years, I decided I wanted to use my skills to argue to a judge or jury. In 1986, the district attorney, the man who held the seat I hold now, offered me a job, and I jumped at the chance to be a beginning prosecutor and learn how to put a case together. That was probably the most fun I had ever had. I was in court every single day, and within four or five months, was handling a jury session. I tried between three to five jury trials a week, worked my way up the ladder, and took more serious cases.

Tom Reilly, who held this seat before me and who is the current attorney general, asked me if I would become chief of the child-abuse unit. It changed my focus as a prosecutor. We worked with child psychologists and medical doctors for kids who have been sexually and physically abused. **I worked with kids who ended up on the autopsy table and parents or caretakers who said, "Gee, we don't know what happened, they just took a minor fall." That laid the groundwork for how I came to be one of the prosecutors in the well-known Louise Woodward "nanny" case.** Things happened pretty fast. We tried that case, and she was found guilty of second-degree murder, and then the judge reduced the verdict to manslaughter.

I had run for a state representative seat in Dorchester. I liked politics, watched it from afar, read it, talked it, so I thought, "Here is a chance at a fairly local level to throw my hat into the ring and see what happens." **I didn't win, but I learned a lot about what I have to do to run for office.**

Shortly after the Louise Woodward case, when Tom Reilly decided he was going to run for attorney general, people encouraged me to run for the district attorney seat. I sold my house in Boston, left the job there, which I had to do in order to raise money for the campaign, moved to Middlesex County, and then spent the next nine months, seven days a week, twelve hours a day, appearing at functions, shaking hands, and kissing babies. We were able to win in a very difficult Democratic primary with 47 percent of the vote. There were two men who had gotten into the race before me, and one who had already raised $100,000. After that I faced a Republican candidate, but ours is a Democratic county, so the primary was most important. I was sworn in as district attorney on January 6, 1999.

I'm close to my three sisters. After both of my parents died (my father died of a heart attack in 1993, and my mother of leukemia in 1995), my only brother, Edward, who was probably the brightest in the family but who suffered from mental illness and depression, committed suicide. He'd been a very difficult child for my parents because as he matured, it became harder and harder to cope with his mental illness. **That has influenced all of us in our perspective on families. My brother influenced the way I see the criminal justice system.** As I do my job in a county with fairly sophisticated communities, we still have parents who fail to recognize that their kids are showing signs of depression and mental illness. I want to change that.

My sisters and I knew we wanted to have careers. But we also realized how hard it can be to balance the competing demands of family and career, particularly for women in high-pressure, heavy-workload jobs. I have continued to wrestle with that throughout my adult life and have always been in awe of people who are able to have both. I recently became engaged to the deputy superintendent of the Cambridge Police Department. He's fifty-one; I'm forty-six. He's never been married either. We started dating before my primary last year and went out for about nine or ten months. Although we had never talked about getting married, one day he produced a diamond. I was surprised, but I'm pleased, so we're getting married soon.

# Girl Scouting, Ballroom Dancing, and Battling Dyslexia Gave Her Confidence

## Martha Lindner

### MANAGING LAW PARTNER

*Attorney Martha Lindner struggled to read, but she overcame that obstacle to graduate from Trenton State College with highest honors and pass a multistate bar examination in the top 10 percent nationally. Her successful law practice specializes in family law and immigration. She has been a leader in political action and has managed to combine her career successes with her family successes. All three of her children have found successful direction, but Martha is especially proud that her son has chosen to be part of her firm, Lindner and Lindner.*

I've run a successful law office as a managing law partner for over twenty-five years. I specialize in family law, and when people are going through crises, I help them put their lives together. I've been involved in Republican politics for the last ten years. I am currently a trustee on the board for the Bucks County Community College.

When I was in elementary school, I was really lost because I'm dyslexic. I could never keep up with my classmates. I knew I should have been able to do things, but I couldn't. I couldn't remember my telephone number, and I didn't know why. I felt like there was a person trapped inside me that couldn't get out. I was very shy.

An incident in fifth grade taught me an important lesson. I was very musical. I played piano, and I could sing. The music teacher asked each of us to sing a song because she was selecting people to sing solos. I didn't project my voice because I was afraid. My girlfriend was chosen instead. I went home, angry at myself. I knew I could sing better than she could, and I blamed myself because I didn't do my best. **I learned if I don't take the risk of doing my best, I'll lose opportunities.** Not getting that solo was a turning point.

When I moved to a different school, I decided it was time to give it my best. **No one in the new school knew how I had done be-**

fore, and I decided to push myself as far as I could. In sixth grade, I had a teacher who took the time to encourage me to be successful. By eighth grade, I began to understand that I was a smart human being, and if I tried hard enough, I could make great grades. Other people in the class would do homework in an hour; I'd be struggling for three hours. I never had time to reread chapters because I was so slow. I developed a special skill because I had to understand and remember what I read the first time, so I could retrieve it for an exam. My reading problem actually led me to better comprehension and memory.

My father, who died recently at the age of ninety-seven, had a sixth-grade education and was a businessman, and my mother was a high school graduate but wore the pants in the family. I remember a story from when I was about five. We were looking for a car. Men usually did all the negotiating, and my mother was coaching my father, "Now you go in there and you tell them this, and tell them that so you can get us a good deal." I was in the backseat, and I knew that if my mother talked to that salesman, she would get what she wanted. My father, whom she was pushing as a front, couldn't do it. He was a gentle, kind person. I think I saw him upset only four or five times in my life. He didn't know how to push or be competitive, but my mother intuitively did.

My brother is seven years older than I am. I had the advantages of being a second child and yet like an only child. My mother used to take me places every Sunday. We didn't have money to travel far, but she took me to museums, and we went to Washington, D.C. Those trips compensated for what I couldn't learn from reading. Through them I found the joy of learning and developed great curiosity. My mother has her own natural curiosity, and although she is ninety-one, we continue to go to museums.

I often wonder now where I found the courage to come out of my shyness. Scouting was very important in my life—Girl Scouts, Senior Scouts, and Mariners. I earned all the different badges, and I couldn't get enough of them. Music was also important because I was good at it. I composed and was active in every musical activity in junior and senior high school. That helped build my confidence.

In junior and senior high, I was awkward and felt ugly. I

remember walking home from eighth grade saying, "My feet are too big, my stomach is too big, I have a terrible waistline, I have a big nose, and I'm ugly. What can I do about it?" I thought I was also un-popular, gangly, and unwanted. **Now I look at my pictures from then, and I really wasn't so bad. It was very difficult going through that.**

I had a friend in middle school that I was very close to, who was very competitive with me. I remember we were involved in Girl Scouts together, learning navigation. Our project was to go to the Coast Guard and write a report about it. **She took all my informa-tion, submitted it as her own, and took full credit for what I had done.** I was aghast and upset for a long time. Nothing like that had ever happened to me. I was very angry, and **I told her so.** I went to her mother, who, incidentally, was the one who had taken us to the Coast Guard to learn the course, and she stood by her daughter. **That was another lesson in life.**

This girl and I were in competition with everything. Piano was my main instrument. I also played violin, and it seemed like in everything we did, she was first chair and I was second chair. There were a lot of things in my life that I came in second on, and I believe I really deserved first. That was part of the person inside me trying to come out. **I was holding myself back. When I look back on it, I wasn't willing to take the risk, to move out and give it my all so I could come in first.** Then when someone else came in first, I was angry at myself.

I had another defining moment in high school. I wanted to go to college, and my parents and I had a conference with the guidance counselor. I had taken my SATs, and I was still struggling at that time because I was a slow reader. My counselor looked at the test scores and said to my parents, "Your daughter is an overachiever. She's making good grades, but that's because she works so hard. If she goes to college, she's going to flunk out in the first year. Girls don't need to go to college. They're better off getting married any-way." She killed the little enthusiasm my parents had about sending me to college. That guidance counselor set me back many years be-cause I didn't go to college directly out of high school as a result of that conference.

At nineteen, I went into dancing with the Arthur Murray Dance

Studio. I became a very good ballroom dancer. I taught other ball-room teachers and did exhibition work. **When I did exhibition shows, I had to bring myself out. Dancing taught me skills I use as an attorney. I lost my fear and began to realize that I was a nice-looking person.** It was as if I were a butterfly coming out of a cocoon that had trapped me all my life. **Being able to speak in a courtroom came through my ballroom dancing experience.**

**I had a very good friend from ballroom dancing who was a great listener.** I told her I felt like Gulliver in the land of Lil-liputians, when they tied him down with tiny strings and held him captive. I felt the tiny strings that were holding me back were break-ing one at a time. I was ready to fly.

I remember when my husband asked me to marry him. He wanted to become engaged right away. I had some reservations. About three months into our courtship, he gave me an ultimatum. Either I was going to agree to marry him, or he was going back to California. I really loved him, but I couldn't have said that then. **I went to New York City to hunt down my good friend, who was now a nurse in a hospital, and I said, "I must talk to you."** I hadn't seen her in about a year. We went back to her room, and **sat there for three hours as I talked my whole mind out about this guy who wanted to marry me.** I didn't know what to do. I walked out say-ing, "I've made up my mind. I'm going to marry him." I thanked my friend for having talked with me, and she responded, "Martha, I never said a word." My husband and I have been happily married for thirty-eight years.

Shortly after we were married, I became pregnant with my first child. I was battling morning sickness. Instead of offering me crack-ers and ginger ale, my husband's response was, "Why don't you go to college now and take as many courses as you can take?" That was the beginning. When I finally went to college, my reading skills had caught up. I was given a battery of tests and called into the dean's of-fice. The dean said I had done extremely well in math, scoring the highest in the college and at the ninety-ninth percentile nationally. **I launched my career as a student and went to college while raising my young children.** The children had to go to bed at eight because I had to study. I studied into the night and was determined to earn a doctorate degree in something. I took many math and science courses, and I ultimately graduated from Trenton State College. It took me six years because I had three children at the time.

When I graduated, I tied for first out of a class of thirteen hundred students. I had a 3.96 average. I wanted to become a nuclear physicist, but the department chairman for science warned me that I would never get a job in their college and probably never with the government because they didn't hire women in nuclear physics. They said that all the time and effort that is put into women would be wasted because they would have children and quit, or they would move away to follow their husbands' careers. I had passed the biology final exam with a higher score than anyone else who had ever taken it, but they didn't think I could ever get a job! I was very disappointed. **I went to a college library and went through books about different professions.** I was interested in medicine and law. I believed medicine was a closed door to me because I was over thirty. There seemed to be some break in law because at that time they were accepting a few more women. I went for law, and I have never regretted that decision.

My husband was very supportive. I had to take the LSAT admissions exam before I even applied to law school. That was a big step. He urged me, "Go. You have nothing to lose. You can do it." If he hadn't said that, I don't think I would have walked out the door to take the exam. He was supportive throughout law school and my career. It was difficult for him because he'd been brought up as a traditional male. **We were making a change in the way people looked at family in our society.** People would come up to him and say, "How are you going to feel when your wife is making more money than you?" He had a strong self-concept. **He never let those comments get him down, and together we took care of the children.** My husband's a teacher, so he could be home at a reasonable hour after school for the kids. I would come home around six and spend time with the children until they went to bed, and then I would study. I started after their bedtime and studied until three in the morning. I'd get four hours of sleep, and that's what I did for three years, seven days a week. That was part of the reason my health broke. The habit of getting by on less sleep stayed with me for quite a while. Even today, I probably do best with about five to six hours of sleep, but I can't go on four hours anymore.

My youngest child was four, my middle one was seven, and my oldest one was nine when I started law school. I learned later I was among the first women (there were three of us) with children they admitted that year because they were not sure anyone could do both. Villanova University Law School was about an hour away, so it also meant traveling.

When I went to law school in 1972, nobody had ever heard of a woman becoming an attorney. Strangers attacked me verbally at parties, saying, "How does it feel to be neglecting your children and going to law school?" I had to be strong to ignore the hostility and continue. **"Just do it," I would repeat to myself.** I had faith that the kids would grow up great. They did, and my son is now my law partner.

I had to complete law school by the normal three-year schedule. Law school accepts no excuses under any circumstances. It was physically hell. I ran my health to the ground and had tremendous lung problems. One semester, the doctors wanted me in the hospital. I simply said, "No, I'm going to law school, and there's no time for the hospital." The hardest challenge was getting up the steps from the parking lot with my books. I would make it up one step, then pull up my briefcase and sit on it to catch my breath. I just didn't have the strength because I didn't have the oxygen.

When I graduated from law school, nobody wanted to hire me. That's why I went into my own practice. **It's important for all young people, particularly women, to realize that sometimes what you think is the worst thing that ever happened to you turns out to be the best thing.** That happened to me with my practice. After the first couple of years, I was way ahead of my classmates in earning money. Even more important, it allowed me to combine my roles as a mother and as a professional woman. I didn't have to answer to anyone. If I wanted to take off an afternoon and go to see my kids in a play at school, I could go. I could have it all—career, kids, and family.

# 3

# The Shatterers of Glass Ceilings

$\mathcal{M}$ORE women today are seizing opportunities to be business leaders; glass ceilings are being shattered on a daily basis. The successful women in our study included executives and entrepreneurs from for-profit businesses as well as administrators of not-for-profit organizations. What they all shared is a certain determination and self-efficacy—a sense that they could overcome the obstacles in their way.

## *Results from the* See Jane Win *Study*

Businesswomen in our survey tended to be more socially involved than women in some of the other career groups. They often described themselves as leaders while they were growing up, and many had a colorful history of entrepreneurial activities. They included, but went far beyond, lemonade stands and Girl Scout cookies.

Women executives in for-profit business often picked math as their strong subject, while for those in not-for-profit business favored social studies and history. High percentages of the women in business went to women's colleges and received leadership opportunities there.

The women in for-profit business in the *See Jane Win* study indicated the most financial job satisfaction but were the least happy in their home lives and had the highest divorce rate compared to other career categories. None of these findings held for the women who led not-for-profit organizations. It may well be that the very competitiveness and achievement orientation that led to their extreme success in the career world could have interfered with their other relationships. Despite the negative comparisons to other groups, remember that we're speaking relatively; to be included in our study, these women needed to consider themselves happy in their home lives, so it would be inappropriate to draw too many conclusions from this comparison. I definitely don't want to suggest that women in business can't be happy at home and on the job; that certainly wasn't true for the women you'll meet in these pages.

## *How Jane Won*

Most of the businesswomen we interviewed were quite social as girls. CEO Marilyn Carlson Nelson was accepted by both the popular group and the brainy kids. Cathleen Black, president of Hearst Magazines, enjoyed the social part of school as much as the academic. Both Marsha Evans, executive director of Girl Scouts USA, and Charlotte Otto, senior vice president of Procter & Gamble, had to navigate the social whirl over and over each time their families moved, but both credited moving with teaching them adjustment skills. Sandra Fenwick, COO of Children's Hospital in Boston, considered herself very social but carefully prioritized her schoolwork before her social life. Associate Dean Merle Waxman found that her academic achievement was helpful in establishing social success, and she played a mediating role even as a child. Although CEO Katherine Hudson's parents worried that she wasn't social enough, Katherine was content with her small group of friends. She felt validated when her class elected her to give the valedictory address.

The women we interviewed were born entrepreneurs. Charlotte Otto credited Girl Scouts for helping her set goals and accomplish them. Tamara Minick-Scokalo, marketing director of Procter & Gamble, established a business on her own school grounds selling snacks, and Cathleen Black managed to sell Catholic newspapers to her Protestant neighbors! Marva Collins played an important role in her parents' many businesses and worked alongside adults on a daily basis. CEO Patricia Seybold and her friends created plays and circuses; they charged admission, then contributed the proceeds to charities.

Like the women in our *See Jane Win* study, quite a few of the women interviewed for *How Jane Won* attended women's colleges, including Cathleen Black, Marilyn Carlson Nelson, Annik LaFarge, and Phyllis Grann. Contrary to our survey results, the women interviewed for this book seemed to have good marriages and often found innovative approaches to including parenting in their busy schedules. Quite a few had husbands who were extremely active and happy in parenting as well; Marsha Evans and Katherine Hudson even have husbands who are the primary home managers.

As much as I love interviewing these world-beaters, particularly those whose partners have been equally nontraditional as male homemakers, I look forward to the day when women won't have any more ceilings to smash or sticky floors to hold them down. That day continues to be somewhat distant.

# PROTESTANT NEIGHBORS BOUGHT CATHOLIC
# NEWSPAPERS FROM HER

## Cathleen Black

### PRESIDENT OF HEARST MAGAZINES

*In the October 25, 1999, issue of* Fortune *magazine, Cathleen Black was ranked No. 22 among the "Most Powerful Women" in American business. As of 1995, Cathie was the first woman to be named president of Hearst Magazines Division, the world's largest publisher of monthly magazines. Yet, on* Oprah, *when Cathie modestly described her childhood in the Chicago suburbs, she sounded to most people like an ordinary girl. Those who knew her while she was growing up, however, expected great things. She came to Hearst Magazines by way of* Holiday, Travel & Leisure, Ms. *magazine, and eight years as president of the Gannett Company, Inc., and publisher of* USA Today. *With all this success, Cathie and her husband are also managing to raise two children.*

I had a great childhood. I am the youngest of three children and grew up on the not-so-fashionable South Side of Chicago in a very Irish-Catholic neighborhood called South Shore. My mother was Catholic, and my father was Presbyterian. In that era, it was a big deal to have an interfaith marriage. You had to sign on the dotted line to raise your kids as Catholics, so I went to Catholic schools.

In about third grade, we were asked to sell the local Catholic newspaper to our neighbors. One of the Protestant neighbors called my dad, cracking up with laughter. He figured I was going to be great in sales someday because I'd convinced him to buy a subscription even though he wasn't Catholic and hadn't been to church in twenty years.

**Right from the beginning, I had this set of genes that made me an ambitious kid. I was always interested in working.** I wasn't a straight-A student, but **I was always a very good student, and I liked school, my teachers, and my friends,** and the motivation seemed inborn. **Nobody had to sit on me to do my homework. I was naturally responsible.**

I went to an all-girl Catholic high school. I was never the most popular kid in the class, but I had a good circle of friends and was generally a part of the in crowd, although not always the leader. Not long ago, a friend from my childhood sent me a funny birthday card. I must have said something when I was on *Oprah* about not having really known where all of my success came from, and she wrote this very cute note saying, "You may be the only one that didn't think you were destined for success." That was interesting because **I didn't think my life was very different from that of any of the other girls that were part of my group.**

**I always enjoyed sports.** My dad had a theory about sports, which was that **you should learn how to play everything reasonably well so if somebody else in your adult life would ask you to play tennis, for example, you'd be able to hold up your end.** I'm not a ferocious competitor, but **I have always liked competition.** I did a lot of horseback riding when I was young, and I loved the horse shows and winning ribbons and trophies and playing in tennis tournaments. **A pressurized environment has never made me choke.**

**My experience in competition has put me in good stead in the executive role. It allows me to be more comfortable with male executives.** Not that I sit and talk sports on a Monday morning, but **I'm not intimidated by the competitive atmosphere in business meetings.**

**Socializing has always been pretty easy for me. Sometimes I'm quiet,** but I've never been shy. **I liked having a lot of friends and being with people as opposed to being alone.** A few years ago in one of my jobs, a really terrific woman, who had her Ph.D. and was very nice looking, said to me, "Cathie, I watch you come into a group, and you are always so comfortable, even if it's a group of strangers. When I walk into a group, I'm sometimes literally ignored. Do you think it's because I'm small?" I had never really thought about it before. I said to her, "**It's no easier for me to walk into a cocktail party where I don't know anybody than it is for you, but I learned a long time ago, if I walk up to a group of people and wait there for a second or two, then say, 'Hi, I'm Cathie Black,' generally, people will offer their name, and they will be pleasant and friendly.**" It was interesting that she thought it was so much easier for me. Being tall is an asset for a woman or a man. My family is tall. I'm five feet seven and a half, my dad was six-two, my brother is six-five, my sister is five-seven, and my mother was five-seven. **There is a sense of confidence that comes from that. I never felt small anywhere.**

I don't remember anything terribly difficult in middle school and high school. I had a couple of boyfriends, but **I never went off the deep end in terms of being rebellious. I was a fairly typical teenager, if one assumes that not being rebellious is typical.** I'm sure I was moody, but by today's parlance, I didn't have blue hair or seven pierced ears or rings through my nose or anything like that. **I was a good kid, obeyed my parents, went out socially, and had nice friends.**

**During the summers, I always found jobs, even though I could have been just a "country club kid," playing tennis and going to the beach.** I did everything from cashiering to gift wrapping at Marshall Field and Co. I remember earning exactly $1.07½ an hour, paid in cash. (It was the early sixties!) I chose the gift wrapping over operating the elevator, which paid $1.33 an hour. If I were really money-driven, I suppose I would have gone for more money, but it was one of those big, old-fashioned elevators with the clanging gates, and the operator had to adjust the elevator cage to the floor. I thought, "Oh no. I'll be throwing up all day long."

During high school I also worked at Saks Fifth Avenue on the "College Board" (a glorified sales job) and in a variety of offices. I thought it was fun to get on the train to go to work. **The independence was even more important than earning the money.**

**I went to a women's Catholic college** in Washington, D.C., and I've been involved in women's issues over the years. **The achievement statistics for women who have graduated from women's colleges are pretty compelling because we were surrounded by female role models.** If the editor of the paper, the coach, and the head of the basketball team were all women, we never thought there was anything we couldn't do.

**I always dreamed of coming to New York City.** I'd have a roommate and a job. I'd say to my mother that I knew I wanted my life to be different than hers. It hurt her feelings that I didn't want to be a traditional mom at home. **I wanted children and a spouse,**

but those would come along with a career. My mother died a long time ago, and my father died when I was twenty-three. My dad would have loved my career and how my life turned out, but my mother would have had difficulty understanding it.

I'm much more like my dad. He had his own private-label food-manufacturing company of high-end gourmet specialty items before gourmet foods were what they are today. Unfortunately, he went through a progression of eye diseases, resulting in the loss of his eyesight when he was about fifty. He died at sixty-three.

**Having a parent who has a severe disability like blindness puts you into a different crowd in your mind. I wanted my family to be like everybody else's.** If I had any advice to girls on that, it would be to **try to be as understanding as possible of other people and appreciative that no one's situation is perfect.**

My father's blindness only became apparent in my junior year of high school. **Going away to college was a given,** but it was certainly very hard on my mother. I came home holidays and summer, but she shouldered the burden of his deteriorating health. The last decade of his life was heartbreak for all of us, but certainly it was most difficult for my mother, who was there on a daily basis.

Despite my dad's worsening eyesight and health, **my parents always encouraged me to move beyond dealing with home problems.** For example, I spent my junior year of college abroad in Rome. My mother had had a bad accident that summer, and my father was blind. My dad said, "Honey, you're only twenty years old, and your whole life is ahead of you, and we think you should go anyway." My parents wouldn't let their situation hold me back.

In my freshman year of college, a shock for me was walking by a line of telephone booths in my dormitory and hearing girls screaming, shouting, and fighting with their parents on the phone, night after night. I was flabbergasted girls could have such bad relationships with their parents. **I might have been feeling a little bad for myself because my father was blind, and he couldn't participate the way a lot of dads did, but I realized that other parents and other homes weren't perfect either.**

I wanted to come to New York because media, publishing, communications, and advertising were all there. My dad wouldn't allow me to sign a lease with roommates until I had a paying job. He could have afforded it, but he had no intention of paying my rent, so my parents gave me a little money for the first six months to help me get established on my own. He said, "I know there are other parents who will support their kids, but I believe that once kids are out of college, they should be supporting themselves." I think he hoped that I would come back to Chicago, but he knew deep in his heart that I wouldn't.

The job market was a rude awakening. To placate my folks, I interviewed in Chicago first, but it was hard for women to find a job in 1966. I naively thought I could find an executive training program at a big advertising agency. The interviewer said, "Why would we put somebody like you in our executive training program? You're an attractive young woman, and you'll be getting married in a couple of years. We'll have wasted all we've invested in you." I nearly flipped! It made me more determined to go to New York.

**My cousin arranged for me to have a temporary job as a receptionist** (her way of getting me to New York), **and I used that time for interviewing.** In a very short time I found a good job as an advertising sales assistant at a large magazine publishing company.

**I really liked what I was doing and knew that I was good at it.** My first boss was a woman, and **I remember thinking to myself, "I can do her job."** I would get in one job and look at who was around me, who had the offices (usually the men), and I would say, "I can do that." Then I'd get into that job, and I'd say, "How about the next one?" Then I'd think, "They're all so smart." **I'd get up to their job and think, "Well, I'm as smart as they are. I can do that."**

More than twenty years have passed since I got my first job. When I talk to teenage girls, **it's hard for them to imagine that these opportunities didn't always exist.** I don't know that it's real for them. They're skeptical when I tell them they **couldn't have gotten a loan or gone to Harvard in my era.** It's exciting for me today to think about all the opportunities that are going to be available for my eight-year-old daughter. As for her future, it's unlimited. She may decide to be a writer, or maybe she'll be a musician or mathematician. **I just want her to be happy and fulfilled.**

**I have fulfilled my dreams and more.** Who thought that a young girl from the South Side of Chicago with no family in the media business and very little exposure to New York City could come here on her own and get started and love it, and become president of a large division of a corporation? **I get up in the morning and am excited about what I'm going to do that day. I have a wonderful marriage, two great kids, and a very interesting career. I feel like I have it all.**

# "*I* CAN" BECAME HER MANTRA

## Marva Collins

FOUNDER OF URBAN PREPARATORY SCHOOL, CHICAGO

*Marva Collins started the Westside Preparatory School in 1975 on the second floor of her home in inner-city Chicago with her own children and four others. At the end of the first year, each child scored at least five grade levels higher than when they'd started. She was later offered the position of secretary of education by then-president Ronald Reagan but declined in order to stay with her school. The schools that embraced her methods enthusiastically have enjoyed greatly improved Iowa Basic Skills Test scores. Marva has been awarded over forty-two honorary doctoral degrees and has received many prestigious awards, including the Jefferson Award for the Greatest Public Service Benefiting the Disadvantaged. She has made an impressive difference for thousands of children as both an administrator and a teacher.*

I grew up as an African-American during the worst period of racism in Alabama. If I was called a racist name and I told my dad and my grandfather, they would just look at me without surprise and say, "And . . . ?" **Nevertheless, we believed that the world was a wonderful place, and our lives would be what we made of them.** People would say to me as a child, "Don't you know? Black kids can't do those things." **It never dawned on me that because I was a black kid, I was inferior to anyone.** I never believed the word "can't." It's a word I don't use. Everything I've done in my life I've been told I couldn't do, so **when someone tells me what I can't do, I know I'm on the right track. "I can" has become my mantra.**

**I believe that God and I can do anything.** One Sunday at Sunday school, when the pianist wasn't there, the minister said, "Who can play the piano?" I said, "I can." In fact I had only just started taking lessons. Now that I look back, it was very embarrassing. I actually got up there and made a mess, and the people in church sang right along with me. The minister said, "That kid is so bright. She's going to do great things one day."

I had a grandmother with a fifth-grade education who taught me to read and spell the books of the Bible when I was four. She taught me the Proverbs and to love poetry. **She said, "A good name will go farther than you will ever go." The words of my grandmother come back to me now.**

I was constantly curious and forever asking questions. My parents would say to me, "We'll give you ten dollars if you don't ask any more questions for the next hour." My parents said I was a different child because I was headstrong. I liked to play school, but if I couldn't be the teacher, I wouldn't play.

I lived in a small town, but **because of my reading and exposure, I knew there was a bigger world out there.** There were no libraries or bookstores, but my parents and I traveled to larger cities, where I could buy books. While my mother shopped, she would find me sitting on the floor in the book department reading books. If we visited someone, the first thing I'd look for in their house was a book. I've always been an avid reader and writer, and I would look through magazines for the kind of house that I was going to have one day. I'd tear photos of furniture from catalogs, and I kept a travel journal. I would say, "I visited Germany today, and I went to the Rhine River yesterday, and I went to Greece and saw the Acropolis," all based on my reading. I would read books from all over the world and would create imaginary friends that I knew in those countries.

Many of the adults in my town were illiterate. When I was seven, I would go from house to house to read and answer their letters to relatives in the North, carrying my paper bag with pens and paper. On Fridays, I would help them read their Sunday school lesson.

Schools in those days were all segregated. All black schools had wood-burning stoves, terrible books, and no libraries. When I sat in a third-grade classroom, I was in class with fifth-, sixth-, seventh-, and eighth-grade children. While they were teaching the eighth graders, I learned all the eighth-grade work. I skipped from fourth to sixth grade and sixth to eighth grade. I used to read my teacher's *Instructor Magazine* when she was teaching the other kids.

Kids picked on me a lot. They'd say, "You think you're more than us because your parents have this or that." My parents had to pick me up from high school every day because kids would want to fight me, scratching and pulling my hair.

My parents were entrepreneurial and very successful businesspeople. They had grocery stores, cattle farms, funeral parlors, and flower shops. The smartest person I've ever known was my grandfather. He could add a column of figures faster than we can today with a computer. I always earned my own money from my parents and grandparents.

When my parents got business mail, I would read all of it, and I would circle what I thought were errors and send it back to the company. **My parents involved me.** My first job was rolling and counting the pennies in the store. I graduated from that to the nickels. My grandfather would say to me, "If a case of peas costs twenty-four dollars, how much must I sell them for to make a twenty-cent profit on each can?" My grandfather took me to the bank when I was seven to help me get my first loan. That was hot stuff to walk in the bank and borrow $200. I used it to buy cattle and rear them, then take them to the cattle sales, sell them, pay the loan back, and buy some more. My grandfather, my dad, and I would go to the woods and cut down pine trees. I sold them outside our grocery store at Christmastime. **I don't know anything but a work ethic.**

I had a literature teacher who really taught me to love Shakespeare. My mom would hear me talking to myself in my room, and she would say, "Who are you talking to?" I would be emulating Miss Lowell. I thought she was the prettiest woman. I loved the way she dressed, walked, and carried herself.

As a student, I had to be the best. If I got less than an A, I would pester the teacher until she gave me something extra to change it, just to keep me from aggravating her. My friend and I competed against each other. If she got an A and I got a B, I would go to the teacher and say, "Please, I just can't have this B. You don't want me to go crazy, do you?" I would just continue until they would give me some extra projects. **I was always willing to work for that A. I grew up in a family where I didn't expect to get anything for nothing.**

I graduated from a segregated high school in 1953 and had only one close friend in my school. **When you succeed, you're going to** have a lot of people that don't like you. I always felt different. I worked in the florist shop, wired flowers, drove funeral cars, and unpacked groceries in the store. There wasn't a lot of time to feel bad. I'm comfortable with people, but being alone was never a problem for me.

I was the first in my family to go to college. I cried every day my freshman year in college because I was sixteen, and it was my first time away from my parents. After college, I taught for two years in Alabama. I was born a teacher. I know exactly the right things to say and do, and I think it's a gift given to me from God.

I moved to Chicago to be on my own, and I taught in the Chicago public schools for fourteen years. My training was in secondary education, but I taught everything from Head Start to high school to grown-ups. I married and had three children. I became disgruntled with the education my kids were getting in the public schools, so I took $5,000 and opened a school on the second floor of my home. It was frightening because I had children and a mortgage, but my husband was a draftsman, and he supported us until our school got going. There were some difficult times. I look back, and it gives me faith to do other things because I know that's what God meant me to do.

I started Urban Preparatory School with my kids and four other children. There was an article in the paper about some high school kids and how poorly they were doing with Shakespeare and what they didn't know. My students wrote letters to the paper, and the *Chicago Sun-Times* came out and did a story about our school. Then I did *Good Morning America* and *60 Minutes*. After five years, we bought a building, and we now have an entire block. We're planning to open a high school, and we've trained over 300,000 teachers in our methodology.

I believe that children should be literate and self-disciplined. Our kids discipline themselves, and they love the classics, great poetry, and great thoughts. We can never teach children all they need to know, so we really must teach them how to think and how to love learning.

We stand at the door every morning, and we greet all two hundred students. We have schools in Milwaukee and Kenosha, Wisconsin, and in Cincinnati, Ohio. We started thirty public schools in Florida, and those schools have turned their achievement around in just three months. I took the lowest-achieving public schools on probation in Chicago and turned their achievement around in four months.

I have taken on my grandfather's and father's roles. I have a deep family pride. **I don't want anyone in the family to fail.** My sister and my niece work for me. My thirty-year-old daughter is now running the Marva Collins Preparatory School that I started twenty-eight years ago and doing a wonderful job. My second son helps me set up the schools across the country, and he trains teachers. Our oldest son does the computer, printing, and business activities. My children have never worked for anyone else, and I hope they will pass that legacy on to their children.

My first husband died six years ago, and I'm now remarried. My husband says I'm very gullible because I'm very trusting. I don't believe you can ever hurt a good person. There was a big controversy about twelve years ago when the teachers' union and the Chicago public schools said our test scores were not what we said. We tracked down our graduates, all of whom had gone on to college. None of them were on welfare. None had unwed children. **I never get back at my enemies. I believe success is the best revenge.**

My faith is insurmountable. I am God-centered. I saw my mother and my grandmother praying on their knees at night. I always walk school hallways very prayerfully. I ask God to let me be just the limb of the teacher that he wants. I realize that it's not my brightness, it's not my being accomplished or wonderful; it's really fulfilling the destiny of why I was put on this earth. **Everything I have achieved is a gift that I give back to God for my days on this earth.**

# SELLING JELLY-BEANS AT RECESS WAS HER FIRST MARKETING EXPERIENCE

### Tamara Minick-Scokalo

MARKETING DIRECTOR, PROCTER & GAMBLE

*Marketing was a natural choice for Tamara Minick-Scokalo, who was entrepreneurial from childhood. The lessons given by both her parents will be forever useful. A lot of Tamara's strength today came from coping with psychological pain in childhood as a result of a handicap, or overcoming her fainting when speaking to groups. She is married to Petr Scokalo, and they have a son and were expecting a second child at the time of our interview.*

I'm the youngest of four daughters. My father and my oldest sister taught me my addition, subtraction, multiplication, and division tables when I was four years old. My mother taught me to read. **I had some early successes in school, and they fueled my desire to learn more.**

I was the son my father didn't have and received extra time and attention. When I was little, one of the very few television programs I was allowed to watch was *Watch Mr. Wizard,* hosted by a physics professor. My father was an engineer and was introverted. My mother was Greek, a stay-at-home mom, and more extroverted. **These diverse role models of my father teaching me academics and my mother teaching me love, respect for people, and enjoyment of life gave me a very well rounded childhood. Both my parents encouraged me to be everything I could be.**

I was born with a dislocated hip and unformed socket, so I was in a body cast, then leg braces. Sometimes children would push me down, and I'd be like a turtle on my back and couldn't get up. That was psychologically painful. A neighborhood woman looking out the window would see me, be horrified, and run to help me. It made me a champion of underdogs, protector of the "picked on." **Some of my insecurity goes back to that experience.**

**I was incredibly fortunate to have some exceptional teachers who took the time to give me individual attention. I was part of**

the accelerated program in a small-town public school in Pennsylvania. Everyone knew everyone's parents, sisters, and brothers. **I actually skipped seventh grade,** so in my senior year I took college-level courses in math and science. **When I was singled out in the acceleration program, it boosted my self-esteem and caused me to expect more of myself.**

**I was entrepreneurial from about third grade,** selling pot holders I made or running lemonade stands with my girlfriends. One time, I had a bag of jelly beans at recess, and everyone wanted some. I thought, "There's a real market for jelly beans." When I asked my father for twenty-five dollars, he was shocked and asked, "What do you want that for?" I said, "I'd like to start a little business at school because there are other children who would like snacks who don't bring snacks." We drew up a contract, including an interest payment, and I bought big bags of jelly beans and other snacks, broke them up into little bags, and sold them. I made money and paid back the loan early in order to pay less interest. I did that for two years and saved my money.

When I was about eight years old, my father taught me about the stock market. He had me pick stocks and play them on paper. I learned that stock values were a combination of the actual results of a company and the emotional reactions to those results. When I went to college, I took the money I had earned previously in jobs and invested it and spent time understanding the stock market.

My father also taught me how to play chess. **He didn't just let me win, but very early on made it clear that it was unacceptable to throw a tantrum and walk away if I was losing.** He would try to reinforce in me that a mistake was only a mistake if I didn't learn from it. **That focused my energy and anger away from my loss to a learning experience.** It was years before I won, and I screamed, yelled, and danced when I finally did. **I'm very competitive, and I like winning.** If I didn't win, I could put it in perspective: "I'm still doing well; I shouldn't throw in the towel; I can work this out and do better. **It's okay not to be first in everything.**"

I was in ballet for eight years, taking twelve to fifteen hours of classes a week. **I had to come to grips with the fact that I wasn't one of the top ballerinas in the class.** One of my sisters danced with the New York City Ballet. If I wanted to be the top, I was going to have to dedicate more of my life to doing that, or I could choose a different route, which was a combination of academics, social life, and involvement in school activities. **I learned that life is a series of trade-offs, but I needed to consciously realize what I was trading,** and that the path I selected was the one I wanted to take. I loved ballet, but I chose a different route. My sister didn't have much of a social life at school, was average academically, but her energy and attention was in ballet. I couldn't count on being a prima ballerina of the American Ballet Theater, but I could work my little heart out and make it somewhere because I would be so focused and dedicated. It was my belief that if I really wanted something, I could get it. **The questions were, What would I be giving up? How hard would I have to work to get there? Was it really what I wanted when I looked at the trade-offs I would have to make?**

When I was fifteen, friends of my parents who lived in England and had no children said to them, "We'd really love to have Tamara over for the summer." At first, I didn't want to go because I'd miss all the social life with my friends. I went anyway and spent most of the time in England, but we went to Paris, Italy, and Holland. **That trip opened my eyes to the world. I wanted to understand different cultures and experience things I had never thought about before. I realized my world was bigger than the town I grew up in, and I wanted to be part of the bigger world.**

I asked my father for a car when I was sixteen. We were a middle-income family, but I went to school with some kids whose parents bought them new cars. My father said, "Even if I had the money, I wouldn't buy you a car. It would be easy, and you would like me, but I'd be doing you a disservice because you wouldn't value it. What would you have to look forward to if you hadn't earned it?" **At the time I thought that was a horrible answer. Much later I learned it was an incredibly smart answer because I was always stretching to be independent, to earn my way.**

When I graduated from high school, where I'd been a National Merit scholar, I said to my father, "I don't want to go to college. I want to work for a while, save my money, and start my own business," whereupon he panicked and said, "Try it out. If you don't like it after two years, I'll give you the tuition for the other two years, and you can take that money and travel, because I think seeing the world and traveling is an education sometimes." **His prompting me to at least try school was important.**

**I decided to earn my way through college, even though my father offered to pay.** I had student loans, scholarships, a job in a college bar as a waitress, and a co-op job with Union Carbide. I took a semester off twice to work for two nine-month periods as a chemical engineer for Union Carbide. **I was always a hands-on person and wanted to roll up my sleeves and practice.**

I majored in chemical engineering at Lehigh University. Dr. Leonard Wenzel, chair of the chemical engineering department, made a real difference. **I failed my first chemical engineering exam. I had never failed anything, and it was a big blow.** He took me aside and said, "You're trying to be a perfectionist. Stop being so hard on yourself. You start the test, and unless you finish the first answer perfectly, you never even get to the rest. **Everybody's going through the whole thing and scribbling down as many of the thinking-logic formulas, so they can show that they know how to start these things.**" Chemical engineering started with 120 students, and fewer than 60 graduated. **I stuck it out primarily because of his encouragement.**

I went straight through college and took heavy course loads to accelerate graduation. **I liked school, but I liked its application better. I liked the challenges of the real workplace.**

My first job after graduation was as a process engineer at a paper plant with Procter & Gamble in Mehoopany, Pennsylvania. I was testing the quality of what came off the machines. I liked the people and learned so much from the technicians on those machines and never felt at a disadvantage being a woman. There were only seven of us out of three thousand, but **I rolled up my sleeves, worked hard, and earned the men's respect.**

**I did have one big problem: a deep fear of public speaking.** Whenever I gave a talk, had the lead in the school play, or sang in a rock and roll band, I could perform if it was behind lights and I was divorced from the audience, but if I didn't have a set speech, I'd be afraid there was something I wouldn't know. It would get cloudy in front of me, and I'd faint and fall on the floor. **My superiors at Procter & Gamble decided they were going to break me of stage fright by making me give a division manager talk every**

four to six weeks until I stopped fainting. Now I speak without fainting. It doesn't mean I don't have sweaty palms occasionally. Someone said to me, "**People are in that audience because you have accomplished a piece of work they are interested in learning about. No one knows more about the subject than you, so speak with confidence about it.**" That helped me a lot, but it didn't totally erase my fears.

After fifteen months, I decided I loved Procter & Gamble, but manufacturing was not where I wanted to stay. I transferred to product development and was working on a rectangular diaper with a breathable cuff that went into a test market in Buffalo, New York. I was designing the process for producing this diaper. I found myself with a group of executives and a vice president at our R&D management dinner. We were introducing ourselves: "My name is . . . and I'm working on . . .," so I said my name and that I was working on the diaper, and one of the executives said, "That's an important project to us. What do you think if it?" I responded, "Well, I think we're putting bells and whistles on an Edsel." He turned back to me and said, "What?" His jaw dropped, and I explained, "If we technically have this rectangular diaper that outperforms the shaped diaper two to one, but in a blind test consumers will tell us that the shaped one outperforms the rectangular diaper two to one, we have one of two choices. We can either go with the flow and upgrade the shaped diaper until it outperforms the rectangular one, or we can change their mind through advertising. I think this is one where we ought to go with the flow and change the shape."

We spent the rest of the evening debating whether or not we should move to shape up Pampers. I went home that night in tears. I called my father and said, "I think I lost my job." He said, "Did you say what you thought?" I said, "Yes." He said, "Well, if you lost your job for that, that's not a place where you belong." I thought, "That's easy for you to say." The next day I received a call and was told to put together five handmade diapers the way I thought the diaper should look and get it on CEO John Smale's desk by Monday morning. My technician and I made five diapers over the weekend and got them on John Smale's desk, and that was the beginning of a huge project that totally changed what Pampers were all about. **That taught me that I could be anywhere in the organization, and if I really** believed something was important and voiced it and was persistent in expressing what I thought was the right thing for the business, I could be heard and make a difference. That was a huge feeling. That allowed me to take risks I wouldn't have taken as an entry-level engineer. It also empowered me and energized me, causing me to love my company even more.

I moved to marketing, and it was like a chess game with real money. I had a series of early successes. My definition of success is I'm always learning, always challenged, and with that, hopefully, comes increased responsibility. Success doesn't mean certain titles by X date.

During that period, **I was struggling internally with whether I should be getting married.** I saw that guys my age were struggling, too, and tended to fall in one of two camps. The first were those that wanted to marry someone like their mother. If we got married, I'd have to stay home and support my husband's climb up the career track. The second were those who believed we're going to be totally equal, that there's no difference between men and women. I like my work, and I like being a woman. I came in on the cusp of change when **I could actually be feminine and do my job,** but men weren't necessarily ready to accept me as a partner yet. I dated quite a bit, but it took a long time before I found anyone who would be a great lifetime partner, where we could be cheerleaders for each other.

My husband's from the Czech Republic and grew up under communism. We have a year-old boy, and I'm pregnant with number two. **That has added a new dimension to life and to work. It's more wonderful and incredible than anybody could ever possibly describe. I thought I understood the term "unconditional love," but I really didn't until they placed that baby in my arms, and I knew I would walk through fire for him.** Before the baby, sleep felt like a waste of time. I wanted to maximize work, travel, adventure, and fun. I had climbed mountains, traveled to Africa, cycled around Bali, and toured Vietnam by myself for five weeks. **Now that we have children, we have cut out a lot in life, and it's okay that some things don't get done. It's a whole new feeling.**

Today I'm marketing director in the North American global business unit for Procter & Gamble's bath and facial tissue businesses.

I'm incredibly disciplined about my hours at work because I want some significant time with my son and my husband in the evening and on weekends. My people know, "Here are the times I'm in the office." Late at night, I'll answer some of my E-mail, but I pretty much leave the office in the office. I'm disciplined about hours, so that my husband and son don't just get my leftover energy. When our baby entered our lives, and he beams up at us, takes his first step, says his first word, somehow talking about bath tissue doesn't seem quite so important.

# THE RIGHT PERSON IN THE RIGHT PLACE AT THE RIGHT TIME

## Phyllis Grann

### CEO, PENGUIN/PUTNAM WORLDWIDE PUBLISHING GROUP

*Phyllis Grann's description of how she escalated to the highest level in book publishing makes it sound easy—just being there at the right time. She reminds us that indeed women were attracted to publishing early; but they only had entrée because salaries were so low! However, not all those women were continually promoted. Perhaps Phyllis gives her real secret away when she mentions at the end of her story that her three successful children always accuse her and her husband of being workaholics. Maybe it wasn't as easy as Phyllis tells it, after all.*

Even in my family, **I was in the right place at the right time.** My brother and sister were much older and were basically out of our home by the time I came along. **I was raised almost as an only child.** My parents had already been through parenting a young family, so **they included me much more in adult activities than they would have when they were younger.**

I was brought up in New York, although my parents had emigrated from England. I got rid of my English accent when I was ten; **that was the only thing that had made me feel different. In New York, it's hard to feel different.** My father traveled a great deal, so I was very close to my mother. **My father thought anything I did was perfect, and my mother expected me do well in everything. My mother spent a lot of time reading to me** and had taught me to read before I entered school. **She taught me a lot in addition to whatever I learned in school.**

I don't remember being told that I was particularly talented in my writing. I was terrible at music. They tried me on the piano, and that didn't work. Then they tried me on violin, and the violin teacher begged my mother to stop my lessons. I danced in New York for a long time, and there never was any question that I wasn't good enough to be a professional dancer, but I liked it.

**I was good at keeping friends.** I went to private schools. I had a best friend with whom I did everything. Unfortunately, she died when she was in her early thirties, but we were best friends for all that time. **I was spared peer pressure because I did so much with adults.**

I didn't love school in college; it was a lot of hard work. I studied for the result, not for the love of learning. At Barnard you could study at the Butler Library at Columbia, which had a lending library, and I spent a tremendous amount of time there because I disliked studying. **I'd read my way through all the best-sellers. I read all popular fiction from the time I was small. Reading and my taste for popular books led me to writing and editing.**

I had a wonderful professor at Barnard, and I loved him so much that I majored in English history. I lived with another girl in an apartment on the Upper West Side, and I had a boyfriend. I had some friends who were very active in leadership at the college, but I wasn't.

I was planning to get a Ph.D. in history but wanted to have some fun first, so I took a year off. The placement office accidentally sent my name to the Doubleday training program, and in the middle of finals they begged me to go there for an interview. The graduate school was willing to postpone my admission for a year, so I came to the Doubleday training program, to the right place, at the right time.

The men in the Doubleday training program were trained to become either sales representatives or editorial assistants, while the women were trained to be bookstore clerks or to work in the mail room. In those days the training program was not woman-friendly, and I lucked out by becoming Nelson Doubleday's secretary (maybe it was because I looked nice; my mom had promised to buy me two outfits a year, and she had very good taste). **I was in the right place at the right time. I wanted to become an editor. He helped me get a job in another company, where I could reach that goal.**

I did well as an editor, but I had to give up my job because I got married and followed my husband to his medical internship in Chicago. I had three children pretty quickly, and we moved back east. I kept working as an editor, but only three or four days a week. When my youngest child was two, I commuted from Connecticut to work for Dick Snyder at Simon & Schuster.

Dick Snyder, who was sometimes a harsh mentor, certainly had a great impact on my career. He actually fired me, though he denies this to this day. Then I was hired by MCA Universal, and I worked twenty years for Lou Wasserman and Sid Sheinberg, which was just great. **Stanley Newman to whom I reported forced me to learn the business end of the business. He taught me how to read a balance sheet** and said, "You have to learn this, even if you remain an editor." **He interested me in numbers, and I found that I liked numbers a lot.** I'd been good at math until ninth grade, when girls were no longer supposed to be good at math.

There were always tons of women in publishing because it was a very underpaid profession, **but I was a woman at the right time for women.** I was promoted to my first executive position because **there was pressure on corporations to move women up.** It was an asset to be a woman by the time I was thirty-five, **and it felt good.** I was in the right place at the right time.

My husband is an oncologist. We've been married thirty-eight years and have known most of our friends for over thirty years. I have a daughter, who is a radiation oncologist, and two sons; one is a journalist and the other produces TV commercials. **They would tell you that they are all workaholics because that is what we made them.**

# VISUALIZING SUCCESS MADE A DIFFERENCE

## Charlotte Otto

### SENIOR VICE PRESIDENT AND GLOBAL PUBLIC
### AFFAIRS OFFICER, PROCTER & GAMBLE

*Procter & Gamble's first female corporate officer, Charlotte Otto, tells how the Girl Scouts taught her early lessons in setting and accomplishing goals. A childhood of projects and entrepreneurial accomplishments preceded the not-so-gradual steps upward on the ladder at Procter & Gamble. Charlotte candidly explains how perfectionism and the impulse to blame herself for work problems— traits so many women share—have been her most formidable obstacles.*

I am the only child of absolutely wonderful, devoted parents, and I think that has a lot to do with how I turned out; I was their singular project. They gave me a really good start, and every reason to be confident.

As an undergraduate at Purdue University, I was in a "make-up-your-own major" program that included course work in communications, consumer relations, and business, which reflects exactly what I do today. After earning my master's degree in management, I came right to Procter & Gamble to get a few years of marketing training. The "few years" became thirteen years, and that provided a stepping-stone to my present position as global public affairs officer. In 1996, I became the first female corporate officer in Procter & Gamble's 160-year history. My responsibilities include our communications, government relations, and consumer relations around the world. I've been here for twenty-four years.

**My marketing sense began as a kid. I liked to sell things.** Once I dug up my mother's garden and sold her plants. She was not pleased about that. I made and sold aprons to earn money to pay for a trip to visit my grandmother. I made my little sample aprons, packaged them, and sold them house-to-house in the neighborhood. I'm sure I didn't come close to earning the money that was needed for the airplane ticket, but my parents made me feel that I contributed; I learned there was a value in making and selling goods.

I loved selling Girl Scout cookies and developed a distributor system with my father as my chief salesperson. He accepted his quota from me to sell at work. **I always tried to sell the most cookies; I didn't always do it, but I was motivated to be in the top sales group.**

**Girl Scouts was the center of my social existence.** I was a Girl Scout from Brownies all the way to Senior Scouts and was proud of my Girl Scout badges. My framed sash with badges down the front and up the back still hangs on the wall. **Earning badges helped me set goals, understand the steps, accomplish them, and be rewarded. It was great business training. Girl Scouts also taught me teamwork,** particularly with camping and being buddies whenever we went off in the woods. **As an only child, it was especially important to me.**

In Senior Scouts, we had to earn money to go places, and we made paper dogwoods that we sold at the local spring festival so we could attend Mystic Seaport Sailing School. **I made them, I sold them, I earned my money, and I went to sailing school—all tangible results of my efforts. In my work today, I take great pride in building a strong team of women, and that came directly from my Girl Scout activities.**

**My childhood prepared me for being in new situations. We moved around a lot.** I went to four public schools because I moved in fifth grade, again after junior high, and then again in high school. **The transitions weren't difficult because my parents planned them.** For example, they let me stay in school to finish my sophomore year in Cleveland, although they had already moved. **Moving taught me how to be comfortable fitting in because I was always in a new situation and had to learn to adapt.** At Procter & Gamble, even though I was the only woman in many situations for a long time, I rarely felt uncomfortable.

My parents concentrated all their efforts on me. If I had a school project, we all did it. For example, in anticipation of California history, we went to most of the California missions the summer before. Then we made one of the missions out of salt and flour and cardboard. **I always tried to do something distinctive, above and** beyond, that set me apart from others. It was unsatisfying for me to be ordinary. Yet sometimes I had difficulty separating out what I contributed from what my parents did.

I identified with both my parents. My dad worked incredibly hard. He was always working on a project at home, like landscaping or building something. My mother was determined, outspoken, and strong-willed. She was brought up on a sheep farm and had lots of responsibility and a very strong work ethic as a child. She had leadership roles in community activities, although she didn't work for pay while I was in school. My parents always conveyed to me that I could accomplish whatever I wanted. Leadership and accomplishment were high priorities in our family.

I was a good student in high school, near the top of my class but not the valedictorian. I distinctly recall being afraid I might not get all A's. Somehow I was indoctrinated with "I can't do math or science," but I discovered there was no truth to that prejudice. I took chemistry in high school and was surprised I actually did well. In fact, one of my favorite courses in college was organic chemistry.

I see now that I lacked confidence growing up. I was always surprised when good things came my way. I had a real fear that I couldn't be perfect. I lived in constant fear of failure, of disappointing my parents, of falling short. I lived in fear that someone would figure out it was luck, not skill, that created my accomplishments.

In my sophomore year in high school, I tried out for a girls' athletic group called "The Leaders." I was sure I wouldn't qualify because I wasn't particularly athletic. Surprisingly, I passed the tryouts and became a member. They seemed to see something in me that I didn't see.

When my high school senior class voted me the girl most likely to succeed, I was astounded. I never thought of myself as successful, despite the fact that I was involved in lots of school activities and I enjoyed leadership. I was in the school play and was the yearbook editor, yet I had a nagging doubt that if Mom and Dad weren't there, I couldn't be successful on my own. That seed of doubt was there for a long time.

My parents filled me with affirmation, but I felt too

dependent on their affirmation. When I did well in college, I realized that there must be something I had because my parents weren't there, and I still did okay. I had all A's, and Purdue is not a party school. I was very surprised.

I continued to surprise myself. I recall worrying whether I was going to have any job offers, and I had fifteen of them when I graduated from business school. Then I wasn't sure if I was actually going to get any of the jobs. The only job offer I didn't get was the very first one I tried for, at AT&T.

A big part of that interview was a business case study. I was paralyzed. I couldn't think. I was full of fear and anxiety. I remember the interviewer saying, "I know that you'd be very successful here, but you flunked the case." My confidence was shaken, but after that I was accepted for every other job for which I interviewed.

**Being a woman at Procter & Gamble has been an advantage for me. It's a company that relies very heavily on results. I've benefited from their commitment to developing people.** I've had bosses here who have been straight shooters with me. I was absolutely sure that at my first performance review, I was going to be fired because I had a really difficult time doing my first business analysis. My brand manager sat me down and said, "Well, you are really a quick study at this. You're doing very well." I just about fell off my chair. I had very little understanding of how my ability stacked up against his expectations.

I've always had doubts and a difficult time accepting criticism. I had one boss who told me I was terminally naive. Devastated is probably a good way to describe my feelings at that point. I wanted to argue with him, except at least I knew it was naive to do that. **But with that boss I learned an important lesson about trust, and trust is part of confidence. I started to tell myself, "He is telling me this to help me, not to punish me, and if I can just put down my defenses and say, 'This is clearly a problem that I should fix,' then he can help me fix it."** I finally set aside hope that no one would ever find out what was wrong with me, and I decided to be more open and trusting and let people help me.

I tend to internalize blame and spend an inordinate amount of energy talking negatively to myself, criticizing and punishing myself. Men are different from women in this regard. They tend to externalize failure, learn from it, and move on. I remember some-time during this period realizing, "**I can't afford to expend all this energy on beating myself up. I'm going to allow myself to learn and try not to make the same mistake twice. I'm going to ex-amine things and understand why they happen.**" I reached that conclusion by observing my husband, Bob. He doesn't waste an instant blaming himself for anything. I would be accepting blame for every situation, and he coached me by saying, "That's not your problem. The guy's a jerk." I discovered that everything wasn't my fault. Worrying was taking energy and attention out of doing productive things. **When I catch myself worrying, I make my-self sit down and write affirmations that I put by my dresser. When I have doubts, I look at them in the morning before I go to work: "I'm good at what I do." "I have support for my di-rection." "I don't have to figure things out by myself; I can reach out to others." When I write down these affirmations, I feel like I'm digging inside myself to get myself on the right track. These help me focus on dealing positively with the issues.**

**I also use imagery to** *see* **myself being successful.** I learned the technique at a leadership conference at an outdoor learning center. We had to climb on high ropes. I hate heights and was really scared, shaking, so I visualized myself jumping across the ropes, like a squirrel, and enjoying it. It worked. I completed the ropes course without falling. I felt really proud I had conquered a fear.

I use imagery a lot. If I have to make a speech, I envision connect-ing with the audience. If I have to have a difficult conversation, I play it like a movie in my head. It's very powerful. When I see my-self succeed, I do.

# CREATIVE PROJECTS WITH HER DAD GAVE HER A START

⌒

## Patricia Seybold

FOUNDER AND CEO, THE PATRICIA SEYBOLD GROUP

*The Patricia Seybold Group is a Boston-based research and consulting firm that helps businesses take advantage of the Internet to create vital connections with their customers. Patricia's Quaker heritage influenced her noncompetitive approach to organizing her business. Her love of writing from childhood continues, and she is the author of the best-selling book* Customers.com. *At fifty, she is married and has a young adult son.*

I was the youngest of three children. My brothers are three and six years older than me, and my father spent a lot of time with us. He set a pretty high bar for our behavior and intellectual activities and had a very strong early influence on me. One of my earliest recollections was of playing piano with him. **He was a taskmaster.** He sat down at the piano and practiced with me. **I eventually gave up piano lessons because he'd make me do things so many times, and I'd end up in tears.**

Other than that, **I had a very happy childhood. My dad loved to organize play activities he called "projects."** For instance, he built a crazy house in our basement for Halloween. It was elaborate, with spooky things like spaghetti that hung down in our faces, a shifting floor, and strange sounds and lights. We brought our friends in to walk through it. For the Fourth of July, he made elaborate costumes and props and entered my brothers and me into the parade. One year I was Little Bo Peep, and my brothers were the sheep; another year the three of us were "The Little Engine That Could." The creation of these costumes was a family effort. **While my dad was the taskmaster, my mom was the one who was very encouraging. She was very enthusiastic about whatever we did.**

My mom was a full-time homemaker until I was in junior high, at which point she asked me if I minded if she went to work. I said, "Okay," and she went to library school and began working at the local library. By then we were pretty much self-propelled, and she was still there for us all the time.

**I did entrepreneurial things like organize the neighborhood kids into doing plays and benefit performances.** We'd put on a circus or a play, invite people, and charge a nickel. **Then we'd take the money and donate it to some worthy cause.**

**We were Quakers and went to Meeting every Sunday, which created a very important community for me from childhood through high school.** The Quaker philosophy states that everyone has a part of God within them. We believe that everyone is essentially good, and all have creativity within them. **We had a strong feeling of community and learned that by working together we're more powerful than by working on our own.** We'd get together and fix houses for people or donate our used clothes to refugees. **We made decisions based on consensus,** and learned to be sure that everyone was comfortable with the decisions we made. **I've tried to carry this style of decision making into business life, but it isn't always very successful because it takes too long to get anything done.** Finally, we valued pacifism, the idea that **conflict can be resolved by talking and listening as opposed to striking out at people. This value was pervasive in our home and affects me still.**

School was great and I was an A student. I grew up in Swarthmore, Pennsylvania, a college town, and the school that I attended from elementary through high school was a very close-knit, small public school. Ninety-five percent of us were college-bound. **We had great school spirit and very good teachers. I was involved in a lot of school activities, including orchestra, band, chorus, yearbook, and the literary magazine. Writing was important to me.** I typically gravitated toward my English and language teachers all the way through school. I took French, Latin, Spanish, and German and loved writing and literature. Like my father, who has been a prolific writer all his life, I felt like writing was my natural vent.

It was a vibrant school community, and I had a great group of friends, the nonjocks. **We were the intellectual prehippie, hangout-and-sing-folk-songs-and-go-on-picnics-together type. We were predrinking and predrugs and very wholesome.**

I didn't participate in a lot of competitive sports, although I liked playing on the lacrosse team. **I swam competitively but enjoyed the swimming more than the competition. I liked working out, having a coach, and being egged on. My childhood was about collaboration more than competition, except within my family. We competed for my parents' attention—which one of us was the golden boy or golden girl.** I always tried to be the golden girl and the peacemaker whenever conflicts would break out between my brothers.

My family moved to Paris for almost two years when I was in fifth grade. My dad took a sabbatical and did volunteer work for a year and a half. I spent eighteen months going to a French school in Paris, a formative experience in my life. Not only did I learn a new language, I was indoctrinated into a whole new culture. We lived at the Quaker Center in Paris, a wonderful communal place with incredibly interesting people coming through all the time.

My college career was checkered. I went to three colleges, and it took me a while to finally finish school. I went to Pembroke College, which is part of Brown, on early decision. **I liked Pembroke because it was coed, and I knew there'd be a lot of men around.** I stayed there for two years, met my first husband at the end of my freshman year, moved in with him, got married after that first year of college, and moved into an off-campus apartment. He finished school, graduated while I was a sophomore, and took a teaching job in a little town in Maine. We moved there, and I transferred to Bates College, which, in comparison to Brown, was a much smaller and less challenging liberal arts college. I stayed there for a year and a half, but didn't find it intellectually stimulating. Also, I fell out of the student scene because I was married and was commuting. I dropped out and taught French in a local Quaker school, a free-spirit place where all the kids turned up and did whatever they felt like.

I had my son, Jesse, at age twenty-one, and when he was one, we went to live in Germany. After our return, I enrolled in Goddard College's Adult Degree Program, **which was my favorite educational experience because it was an independent-study program** in comparative literature. I went to the campus in Vermont for two weeks every six months. I picked my professor and subject matter and did one major project each six months. **I found that doing work on my own was more fulfilling intellectually.** I wanted to follow my own nose and do my own thing. My professor and I talked on the phone, I'd send him papers, and he'd critique them. We'd get together every six months. I did that for two years to finish my degree while I took care of my young son and worked full-time in a bank. It was exhausting and busy but intellectually challenging and fun. **It was project-oriented.**

At this point, my husband decided that teaching school was not going to work for him in the long run, so he applied and was accepted into the Wharton Business School in Philadelphia. I called my dad, who had just started his own business consulting firm, and said I needed a job. He, of course, gave me one, and I apprenticed with my dad and my older brother for five years. **That was a very important experience for me, and now I'm a big fan of apprenticeships. My dad was a good boss and mentor. He gave me projects, I did them, and he critiqued them. I tagged along with him on consulting projects. Eventually, I asked questions, and he'd nod encouragingly when I was on the right line of questioning. He modeled appropriate behaviors and gave me opportunities to try them out. He nudged me along without being critical. He was this way throughout my life in all areas except music, where he had been too heavy-handed. I think he'd learned from that experience.**

I continued to work with my dad, although I left Pennsylvania. My husband had graduated from Wharton. He took a job in western Massachusetts, and I said, "Hell no, I won't go." I'd developed a pretty serious career while he was changing his. He assumed that I would always follow him wherever he went, and **I was clear about the fact that working in my field was what I needed to do. I didn't feel particularly respected by my husband at this point, either professionally or romantically, so it seemed like a good breaking point for us.** We divorced. It was traumatic, especially because our son was six. **We survived it and are still friends.** I would say that as divorces go, it was probably among the more amicable.

**My conflict-resolution experience was helpful in my divorce.** My son went to live with his father for the first couple of years because we wanted to be sure that there would never be a custody problem. We decided to set a precedent by having joint custody and agreed that he would take Jesse first. **I bent over backward to make sure that things were fair.** It was a hard decision for me, but it enabled me to put my career first. I hadn't had an opportunity to establish my career before I became a mother, and I don't think I was a particularly good one. I didn't know what to do and just bumbled along. Luckily, when we were living in Pennsylvania, my mom was there as backup.

My son came back to live with me when he was ten. I continued to work for my dad but moved to Boston, where I met the man who became my second husband. At the time, I edited my own technology newsletter and did more consulting for my father, since most of the action in my field was in New England. Two years after I'd set up my little satellite office, my father called me and said, "You act like you're trying to set yourself up as an independent business." He was right; I realized that I'd be happier going out on my own. I raised some money locally in Boston and found some investors to buy myself out of the family business, and I've had my own business ever since. I started in word processing and office systems and kept delving into how companies used computers to run their businesses. I've always followed the leading technology. My customers are primarily the early adopters of technology in large corporations. **I try to run in front of the parade they are already leading and give them advice as they go.**

**I've had quite a few mentors during my adult life. I've managed to hire people who are tops in their game so I can learn from them. My current vice president in sales and marketing has taught me a lot. I've been apprenticing with her in sales and marketing, areas that I knew nothing about. I hired a merchandising consultant and started learning about merchandising from her. I have switched from going outside to find gurus to hiring people who know something I need to learn.**

I've noticed one thing that differentiates me from other women in business: **I am extremely self-assured. I get scared a lot and often feel like I don't know as much as I should, but underneath I have a very strong sense of myself. I know I have what it takes. I think this comes from my mom always being there and encouraging me.** Some other women with whom I've been in business seem to have a victim mentality. When something goes wrong, they blame the men for doing it to them. **I grew up with a very strong father and two very strong older brothers, and I've always felt equal with them and that I could stand on my own two feet.**

I don't feel like a very competitive person. I strongly believe in having a heartfelt connection with the people I work with and those I am consulting with. I rely very heavily on my intuition, a quality I attribute to my Quaker upbringing. I don't always say this aloud, but the people I work with know that's the case, and they trust me. **That's what keeps our business together.**

# *H*ER WISH IS TO MAKE AN ENDURING
## CONTRIBUTION

### Annik LaFarge

SENIOR VICE PRESIDENT AND E-PUBLISHER
OF CONTENTVILLE.COM

*As senior vice president, Annik LaFarge is in charge of everything
to do with books on Contentville.com, a Web site that sells every form
of written content—books, e-books, magazines, speeches, legal documents, doctoral dissertations, transcripts, and screenplays. She is
doing both original e-books and selling e-books from other publishers.
Annik is on the cutting edge of e-commerce and the technological
world, a place where only a few women had ventured initially.*

A day doesn't go by when I don't remember how lucky I am to have
grown up as I did and how much my upbringing has to do with my
successes. I grew up in New York City and went to an all-girl school,
Brearley, one of the best schools in the country, and to an all-girl
summer camp in Vermont. **I'm a very big believer in women's
education.**

I liked school enormously. In my younger days I was quite distracted, a little bit of a clown, and got in trouble periodically. I'd distract the class and be told to focus. **I felt that everyone was
smarter than I was because the student body included some of
the smartest kids in the city. I learned I had to work harder if
I wanted to do well, but I also had to rely on my ability to be
charming, friendly, funny, and someone whom people would
like. Being in a place where everyone was so smart challenged
me to develop other parts of myself in an entrepreneurial way.**

I had a lot of good teachers. I've never been good at math, but
there was a math teacher, Judy Conant, who was tough on me. Some
of the bosses I've had in my career remind me a bit of her. Even if I
got things wrong, as long as I was paying attention and was working, she was enormously supportive, but always tough and exacting.
She taught me that working hard was a great virtue in itself, and if
I didn't get it right, I'd be rewarded for the hard work. In the

eleventh grade I had a teacher, Susan Knox, who completely turned me on and made me feel like some of the off-the-wall ideas I had were legitimate and interesting. **The teachers in the school had a seemingly unending amount of patience and generosity toward all the students there. Even if I wasn't doing well, I felt that whatever I was working on was legitimate and appreciated.** We were being custom-taught. **I felt different from the other girls, but the school was a place where being different wasn't a terrible thing, and I thrived on it.**

I kept diaries for every year of my life from the time I was eight years old. I recently found them when I was packing for a move, and they are my prized possessions. I wrote a lot, and not always particularly well. But the diary I wrote when I was eight is really quite marvelous. I also wrote short stories and in my thirties had a letter I wrote (about gays in the military) published in the *New York Times.*

My parents were divorced when I was about thirteen. I was forced to juggle between the two of them. All four of us kids shuttled back and forth from Mom's house (on East 78th Street), which was a little chaotic but fairly normal, to Dad's house (on West 78th Street), which was a kind of menagerie: seven kids, a chimpanzee, and a large German shepherd. My dad had remarried. He was an extraordinary man but confused, I think, about where his own talent lay. His family includes a number of well-known artists and writers. My great-uncle, Oliver LaFarge, was a Pulitzer Prize winner. I think my father felt stultified by the talent that came before him. He believed that publishing was commercial and crass, beneath him, somehow. He was a writer and playwright but thought that the theater should be performed in basketball courts or city parks. It wasn't until a few years before he died that he came to me and said, "I'm working on this novel and thinking about publishing it." He struggled all his life with what it meant to be successful. I felt sad that he didn't figure that out before he died. I've always felt that he missed out in some way.

The divorce was hard on us because my mother was devastated. My father changed so much, and for her it was a refutation of everything they'd had together and everything she believed in. My dad grew his hair long, wore a ponytail and bell-bottoms. He went to Big Sur, did meditation and yoga, and became a vegetarian. My mother felt driven to talk about everything to me because that's the way she worked through it. It was hard for me to understand it, but she and I were very close.

Both my parents were easygoing about my three siblings and me running around the way we did. I was popular. I had a lot of freedom and a sense of responsibility, but every weekend I was out partying. I went to bars when I was thirteen and fourteen. I had lots of boyfriends, smoked pot and cigarettes, and had a great time. I threw myself into life with my friends because my home life was so difficult.

**I had very good role models, including my mother. I don't remember a time when she was not at work,** whether she was teaching school or working as a book editor, writing novels, or a syndicated book review column. Usually she was doing two things at once. Gail Sheehy wrote about her in *Passages.* My father was very dark at times, but smart, handsome, and the center of attention. He was hugely kind, drew people out, and always wanted to talk about how other people were feeling. He was an enormously appealing, remarkable guy. **I identified with both my parents very strongly, but more with my mother as I've grown older.**

At Vassar I worked hard. I had partied all of my teenage years. I met a brilliant English professor there who became my thesis adviser. I studied Shakespeare to the exclusion of almost everything else and wrote my thesis on the issue of manhood in three of his plays. In my junior year, I went to Williams College but came back to Vassar to write my thesis because I missed my adviser so much. **My Vassar years weren't particularly happy ones, but I learned to discipline myself. I don't have a lot of close friends from Vassar.** I feel, in retrospect, that I was just passing through. I had a good time, **but I felt impatient to get out and do something.**

I started working three weeks before I graduated from college. I was scheduled to go to Europe in my senior year with a couple of friends when I got a letter informing me that there was a job at Simon & Schuster in the publicity department. My best friend, who was going to Europe with me, applied for the same job. I ended up getting it. She went off to Europe, and I went to Rockefeller Center. I had to get a special dispensation from the dean at Vassar because I had to leave school three weeks early. The dean knew that my thesis had been awarded departmental honors so he decided to cut me some slack, but he didn't tell me that at first. I remember saying to him, "Do you understand that Simon & Schuster is really a very important publishing company and this is really a major job?" I was such a jerk, and so earnest! But he let me go.

I had to study for my exams at lunchtime at my new job and take the train back and forth from New York City to Poughkeepsie. I lived at my mother's apartment during the week and went back to school on the weekends. It was a little nutty. I had no idea what I was getting into. **My boss, Julia Knickerbocker, was extraordinarily charismatic. She was the grande dame of book publicity at the time and a great mentor.** She chain-smoked, was gorgeous, sexy, bawdy, brilliant, and an inspiration to me. She made the whole notion of promoting books seem exciting, challenging, and worth spending huge amounts of energy on. We had a great time, and I learned a lot. I worked with Joan Didion and Leo Rosten and other well-known authors. I went off to Random House a year and a half later and worked there with James Michener, E. L. Doctorow, and Gore Vidal, among many others. It was rewarding, fascinating work but often hard and intense. As a publicist, you're constantly facing rejection. It was challenging and frustrating.

**I was always driven. I had to find my own notion of what success was in response to both my parents. There were plenty of ups and downs, and I worked for some difficult people, but I always felt there was someone who was looking out for me and allowing me to be entrepreneurial.** While I was still in publicity, I started a little business called Random House Large Print. I went to the then-president, Joni Evans, and said, "I'd like to come up with a plan to do this," and she said, "Great, let's do it." Shortly thereafter I decided to leave the company. I had gotten burned out on publicity and wanted to go somewhere else. The CEO of Random House, Alberto Vitale, said, "That's fine, but stay on as consultant." I was moving down to Washington with a woman I was living with who had gotten a job in Virginia. It was a real turning point in my career because what Vitale was saying to me was, "I'll look out for you. You're talented and smart. I'll open all the doors that you need in the company, and you can do this from Washington." I came to New York once a week and started this large-print business and was a little one-man band. I learned how to do a business plan and a

P&L, and after eight months I moved back to New York—the relationship had ended—as associate publisher of Times Books, a division of Random House, where I stayed for three years.

After a brief interlude at Addison-Wesley, I went back to Random House to the Villard imprint and worked with an old friend, David Rosenthal, to revitalize it. We did humor, fiction, nonfiction—everything from *O.J.'s Legal Pad* to Jon Krakauer's *Into the Wild*—and had a lot of fun. We left together after three years and went to Simon & Schuster for another three years. I was the associate publisher, and it was a hard and punishing job—four times the number of books we had published at Villard, and an infamously tough environment.

**I've always been interested in the Internet and computer technology.** I was one of a handful of people in the U.S. who had a Minitel in the early '80s, the first e-mail device that came from France. I was doing e-mail with people in Paris and Washington, mostly in French, with others who had Minitels. I remember sitting on the floor of my bedroom at midnight. My mother would come upstairs with a couple of glasses of scotch, and we'd send e-mails to total strangers. Talking to each other through computers was just the most interesting, bizarre form of communication. As a novelist, my mother was completely transfixed.

Ultimately, after all those years in publishing where I was enabling and serving others—authors, editors, publishers, marketing, sales, and business people—I felt I needed something that was mine. It was about the time that Steven Brill came up with Contentville.com. My new job has given me ownership. E-books are in their infancy now, but it's exciting to be at the edge looking into this future and making early decisions in what will soon become a mature business. I feel like I have a lot of leeway to build the business. Brill is known for being smart, aggressive, and difficult to work for. I've found him to be all those things but, most of all, enabling to me at a time when I really craved that.

**I didn't think of myself as gay.** In my late teens, I was with a woman for three years and still thought it was an exception, an oddity. **It took me a while to figure it out.** When I told both of my parents I was gay, I was in the middle of a very bad relationship in which I was being manipulated. My mother had a terrible reaction to the news, but she said it was because the relationship itself was so destructive. When I found someone who was quite wonderful and kindhearted several years later, my mother completely turned around. This woman that my mother approved of was a lovely person, and I was an exception for her. She was one of those people who had a very involved, passionate relationship with someone of the same sex and then got married to a man. Later she went to law school and had children. I hear she's doing very well.

I told my father I was gay when we were on a trip to Scotland. I was about twenty. He was really great about it. He said, "This is very hard for me, and yet this is something that's important to you. I've always believed ever since I was a young boy that a homosexual relationship would be an inferior relationship. I'm going to learn what I can about what this means to you and try to be supportive."

**I never thought of myself as gay, and I still don't. I think of so many other things first when I think of who I am. It's not a decision to be gay. It's a decision to come out and talk about it.** I made a decision to stop denying it, that this was, in fact, the way I am, and that I was going to be this way forever. It wasn't going to work for me to live a secret.

**I think a lot about what it means to be successful.** Material goods and financial comfort are certainly involved in my idea of success. But I've reached a point where there is nothing I want that I don't have or can't get, which is really a wonderful place to be. To be successful in my job now, **I need to do something in the world of e-books that's going to be enduring, to set up a program that's going to be smart, focused, fiscally responsible, and adaptable as the business changes. I need to be very aggressive and nimble, but I also need to be careful as I make decisions in this fast-moving and volatile business.** When I talk to the press about doing e-books, I find that half the time I talk about how exciting it is and what e-books can do, how we can incorporate music, art, and hyperlinks. The other half of the time I'm saying, "But we have to go slowly; we have to be smart, selective, focused, and careful." **I know a lot about what it means to me to be a success in business terms, but it's as important to me to be successful in human terms: to be patient, fair, gentle, and kind to people who work with me and for me. I think a lot about who is com-**

ing up behind me. I wonder, "Am I doing for others what others have done for me?"

One of the benefits of working at a number of different places (I've changed jobs almost every three years over the past twelve or so years) is that you start to look at how you work. If you're in the same job for years and work for the same person or company, you can always get away with saying, "I'm this way because that person is the way he is or this company is the way it is." When you change jobs, you're forced to look at your own pattern. If you start to hear yourself saying the same thing over and over again, chances are it's you and not the job. It's important to me to be someone who, at the end of the day, can feel that people around her are saying, "That person is smart, driven, aggressive, strong, and tough, but also fair and openhearted and wants to have a good time."

I feel strong, and the older I get, the more I feel that. Maybe it's because the closer I get to CEO, the closer I get to the top of the ceiling, the more I see up close the bad management styles that can crush creativity. I believe every day when I go into my office that if the job gets abusive or too much, I'll just walk out. I can do that. I believe that I'm smart enough and talented enough that I can find something, and there's another job waiting for me. The greatest privilege of all is knowing I have the freedom to say, "I won't take it anymore." Part of that comes from believing in myself and part comes from living as part of a couple without kids to put through college. But mainly it's from being comfortable in my own skin. Again, I feel lucky. But it took a lot of years to get to this point.

# SHE LEARNED TO PASS TESTS FROM THE BOYS

## Katherine Hudson

PRESIDENT AND CEO, BRADY CORPORATION, MILWAUKEE

*Katherine Hudson's excellence led her from a spot as the top female executive, as vice president and director of corporate information systems, at Kodak to becoming the first female president and CEO of a major public company in Wisconsin. The Brady Corporation manufactures approximately thirty thousand industrial items and has yearly revenues of about half a billion dollars. The company has twenty-five hundred employees in twenty countries and under Katherine's leadership is growing rapidly. According to Brady's Internet site, Katherine's salary is $1 million a year. In a business overwhelmingly dominated by men, Katherine is one of a very select few in the highest echelons—a true shatterer of the glass ceiling.*

I was the oldest in my family, so my dad taught me to play baseball, fish, and do all the boy stuff. I was his "son" and a tomboy. We lived in a rural area near Rochester, New York, and the only kids to play with were boys who **were always testing me.** They told me I could play football with them only if I could tackle this kid who was bigger than me. He went too low when he charged me, and even though he hit me in the stomach and it really hurt, I fell on top of him, which they counted as a tackle. **I passed their test, and I could play.**

Later we moved to a new neighborhood in a suburb with both girls and boys. We played baseball on vacant lots. **The test whether we girls could play was if we could hit a ball off their pitcher, Sherm Parker. I played ball only because I passed the test.**

When my dad signed me up for courses at the public high school, I was enrolled in advanced-placement English and social studies because of my excellent grades in the Catholic elementary school I'd attended, but not in a regular math class. I also had an A in math so my dad said, "What happened to algebra?" The counselor said, "Most girls don't like math." My father insisted, "My daughter is taking algebra." If not for my dad, I wouldn't have taken algebra and wouldn't be sitting here today.

Being picked for the Finger Lakes all-star field hockey team was a formative experience for me. I played defense. It was pre–Title IX, so every school had their team decked out in the boys' hand-me-down navy blue sweat suits. It was a sea of navy blue and hard to tell teams apart. I wore the only red stocking cap. I wasn't that good, but I'm sure I made the all-star team because **the kid in the red hat was everywhere. I learned the importance of making myself visible.**

I remember when I was eleven years old being in a drugstore that displayed doorbells. My mom, who always did funny things, rang every one of them. **I remember thinking to myself, "That's my mom and I'm me, and I'm not going to be embarrassed by anything she does."** I made a conscious decision. If people wanted to laugh at my mom, that was okay. **That gave me a greater realization of my own identity. I also learned that it's okay to do crazy things if you want to, and life isn't really a popularity contest. I was never concerned about being popular. I was occasionally excluded from something but learned to "do my own thing."**

My parents and I were very close, and **we had lots of laughs in our family.** They were concerned because I was a real studier and wasn't as social as some kids, although I had a group of good friends. At my high school, the speaker at graduation was chosen by vote of the honor students. I was elected speaker and was very surprised and flattered to have my peers choose me.

When it came time to choose a college, my dad drew a circle with a radius of three hundred miles around our house on a map. He told me I could go to college anywhere in that circle, so I picked Oberlin College, 299 miles away. It was an unusual choice because I was politically conservative, but **the school had an outstanding reputation.**

My goal was to become a high school math teacher because **my math teachers in high school were really good female role models.** Then I fell in love with economics when I took an elective, and my professor was absolutely outstanding. I started thinking about business. Unfortunately, before my junior year, two good professors left, which left me with very few elective choices.

After convincing my dad to give me another three hundred miles, I chose to transfer to Indiana University **because it had one of the top ten undergraduate business schools in the country.** I continued with economics, although my actual degree is in business management, and **I graduated first in my class.** When they handed me the award, they announced "Katherine Mary Nellis, whose academic achievement puts *him* in the upper one percent of the graduating class." There were 783 students in the business school and only a couple of dozen women.

When I wrote my résumé, I wasn't sure what I wanted to do. None of the companies were interested in my doing financial work, despite my graduating first in the class. **The salary offers were for about half of what the guys in class were being offered. This was in 1968, before affirmative action.**

I was standing outside my adviser's office, feeling discouraged, when out of the corner of my eye, I saw an ad for an economics fellowship that would pay for four years of graduate school, a full ride for the same amount of money as one of my job offers. I applied for the fellowship, went to Cornell, and actually saved money. I started in the fall of '68, and in the spring of '69, more than a thousand college campuses across the country, including Cornell, were closed by demonstrations against the Vietnam War. The economics department split in two. I lost all of my advisers, so I applied for a leave of absence and went home to Rochester. My folks said, "Welcome home. Get a job." I went to Kodak because my dad worked there and because it was the largest employer in the county. As a systems analyst, I planned the forecasting of sales. Between the time I graduated from college and when I started at Kodak, **affirmative action had begun, and I received a very competitive salary.** I stayed at Kodak and never went back to Cornell.

After the systems job, my normal career path should have been to rise up the ladder rung by rung. Luckily, however, someone I knew in finance needed an "affirmative-action woman" in his group and offered me the spot. I loved it, and **I set a goal for myself to become the first female corporate officer at Kodak, in a job that wasn't traditional for women,** which meant finance, operations, or marketing—anything but public relations, which is where most of the women got stuck. After I'd been in finance for five years, my boss, Paul, called me and said, "They're forming a new division, and they need an administrative assistant to the vice president. I think you should interview for the job." It was in public relations. I didn't really want it. I had a terrible interview, but it was a done deal. Dave, the corporate vice president, had met with Paul in the locker room after golf and talked me up. That's how I grudgingly took the job working for Dave.

It turned out to be the best thing that ever happened in my life. Dave was great. **He taught and showcased me. He also tested me.** It was a familiar theme. Shortly after I started working for him, he called me when I was home sick and asked me to come to his house and edit some memo. **I realized it was a test, so despite my not feeling well, I went to his house and did the work.** His wife cooked a beautiful Italian meal and I played video games with their daughter. I'd passed another test from the boys.

**Another lesson in my career was the importance of volunteering, especially when everyone else takes a step back.** Kodak was getting ready to celebrate its centennial. Since Rochester was basically a Kodak town, Dave said, "We're going to get a lot of phone calls from car dealers and dry-cleaning places, and they're going to want to give discounts to Kodak employees. We want to discourage them. We want the celebration to be classier and more community-based. Is there anybody who will volunteer to take the phone calls from these people?" Everyone looked down at their papers to avoid eye contact. I said, "I'll do it." I fielded the calls. I put a program together with the local museum, art gallery, theater group, and baseball teams, and it was great. So when the head of the community relations department position became available, a substantial promotion, I got it, and when another higher position opened up, I snagged that one too. In three years, I had gone up five levels in the company. I was working with the vice presidents and chairman of the company.

I became the chief information officer of the company and the first woman to become a corporate officer. The president and chairman of the company took the officers off-site about two or three times a year for either strategic reviews or an educational experience. After I had been on the job a couple of weeks, I was looking forward to my first such meeting in Toronto, but I didn't get invited. On the Monday after the meeting, I had my regularly scheduled meeting with the president. The first thing he said was, "I owe you an apology. I didn't invite you to Toronto because we never had a woman at that meeting, and I didn't feel comfortable. When several other people said, 'Where's Kathy?' I realized I had made a mistake. The next meeting, you will be invited." **That's one of the major barriers that women have in getting through the glass ceiling; the people who are on the other side of it have to feel comfortable with us.**

I came to Milwaukee to run the Brady Corporation in January 1994 after being aggressively head-hunted. I went to meet my management team for breakfast at the University Club. As I walked down the hall, I could see a half dozen men waiting, trying to determine who was coming. I saw the strange look on their faces as they realized, "My God, it's a woman." Since I've been here, we have doubled the size of the company, tripled the market cap, and have done eleven acquisitions. We're having a lot of fun, and I have a great team of people that I work with. I've passed their test, and now they're passing mine.

When I decided to take the job at Brady, my husband and I made a careful decision about the future. His first career was as a professor of biology at the University of Rochester, and his second career was working at Kodak for ten years as the director of strategic intelligence. My loving spouse is now an at-home husband. He fiddles in the stock market, nurtures our twelve-year-old, and manages the home front. He calls himself the CEO of 10357, our address. Thanks to the stock market, he made more money than I did last year. More importantly, he made it possible for me to be a CEO and still have a happy family life.

# Growing Up in the Best of Two Worlds

## Connie Matsui

SENIOR VICE PRESIDENT, PLANNING AND RESOURCE
DEVELOPMENT, IDEC PHARMACEUTICALS, AND NATIONAL
PRESIDENT, GIRL SCOUTS USA

*Connie Matsui, the daughter of servants, learned early to analyze everything incisively from English literature to complex marketing and employee relationships. Her talent and hard work rapidly elevated her first to vice president and manager of employee relations and communications at the Wells Fargo Bank, and then to senior vice president of planning and resource development at IDEC Pharmaceuticals Corporation. How she managed twenty years of volunteer services to the Girl Scouts USA, culminating in her election as president of the board, while raising two children and a loving husband is a fascinating story.*

My parents are both second-generation Japanese-Americans. During World War II, Dad served on a limited basis in the U.S. Army, and my mother was transferred to an internment camp for Japanese-Americans. When they were released, there were few jobs available to Japanese-Americans, usually as maids, butlers, and gardeners. So while I was growing up, my parents worked in the home of a wealthy family. My dad worked fourteen to sixteen hours a day as a domestic servant. My mom was on call as a maid every day except for once a week. We lived in the maid's quarters of the house in a very small space, and it was necessary for us to be quiet and well-behaved so as not to disturb anyone. **I was exposed to culture, privileges, education—much that money can buy, though that exposure wasn't through my parents' money. I didn't have much of my parents' undivided attention, but I was with them a lot and had a happy childhood. I had the best of both worlds.**

My sister was seven years older and was closer in age to the children of the family my parents worked for than I was, so **I was on my own much of the time.** My parents' employers were also my godparents. As I grew up, they helped pay my college tuition, provided me with a car, and have been avid supporters of my success. The material things my parents would never have been able to provide for us came from my godparents. At the same time, the children of the family found warmth and love from my parents and remain close to them.

I was usually one of the few Asians in the public elementary schools. I went to incredibly good schools by virtue of the neighborhoods we lived in and had friends who had many opportunities and resources. Some lived in mansions; yet, who I was or the fact that I was Asian and didn't have as much money as they did didn't come into our relationship. I never felt discriminated against or excluded. It was a fortunate way to grow up, another one of those best of both worlds.

School was easy for me. I was able to excel in all the subjects and loved to read and learn. In fifth grade, I wrote to a children's author, Madeleine L'Engle, because I wanted to be a writer and illustrator like her. I also had an extraordinary sixth-grade teacher who gave us opportunities to learn more about science. She made no distinction between boys and girls and was a very strong influence on me. My seventh-grade science teacher looked like a Barbie doll, and I thought it was striking that someone so beautiful and confident chose science as a career.

My parents saved enough money to buy a small home in a neighboring affluent neighborhood, and I went to junior and senior high in a privileged area. My dad continued to work at my godparents' home part-time, but my mom went to work long hours for a woman's clothing store, eventually becoming one of the managers.

I don't know how we managed. My mom and dad worked hard all the time, in and out of our home. Although I baby-sat, helped as a teacher's assistant, and worked with my mom from time to time at the retail store, our parents raised us to believe that our most important job was to work hard and do well in school. We both took school very seriously.

During junior high, I felt like an outsider, although I had some close girlfriends with whom I spent time. I was extremely self-conscious. My being smart (or maybe being Asian) put off

**some people.** My sister and my mother were very close, and both were very vivacious and beautiful. I was in my most awkward physical stage when my sister was in her most blossoming, beautiful stage. I remember feeling I would never fit the public's image of what an attractive woman should be, because of the TV stereotypes, which were primarily blond and blue-eyed, but also because I was so different from my sister, who was winning beauty contests. My mother said, "Dale's like me and you're like Dad." I thought, "**I can't excel in beauty, so I need to be an excellent student.**"

I felt close to my dad. He and I were quiet and serious. He is the kindest person I know. He always said, "Try to understand what it is like to be the other person." Even during the times when I was having so much self-doubt, **I learned from him that other people were struggling with other things and that I could help them.** That gave me a lot of personal satisfaction as well. I believe this virtue is where my involvement with Girl Scouts came from.

**I didn't fit in socially in high school and wasn't popular.** I was active in school events and programs, but I never dated anyone and never went to a prom in my entire life. **I had a close group of friends who were very interested in social and environmental issues, old movies, and more into the intellectual side of things.** Our socializing was with groups of girls and boys rather than dates. **All of us were outsiders, coming from different cultures or less privileged backgrounds.**

I remember some desperate times, feeling extraordinarily miserable and commiserating with friends. As I look back at it now, **I believe feeling unsuccessful may be a key to becoming successful. Living with self-doubt and self-consciousness, then learning to overcome them, is a very powerful and transforming experience. You become stronger and more resilient than if everything comes easily and without challenge.**

When I asked my teachers to sign my high school yearbook, most of them wrote, "Thank you for teaching me something," or "I learned a lot from you." **That's when I began to realize that maybe there were some things I saw or understood that other people didn't. I had very strong communication skills, particularly in my writing, and people immediately understood what I was trying to convey. That's been an extraordinary asset in** being able to do strategic analysis to integrate disparate pieces of information and see trends or connections between events, people, and experiences.

I graduated at the top of the class from a college prep school and received honors for English and Spanish. Both of my godparents were staunch Stanford supporters. **My sister wasn't accepted at Stanford, so I was very motivated to distinguish myself by getting into Stanford to earn the recognition from my godparents and my parents.** Only two of us in my high school were admitted to Stanford, **which was quite a special achievement.**

In college **I was an observer, not a participant in social life.** As a senior, I had a boyfriend for the first time; both he and I were misfits in many ways. Although we were part of the groups that were popular, we ourselves were not. He and I are still good friends. **We saw each other's differences and appreciated them.**

The first year at Stanford I was in the only all-girl dorm because my parents preferred that. My roommate was from Texas, and her father was one of the founders of Texas Instruments. It was another serendipitous situation where I ended up in a close relationship with someone who was wealthy and privileged. Despite our contrasting backgrounds, we turned out to be compatible in many ways. **We cared about the same things—our friends, our families, our surroundings. We'd work equally hard toward common goals, whether it was decorating our room or throwing a dinner party.** We roomed together all four years. I was welcomed in her home, which was filled with extraordinary art and beauty; she was another daughter in my parents' modest and casual home. **I appreciated what she had, and she became very close to my parents and valued their earthiness and affectionate nature. Again, I lived in dual, yet complementary worlds.**

I majored in English literature and was in the honors program. By this time, my mother was disabled by rheumatoid arthritis and no longer able to work. I needed to find a career that would pay for itself, and an English career, whether writing or teaching, was not going to do that for me. **Two close friends in Stanford Business School said, "Why don't you go to business school?" I really liked and trusted them and thought it would be great to be like them.** As a result, I took a few business courses, applied to Stanford

Business School, and was admitted despite my lack of work experience. **Being a minority Asian woman was probably an advantage because it gave me scholarships that might not have come my way otherwise.**

**I treasured my two years of business school; they helped me understand who I am and move beyond my doubts and self-consciousness.** There were only five of us out of a class of three hundred who had no work experience, and about sixty of us were women. The average age was twenty-six, and most people had successful careers and were coming back to learn more. These people didn't seem to care what I looked like, who I was, or where I came from. **Those external or material things that seemed to matter so much in high school and college didn't mean a thing to my classmates in business school.** It was the first time I felt totally accepted as a colleague by men and women alike, by people of all ages, races, and backgrounds. The second thing I discovered was that **my ability to synthesize information and communicate it clearly allowed me to contribute at the same level as people who had years of business experience.**

Coincidentally, I met my future husband at business school. Although we dated throughout the two years of business school, our top priorities were to learn as much as we could and to launch successful careers. Therefore, we didn't get married until about five years later.

After graduation, the only companies that were willing to train people without work experience were banks. I received offers from five banks and chose Wells Fargo because the people I met there were the happiest and most fulfilled. **Being different—a Stanford M.B.A., a minority, a young woman—helped me at Wells Fargo.** It gave me an opportunity to serve as a spokesperson and on statewide committees. I spent fifteen years there and had a fun time as an "intrapreneur" with the diversity of opportunities. As banking became more and more competitive, it became less and less enjoyable. When I left Wells Fargo, **I wanted to do something that was more socially rewarding.** My husband and I were both excited about biotechnology as a field with huge potential for growth and for improving people's lives. Through a banking colleague of mine, I was referred to my current company, IDEC Pharmaceuticals, as a consultant, to help them with a relocation decision. It was exactly the type of thing I had been doing for Wells Fargo. Eventually, I became an employee of IDEC full-time, and we moved our whole family to San Diego, where we have been for seven years.

We have a fourteen-year-old son and a nine-year-old daughter. **My husband and I are very different but compatible, especially when it comes to values.** Because we met in business school and have been very committed to our careers, we've been partners in everything, especially in raising our children. **He finds a lot of satisfaction in nurturing and being actively involved in our children's school and sports activities.** He's a real estate developer, has his own business, and has been able to adjust his schedule when I haven't been at home. I travel at least one week per month for IDEC and Girl Scouts. I was able to work part-time for the first year with both children, and we have always had a professional caregiver who comes to the house on a daily basis. Sometimes it seems funny to me to be hiring someone to take care of our children because that's exactly what my parents did as their work. I never felt it to be so much of an employer-employee relationship as **it is a partnership, because that's the way it was when I was a kid.** My children are very fortunate to have a strong and loving community of caregivers and family.

My company was more or less of a start-up when I began, and it is now viewed as one of the success stories in biotechnology. The value of the company has made a lot of people wealthy beyond their expectations, but what is most important to me goes back to what my mom and dad used to emphasize: **always treating people with empathy, caring about people's needs, and having a strong family life. Caring about people's needs has brought me to serve on the Girl Scouts Board. Family is always going to be most important, no matter how much money we are fortunate enough to accumulate, and that is how I measure my success.**

# SHE LEARNED TO FIX WHAT SHE DIDN'T LIKE

## Marilyn Carlson Nelson

### CEO, CARLSON COMPANIES

*Marilyn Carlson Nelson, ranked No. 17 in* Fortune *magazine's list of the "Most Powerful Women" in American business, is president and CEO of Carlson Companies and fills the position formerly held by her father with the confidence and leadership she learned from him during her childhood. It all started with her dad's expectation that she bring her Sunday school class up to her high standards. Some Carlson brands include Radisson Hotels Worldwide, TGI Fridays, Radisson Seven Seas Cruises, and Carlson Wagonlit Travel. Carlson Companies is one of the largest privately held corporations in the world.*

It never occurred to my dad that his first child wouldn't be a boy. **I picked up on that and identified with him in all things.** My earliest recollections are of being surrounded by unconditional love from my mom and **slightly more challenging or conditional love from my dad. He taught me to be competitive.** Once he challenged me to a race. He gave me a little tin shovel and told me to shovel dirt off one little square piece of the sidewalk. He bet me he could do the whole sidewalk in the same time, and he beat me. I threw my shovel down and had a fit because I'd lost that competition. **He never just let me win, but he provided challenges.**

One Christmas when I was about ten, my little sister received a doll as big as she was from Santa Claus. I literally found manure in my stocking. I cried, tried to be a good sport, but wondered what I had done wrong. Later that afternoon, my dad gave me my own horse with a Christmas wreath around his neck. I leapt on that horse and was about five miles away before I could slow it down to a walk. It never occurred to my dad that I couldn't ride that horse!

My parents were extraordinarily engaged in our lives, and all four grandparents loved us, believed in us, and spent lots of time reading, talking, and playing with us. Academics and participation in competition were important. My dad helped me write a story about my horse, and my mother helped me put my book together. We entered it in a contest, won a blue ribbon, and celebrated. It was very exciting.

**I learned about goal setting from Girl Scouts.** I set my goal, accomplished it, earned a badge, and celebrated with the family. I spent several years building my sash of badges. **Girl Scouts led me into experiences that went beyond my family.** I remember reading Shakespeare by candlelight in a closet with a girlfriend to get our literature badge. For some reason, being in love with Shakespeare made sense.

Our church, Hennepin Avenue United Methodist, made the decision to take in Border Methodist Church, an African-American congregation that was being closed down by highway development. **Our discussions about our charitable responsibility and role in the city had a profound impact on me.** That was the first time the question of race became part of my experience. We welcomed those new members to our church, and to this day, their children and grandchildren participate with our children and grandchildren in a living nativity that my husband and I helped fund.

When I was twelve, as we were riding home from Sunday school, I told my parents I wouldn't go to Sunday school anymore, that I would either stay home or go with them to the sanctuary, where I could listen to the sermon. I hated Sunday school. The boys shot spit wads and chased the girls around, and the Sunday school teacher couldn't control the class. My father was furious. He declared, "You will go to Sunday school." I retorted, "I won't. You don't want me to. It's a ridiculous waste of time." He said, **"Then fix it."** I cried and said, "What do you mean, 'fix it'?" My mother said, "Curt, leave her alone. You don't understand." "No, I won't," he said. **"If she doesn't like it, she has to fix it."** I kept saying, "I'm only twelve, it's a huge Sunday school. How am I going to change it?" and he said, "That's the story of life. The forces are always bigger than you are, and one person can make a difference. If you don't, better that you go down trying than to not attempt it." It never occurred to him that I couldn't change Sunday school. He sent me to my room to write a list of all the ways I could improve Sunday school. I had to call the superintendent and make an appointment to discuss my recommendations. **We got some other young people involved and fixed Sunday school. It was a very powerful experience.**

I had two groups of friends in my junior high years, which sounds great but was actually socially hard. I was a cheerleader, skated a lot, and was a candidate for homecoming queen, but I also hung out with another nice bunch of friends. The popular group made me choose between sitting at their lunch table or with my other friends, whom they considered nerds and weird. I talked endlessly to my mom and cried a lot. **I decided I couldn't sit at the popular clique's lunch table because they weren't going to dictate who my friends were, so I was ostracized. The group they asked me to stay away from grew up to become architects, lawyers, and other professionals who made profound differences.**

**I loved theater. I won first place in the state doing an interpretation of *Death of a Salesman*. Performance taught me empathy.** It made me think about the lives of the individuals I played, and I tried to get into their skin. **Theater was also my surrogate for team sports. Speaking your lines is like throwing a ball back and forth. You are only as good as you become as a team. Rehearsing, working with people toward a common goal, helping other teammates who need special coaching catch up, and dealing with adversity were all important contributors. In** the individual competitions, **it was an exercise in communicating an idea, and I realized I was successful only when I really forgot about myself and wasn't self-conscious. That became valuable for me in my later leadership.**

We weren't wealthy growing up. When my sister and I were young, my dad told us we could have dessert or invest in the company he had started, the company I now run. He had borrowed a lot of money, so he would talk to us about how if we ate a dessert that cost $1.25, it would be gone, but if we saved the $1.25, it would double and triple because of the compounding effect. It would be worth a certain amount in time, and we were investing in our company. He taught us the power of a self-disciplined decision.

**I edited the school newspaper, which taught me a lot about leadership.** I had to select what went into the paper, what was left out, and who covered what stories. I learned about how the paper was a voice that, on one hand, created a common culture, and on the other, had to lead the high school community.

Our school was debating whether it was democratic to have advanced and accelerated classes, and they determined that students could not be divided by performance. One of our teachers, frustrated by the decision, invited a group of eight of us on his own time to have special classes with him. **We met twice a week for a year and read poetry and advanced literature. We grew in our love of analysis and critical thinking. I loved learning.**

I did a lot of ballet and went on my own, without my parents' permission, to audition for the Aqua Follies, a big extravaganza water and stage show. Much to my surprise, I was accepted as a dancer. Then I had to tell my parents I'd auditioned and convince them to let me dance. I was a year underage. My dad worked out a deal with the producer, which was mortifying to me. I couldn't stay overnight with the other girls who were performing; I had to stay at home with my parents. We performed in Minneapolis, Seattle, and Detroit. It was a professional show, we were all paid, and we became great friends and had an awfully good time.

We've always had a philosophy in our family that it was important to know where we came from. My grandfather was a first-generation American and still spoke with a Swedish accent. We talked about the hardships of coming from the old country, about freedom of religion, and freedom to fail or succeed based on our own initiative. **Our immigrant heritage was held up to us as an example of being able to deal with hardship, pioneering, and having the courage to strike out and accomplish.**

At Smith, like a lot of freshman who go to very competitive schools, **I was overwhelmed by how many other people there were who were smarter and more talented than I was. It was difficult to compete on an even faster track. Without question, an all-women college was helpful. Any time I won or lost an election, an argument, or debate, there was no "out" in gender. I won or lost based on my preparation, my articulation, or the power of my idea. Smith challenged us to make a contribution and make a difference.**

I married Glen in 1961, only days after graduating from Smith, which was typical in those days. When I was first out of college, I let it be known that I didn't type well, so that I wouldn't be hired as a secretary. I was able to get a job as a junior security analyst at PaineWebber, although there were no female registered representatives in Minneapolis at that time. I covered a very hot local market, and they liked what I was doing, but they had me sign all of my publications "M. C. Nelson" because they thought no one would buy stock on the recommendation of a woman.

Then I became pregnant unexpectedly. In those days, you had to leave your job three months into your pregnancy. By that point, however, PaineWebber had a lot invested in me, so they rented an outside office so I wouldn't be seen on the trading floor and let me work until the end. By the time our first child was born, my husband was a surgical resident, so I needed to work part-time. I worked for my dad at Carlson Companies, then still called The Gold Bond Stamp Company. We were having a huge growth spurt. I headed group projects, became involved with the purchasing department, and helped put the catalog together. I had two more kids and was up for a promotion, but instead of sharing my excitement, my dad was furious. He wanted me to go home and raise our three kids. I felt deflated, but in my heart, I knew he was right. Glen was an extremely talented surgeon, expert in triage, so he would get called any time of day or night for trauma cases. Our children needed someone to be dedicated to them. I loved being a mom, so **I spent the better part of the sixties as a volunteer taking on larger roles.**

I came to be good friends with Joyce Hughes, a black attorney married to one of the physicians with whom my husband practiced. **I nominated Joyce for membership in the Junior League.** This was in 1968, and I found myself pregnant with my fourth child, standing up in front of the entire nation of Junior League executives at the Broadmoor Hotel, listening to people from the South asking me, how could I do this? I remember in particular one woman with tears rolling down her face saying, "Y'all don't understand that at my house my dog and cat can come in the front door, but blacks come in the back." **It was emotional for all of us, but we prevailed. Joyce became a member of the Junior League.**

When my kids were older, my dad asked me to be director of community and public affairs for Carlson. This time I surprised him by telling him I would help out only if I could work from home until my last child, Wendy, graduated from high school. I convinced Dad to let me have a secretary and office at home so I could volunteer, parent, and do things on behalf of the company too. After Wendy's graduation, I switched to full-time. I've spent the last twelve years working next to my dad. I became CEO in 1998.

Our daughter Juliet followed in my footsteps and went to Smith College at age nineteen. Smith asked me to chair the inauguration of Mary Maples Dunn, and I asked Juliet how she'd feel about that. She thought it would be great, so I was there the week before school started. She'd come over to my hotel, and we'd sit around talking until late, and then she'd go back to her dorm because she didn't want her roommate to think she wasn't committed to living there. We had the inauguration on Sunday, said good-bye to Juliet, and went back home.

That night, Juliet died in an automobile accident. She'd been the middle child, the one who reminded us to always look at the sunrise. Whenever Father was busy yelling at everyone to set goals, she'd climb up on his lap and say, "Come on, Boppa. Give me a hug." She'd written this beautiful speech and given it at her June graduation. **"What would it be if someday you learned that you weren't going to come home that night? Would it be the A you didn't get, would it be which college you did or didn't get into, or would it be the friend that you didn't stop to help?"** Then in October, she didn't come home.

It's so overwhelming to lose someone you love, and we miss her terribly. When you get through something like that, it changes things that might have overwhelmed you before. Our family members loved each other and supported each other and got through that awful experience together. Juliet taught us what we don't know, and both Glen and I decided that we were going to have to cherish every day in a way as if it were our last. **We both are profoundly aware of the gift of time.**

Juliet's roommates shared with us that they'd all been sitting on the bed at 3:00 A.M., getting to know each other, when she told everyone about how on Christmas Eve our family would read the Christmas story from Luke, and the kids always played the parts. The girls wore their nighties as angels, and our boy usually had a towel wrapped around him as a shepherd. In Juliet's diaries, she wrote about how it made her faith seem more real, and she said things like, "I'm an angel again this year." She was counting the years until she could be Mary. By the time she finally got to be Mary, I'd had Wendy, so she got to hold a real baby. **Glen and I decided that we,** with our other children, Diana, Curtis, and Wendy, **would create a citywide nativity at our church so other families could participate.** The nativity has been performed for thirteen years with a volunteer count of two hundred. We've had five marriages of Marys and Josephs, so I have grandchildren from those families that I won't ever have from Juliet. **Juliet's very much a presence in our lives and in many others' lives.**

# $\mathscr{A}$ Leader in the Navy to a Leader in Girl Scouting

## Marsha Evans

EXECUTIVE DIRECTOR, GIRL SCOUTS USA,
AND RETIRED REAR ADMIRAL, U.S. NAVY

*It's only fitting that Marsha Evans accepted the challenge of being executive director of the Girl Scouts USA. As a girl, she attained the highest achievement in Girl Scouting at the time, the Curved Bar. Furthermore, she accepted this important leadership in a woman's world after proving herself in her male-dominated naval career, where she earned the rank of rear admiral. Her husband, Gerard R. Evans, is a retired navy jet pilot.*

*After interviewing Marty, I had the further privilege of hearing her address an audience of community and Girl Scout leaders. Both her interview and her address were inspiring, and I could readily see that Marty will make a positive and exciting difference for hundreds of thousands of girls and women.*

I am the oldest of five kids. My father made the decision to go back into the navy when I was about four, when there were three of us. My mother had a lot to manage. We moved to Jamestown, Rhode Island, which is on a small island, where my father was stationed on a ship that went overseas. One of my earliest memories is my mother becoming ill with a mild form of polio while my dad was gone. I helped her as much as I could. I can remember leaning over a playpen, changing my little baby brother's diaper. **The experience of seeing my mother cope made a strong impression about how challenging life was for her.**

My mother was a fine seamstress. She started a business making slipcovers for people who lived in elegant summer homes on the island. When I was in kindergarten, I went with her to their homes, where she cut out slipcovers and pinned them to the sofas and the chairs. I helped by handing her pins. My mother had quit the Rhode Island School of Design to marry my dad. This was a significant loss in her life because she'd had promise as an artist; making slipcovers for wealthy people was not her grand plan. I'm sure that's why **I never had a break from the consistent message, "Get your education before you have your family."** The message I received from Dad was, **"You can do it. Education is your key." I was complimented intensely for doing well in school.**

As a junior sailor in the navy, my dad would be gone for eight or nine months, and my mother put him on a pedestal. She portrayed his love for family through his letters. We'd get letters from foreign lands, and he'd bring home dolls from the places he visited. We'd have fabulous celebrations and the recounting of my report cards when he came home.

When I was in second grade, my dad came home and announced, "We're all moving to Africa," and that became an extraordinary adventure. **My fascination with international politics began** when we moved to French Morocco. We went from a penurious existence on a tiny island to North Africa, where we had a full-time maid and traveled as a family to places like Fès, Meknès, and Marrakech. We soaked up the local culture. Another sister was born there, and my mother developed herself as a Girl Scout leader. We had a very active scouting program, and because of my mother's artistic background, we often did crafts.

After four years, we returned to Rhode Island, and my dad went back to sea duty. The sister who was born in North Africa was having severe behavioral problems, and our family was torn apart by her acting out. I can remember pleading with my mother to get some help for the family.

We moved to Arizona when I was twelve. When we'd moved to North Africa, I'd skipped from second to fourth grade. When we'd returned to Rhode Island, I'd been ahead of my peers. Now, in Arizona, I was ahead of my peers again and graduated first in my eighth-grade class. However, high school in Phoenix was the first time I was thrown into a large and very rough inner-city school. I didn't fit in and was seriously unhappy.

Midway in my freshman year, we moved again, to southern California. **I fell in with a nice group of like-minded kids and got involved in speech and debate.** There were military kids from three bases and lots of engineers' kids who were like me and had moved around a lot. It was the beginning of the space race, so there was a lot of excitement. Of the top ten kids in my high school class, six of them were good friends of mine, all in the high track. **I wasn't popular in a social sense, but I was president of a number of clubs and was a leader.** I was a driven perfectionist. I was obsessed when I thought I was going to get an A- instead of an A.

My senior year, my dad was transferred to northern California. My parents said if I could find a suitable place to live, I could stay and finish up school rather than move with them. Finally, an English teacher invited me to stay with her family. **She made getting me into a good college her project. It was an incredible opportunity. She was inspiring and reinforcing and provided me with a stable platform.** I was rewarded for my hard work and graduated first in a class of seven hundred. I interviewed at Occidental College in southern California, where they gave me a wonderful scholarship.

My major there was international relations. I remember a prophetic conversation with my religion professor about whether you should approach life conservatively or with zest and risk. **He said to visualize a rope dangling from the end of a pole. A person can hold on to that rope in any number of places. She can be one foot from where the rope is joined to the pole and she won't get banged around, but it would also be pretty dull and boring. On the other hand, she can hold on to the end of that rope and swing around in unpredictable, exciting ways, but she'll also get bounced around and have more risks. I tucked that away as I continued through college. I wanted a riskier, more exciting life.**

I decided to take a course in Asian history. A graduate student in that major was a fabulous teacher, and **he influenced me to change my major to Asian history.** That one course changed my life. With my new professor's counsel, I applied to top graduate schools.

By the spring of my senior year, I was working two jobs to pay my expenses and was exhausted. I was deciding between the University of Michigan at Ann Arbor and Columbia for graduate school. I was visiting friends when I picked up a newspaper and saw an article about a woman officer in the navy. I suddenly realized there were options other than graduate school. By Monday morning, I had begun to talk myself out of graduate school and into the navy. I called the navy recruiter and decided to join Tuesday. It was not a well-thought-out career decision. What clinched the deal was when I called the admissions office at Ann Arbor and Columbia and asked if I could defer my admission for military service, and both said yes. It was a fabulous opportunity from my perspective. I could get two years off, take advantage of the G.I. Bill, and then go back to graduate school.

Unbelievably, my retired navy dad was opposed to my joining the navy. I wasn't twenty-one and had to have parental permission to join. My dad was concerned about my motivation. In those days, people assumed that nice girls joined the military service only to get a husband. I convinced him it would be good for my graduate school goals, so he gave his permission. My mom wasn't wildly enthusiastic, but she was very proud of my accomplishments.

Just prior to departing for navy officer training, I asked my dad, "Do you ever miss the navy?" and he said, "Only about a hundred times a day." **I carried that conversation for a long time because it taught me a lot.** He was a brokenhearted man the day he left the navy, and he never was happy after that. I hadn't really appreciated how deeply the navy ran in him, and it helped to explain why he was able to go away for long periods of time. **He also taught me how important it was to really love what I do.**

After two years in the navy, I prepared to go to graduate school. My boss asked me what I was going to study, and I told him Asian history and politics. A couple of days later, someone called me from personnel headquarters and said, "I know you're planning to get out of the navy, but we'd love for you to stay in for two more years and go to Japan for an assignment." I accepted and went. While I was there, the navy selected me for graduate education. I could go to any school in the country that offered a graduate program that supported the navy's needs. **It was a huge opportunity for me. I exercised that option, went to graduate school, and got everything I wanted.**

After I'd lived in Japan, I decided I wasn't going to be the world's great Asian scholar. I'm almost six feet tall with blond hair, and every place I went in Japan, I was a spectacle. I became tired of both the cultural differences and the physiological differences and realized they might be barriers. I decided to get a graduate degree in national security studies and changed my focus to Europe and the Middle East. I went to the Fletcher School at Tufts University in Boston.

I'd always thought my height was problematic. I felt I could only date guys who were taller than me. **However, my height was an enormous advantage in the navy because it was a power tool. When I exercised authority, I looked the part.** When I came back to Washington, in addition to my regular assignment, I worked at the White House as a navy social aide. There I came in contact with then-secretary of state Henry Kissinger and his wife, Nancy, and I realized my height didn't matter. Nancy is much taller than her husband! Watching the Kissingers helped me get over my problem.

I met my husband, who is five feet eight, when I came back from Japan. He's a navy jet pilot. **He's brought a wonderful dimension of relaxation and risk taking that's filled in my life's missing pieces.**

**I've had great opportunities in the navy.** As the number of women expanded, more opportunities opened, and **I would go into roles where women had previously not served. As I went into nontraditional jobs** and did well, I became a better candidate for other nontraditional jobs. I became an admiral in 1991.

I was the fifth woman line admiral and the second two-star woman admiral. In 1992, I found myself head of the task force to develop a strategy to change the culture and climate of the navy and Marine Corps after the scandal at Tailhook, where female naval officers had been badly harassed. Then I went on to be the chief recruiter for the navy, and later became head of the navy's graduate school in Monterey, California. That's where I got an unsolicited letter from the Girl Scouts, who were looking for an executive director. I was in my twenty-ninth year of service and realized that someday I was going to get out of the navy. **I was mindful of my father's very difficult transition to civilian life. There isn't a lot of advice on how to make a successful transition from something you love and find great satisfaction in to a new life in an alien culture.** I told my husband I wanted to do something that promotes women, to be in an organization that espouses values that are consistent with mine.

I called the Girl Scouts, and they asked if I had a résumé. I said, "Oh, sure," but I didn't. I'd never had to do one before. **My husband went out to get a book on how to write résumés, and I wrote one.** Then I bought a book about how to get a job and started reading that, and in the very final stages of their search, the Girl Scouts invited me to New York for an interview and offered me the job on the spot. I didn't know how to respond; I hadn't gotten to the point in the book about getting the offer yet! I had a difficult decision to make about whether this was the job I would leave the navy for. Fortunately, my husband is a great analyst, **so we sat down and looked at the pros and cons.** "I'll support you" is always what he says. I decided to take the leap.

One of the biggest things I bring to the role is an extraordinary passion about what Girl Scouting does that comes directly from two aspects of my previous experience. As the chief recruiter in the navy, I tracked very carefully the percentage of men and women applicants that we turned down, and why. **In women's cases, it was pregnancy at an early age and multiple dependents.** A single woman with three kids doesn't have much of a prospect for being a successful sailor. **Drug abuse, multiple infractions of the law, and failure to complete high school also make someone a poor risk for the navy.** As I traveled through large and small cities, I saw young women who didn't have a chance because of poor choices they had made along the way. In Girl Scouts, **we do something about helping girls make better choices in the early years.** Directing the Girl Scouts was another way to shake girls up and say, **"You can do all of these fabulous things that are so exciting and will take you places that you can't even imagine."**

My dad denied to his last day that he ever thought the navy wasn't a fabulous idea for me. From the beginning, he carried a glossy eight-by-ten picture of me in my uniform in his briefcase. He made sure he opened his briefcase often so that people could see that picture of me. He relished recounting my navy experiences, just as I'd loved to hear about his travels when I was a little girl. My mother appreciates how much my career has meant to me, although she was relieved when at thirty-one I decided to get married. She thinks the sun rises and sets on my husband. I do too.

My husband retired in 1984 and basically has been a supportive husband and house spouse. I feel like I'm one of the most fortunate people in the world.

# ℱROM CANDY STRIPER TO HOSPITAL COO

## Sandra Labas Fenwick

CHIEF OPERATING OFFICER OF CHILDREN'S HOSPITAL, BOSTON

*Sandra Fenwick always knew she loved hospitals and admired the doctors and nurses who cared for patients. In her wildest dreams she never expected to be COO of the first-ranked children's hospital in the country—a prestigious position dominated by men. Sandra has also managed to balance her career and family, including two children. Her story offers important insights.*

Neither of my parents went to college. My father worked for the post office, and my mom was a stay-at-home mom until I was twelve, after which she went to work for a local college admissions office. **Both my parents were focused on getting all four of us involved in learning. They made sure education came first.** My mom worked one job and my dad worked two jobs to put us all through college, so we recognized how important it was for us to take advantage of what they were putting before us.

I grew up in New Britain, Connecticut, and went to public schools. We were lucky to be part of the state school system, which was funded for training elementary school teachers. We had wonderful teachers, additional student teachers, and tremendous resources. From fifth grade on, I knew I wanted to do something in the health-care field. I thought it was going to be medicine, and **I hungrily read books about the first women doctors, going back to Elizabeth Blackwell. I was in the top classes, had leadership positions from junior high on, and was involved in student government.**

**My fifth- and sixth-grade teachers were responsible for turning me on to science.** My fifth-grade teacher had us wire a dollhouse electrically so we could actually see how the electricity lit up the house and turned on buzzers. He also had us wire the internal organs of the body on a big board he had colored. We took tests to learn all the internal organs. Science literally lit up for us. **Our teachers were gender-neutral.** They didn't segregate girls from boys in anything, including sports. They pushed us out on the field, and we played kickball and soccer, although there were no organized sports for girls. I'm very petite, five feet two, and I wasn't going to have anyone think I was weak or retiring.

I have been very competitive my whole life, and that's probably what drives me. If the boys beat me up, I beat them up. The first time this happened, I came home crying, and my mother said, "Turn around and punch them back," so I did, and it worked. In both middle school and high school, I tried to be number one in the class. There were some pretty smart guys in my class, so I decided if they could do it, I could do it.

I competed socially, too, and wanted to be in the top social group and have the cutest boyfriend. That was harder for me because I wasn't the prettiest. I had more disappointments socially than in other areas, but I still feel comfortable with and love people.

My parents set a standard that I didn't resist. I came home, did my homework, did the hard stuff first, and saved the easy stuff for later. I had a very active social life through middle and high school, and a lot of friends, but the social life was on my terms when I could fit it in. I was a candy striper at one of the hospitals from age twelve. I loved a hospital setting. I loved watching the nurses and physicians in their work.

The two guidance counselors I went to for advice to select a college didn't give me much encouragement to reach for the highest level. They said, "Your father probably can't afford the top-tier schools, and because you're not number one in the class (I graduated fifth), you probably won't get significant scholarships. We suggest you apply to the second-tier schools." I applied to Russell Sage, Simmons, and Connecticut College and got into all of them. I chose Simmons because I wanted to go to a women's college in Boston. Although I had done well in high school, I didn't want the distraction that comes with big schools. I decided if my parents were going to sacrifice for me to go to college, I really should plow through the next four years.

I was in college at a very difficult time, the late sixties and early seventies, when everyone was protesting the Vietnam War. When everyone else was out marching or storming offices and into drugs, I studied. I went on marches when it didn't interfere with my classes but was focused on doing what I needed to do to get through the course work and pull the grades I needed to have.

I took premed classes and **had some extraordinary female role models in college,** in particular a developmental biologist and a microbiologist. We started out with an enormous class of biology majors and graduated only five. I graduated as a double biology and chemistry major in the honor society. At graduation I thought, "**I've always said I was going to medical school. I should take a year to work and make sure that's what I want to do.**"

One of my professors introduced me to a wonderful physician in microbiology and immunology at the Harvard School of Public Health. I became a research assistant doing clinical research, which I loved, and thought about maybe earning an M.D.-Ph.D. Two months after I got there, they asked me if I wanted to go to their field station in Saudia Arabia to run a laboratory with a team of people from Boston. After about a month in Saudi Arabia, they asked me if I would stay and run the lab while everyone went back to Boston. **That was my first big break, being in a foreign country running both the fieldwork and the laboratory with no one above me and leading a team of five people.**

I had a very hard choice at that point. I had planned on staying a year and then going back to medical school, but the head of the department of microbiology at the Harvard School of Public Health said, "I know talent when I see it, and I see no reason why you can't take this and make it a success." **I was asked to run the program for another year. It was the greatest confidence builder I ever had.**

I stayed in Saudi Arabia for a second year and met my future husband. He was there on a project for England as an engineer working for an oil company. We married when we moved back to the States. I went back to the Harvard School of Public Health, but my husband wasn't able to get a job in Boston, so we relocated to Texas, where he found an engineering job. I was doing consulting work and writing the manuscripts for two research studies we had completed in Saudia Arabia. I earned a master's degree in public health from the University of Texas, completing a two-year master's program in nine months by doubling up on course work, completing my internship, and writing my thesis. I was convinced that even though I kept my hand in research, hospital administration, not medicine, was the area I wanted to pursue.

We returned to Boston, where my husband went to Harvard Business School. I was offered a job at Beth Israel Hospital, building a new department. Before I took the job, **I looked at the person I'd be working with and tried to determine whether he could help me grow, provide me with new opportunities, open doors for me, and teach me as a mentor.** He did. I was promoted as the first woman administrator the hospital had ever had. **Finding a good mentor to help you is as important as your title or salary.**

Through a series of promotions and reorganizations, I became vice president and deputy director of the hospital, the number two person under the chief operating officer. I was virtually running all the clinical operations of the hospital. I also gave birth to my first child, a daughter, during that tenure.

I was absolutely blessed because my widowed mother-in-law came to stay with me and my husband. **She became my support system, caring for our daughter and managing the house.** She allowed me to have the flexibility to be everywhere I needed to be, meeting with doctors at 7:00 A.M. and attending dinner meetings with board members in the evening. **My husband has also always been unwaveringly supportive of my career.** I had a second child, a son, four years later. Two children are definitely many more than one! I was actively involved outside of the institution, on state committees, attending statewide hospital association meetings, and representing the institution on a Blue Cross negotiating committee, so I got tremendous external exposure. It was becoming really very difficult to juggle. I was burning out.

When my son was a year old, I went to my president and executive vice president to talk to them about the possibility of actually stepping down as vice president. The president, Dr. Mitchell T. Rubkin, helped me construct **something that would work for me but would also make a major statement for the institution that they valued women and working mothers.** They were going to be flexible in not only creating a role for me but also keeping me as vice president. Every chief of service told me, "Thank you for doing this and making this statement." The blue-collar workers said, "At least you understand how hard it is for all of us trying to juggle all that we do." I tried to do this new role part-time, but about six months into it, instead of working three days, I'd started to work four because I'd taken on more projects than I should have. Six months later, I abandoned my part-time role and flowed back into a full-time role. I realized how much I loved what I did, even though I was torn about no longer continuing as a part-time role model. It was a little more manageable because I didn't have night and week-end call and operations responsibility. I led the hospital merger activities, and as vice president of Beth Israel, I became the senior vice president of the new $1.1 billion system.

I was there for almost two and a half years when I received a call from the president of Boston Children's Hospital, who tapped me to be senior vice president for strategy, business development, and ambulatory operations. Five months after I took the job, the president stepped down and the board asked me if I would take his role permanently. For the last month, I have been chief operating officer of Children's Hospital and have also filled in for the CEO, who also announced his retirement, as well as continuing my role as senior vice president.

**All the chiefs are still men, the board members are all men, so there are many times when I am still the only woman in the room, but I've done very well and am extremely happy.** I think I'm pretty balanced. I love being with my children and my husband. My parents and family are very important to me. **I organize my work so I do all my phone calls, meetings, all the work I have to do face-to-face, during the day. I put everything into a pile that has to go home, and we all sit at the kitchen table and do our work together.** The kids do their homework, and when they go to bed, **I keep working.**

# Mediator in the Middle

## Merle Waxman

ASSOCIATE DEAN, OMBUDSPERSON, AND DIRECTOR OF THE OFFICE
FOR WOMEN IN MEDICINE, YALE MEDICAL SCHOOL

*Merle Waxman, M.A., serves as the associate dean for academic de-velopment and ombudsperson at Yale University. She is also the di-rector of the Office for Women in Medicine. She shared with us her quiet wisdom about how to take an opportunity and redesign it to fit with your ideal job. Her present broad opportunity to act as om-budsperson at all levels about student, faculty, and women's issues was her gradual creation, much appreciated by the medical school she serves.*

I was the middle child between two brothers, and my birth position may have been an introduction to my ombudsperson career. It gave me a head start as a mediator, even in my childhood. My parents were both first-generation Americans, the children of immigrants who were part of the influx from Eastern Europe just prior to the onset of the First World War. My father never finished high school. He worked hard as a printer in a shop he later owned, and he came home late at night. My mother, like my father, had only a high school education and spent her time running our home. Ours was a "traditional" Jewish family, in which women were supposed to be wives, mothers, and homemakers, and since I was a girl, neither of my parents had significant professional aspirations for me. When I was young, my mother told me she hoped I would marry a rich man (preferably a doctor) who could take care of me.

Despite my milieu, it was important to me to achieve. I learned I could be an outstanding student. I loved to read, and despite my mother's admonitions to "Turn off the lights, go to bed, and don't strain your eyes," I spent a lot of nights under the blankets with my flashlight.

**One teacher after another liked me because I loved school.** I always wanted to teach every grade I was in. My teachers motivated me. I was kidded about being a goody-goody. I was also kidded about being a tomboy. I was bigger than most girls and could play games and rough-and-tumble with the boys.

I had one really good friend all through school. She was bright and her parents pushed her, and she and I would study together a lot. **We competed with each other; sometimes she would get the top mark, and other times I would, so it balanced out. During adolescence we both felt we weren't part of the in group.** If one of us got more attention by the in crowd, we flaunted it, which produced some tension between us. We were both a little tall for our age. I'm five feet six now but I felt like I was six-ten growing up. I was invited to all the parties, but I never felt like part of the group.

**Being an excellent student helped because it gave me some prestige in school.** Kids would say, "Merle, can you help me with this problem?" or "Merle, can you explain this to me?" I liked the attention. However, I received little guidance and little encouragement from my parents; their traditional background prevented them from pushing me too hard, and in fact, they encouraged me not to excel. I was told, "Women aren't supposed to be smart. They are meant to be taken care of." Although I didn't understand why, this didn't seem right to me.

**I always belonged to service groups at school.** I was a class officer every year, mostly vice president or secretary or treasurer because I didn't want to be the president. Maybe it was because I was a middle child or a girl. **I loved being behind the scenes and putting things together, which meant organizing and mediating.**

An important motif—and one that I think had an enduring influence on me—emerged when I was about to enter college. **This was a desire, or even a need, to be associated with interesting people who challenged me.** I always chose slightly offbeat friends and found myself attracted to the nerdy crowd.

Once I was at Boston University, I spent more of my time at Harvard, where my boyfriend, Steve, and his friends were. Steve and I had met in junior high school and dated in high school. He's one of the brightest people I've ever met. We started dating when I was sixteen, and I still have the little heart locket he gave me for my sixteenth birthday. We stopped dating for a while, and after nine months, I realized, "Oh, you fool." **Steve was so right for me, and he made me so happy. I called him up and asked if we could**

**see each other again.** He had let his hair grow, gotten contact lenses, and was feeling his oats. He didn't say, "Oh yes, of course." He kept me at arm's length for a while, went off to University College in London for a semester, missed me a lot, and when he came back at the end of his junior year, we became a couple again. We were engaged my senior year in college and married within a month of my graduation.

Steve is a brilliant neuroscientist and neurologist. He has always worked in medical schools rather than private practice, so my mother bemoaned the fact that I "did not marry a real doctor"! In some ways, my marriage to him reflects my need to be challenged. I chose a mate who wanted me to travel with him into the intellectual fray. We play off each other, support and complement each other, and we have both enjoyed it immensely. This theme of being challenged, surrounded by people who are smarter, more gifted than me, has shaped my life during college and thereafter.

For four years after college graduation, I taught language development in an inner-city school district and earned my graduate degree in speech and language pathology in the evenings at the City University of New York. I had the choice of working in urban Yonkers or in more well-to-do suburban Mamaroneck. **I was idealistic and wanted to go to Yonkers. I wanted to try to change the world and make a difference.** It was an eye opener for me because I wasn't trained in working with inner-city families. It was learning on the spot, but I loved the children and was able to relate to them well.

Steve and I had two sons, and I divided my time between my job and raising the boys. Sometimes it was hard to watch Steve's career rocket ahead while mine lagged. In retrospect, I'm glad we staggered our career development in this way. My mother voiced some concern when I picked up the pace and began to launch my career in earnest when the boys were four and six years old. My husband tells me that, even prior to my entering the professional workforce when our children reached school age, it was clear I was repositioning myself. I had begun to jog, sometimes with my husband, and he noticed I was running well ahead of him!

When my children entered nursery and elementary school, I got a job as managing editor of a consumer newsletter. It didn't pay well, but it allowed me to use my negotiating talents and hone my management skills, and I liked it. After a few years, I felt I needed more.

I applied for and obtained the position of assistant ombudsperson at Stanford Medical School. In retrospect, my timing had been lucky; the field of "ombudsing"—of resolving conflictual issues, such as complaints and grievances, in a nonlitigational way—was just beginning to emerge within American universities. Despite my interest in conflict resolution, I was new to the field, and few formal training programs were available at that time. I fell back on my much-used coping mechanism of associating with challenging people. In my case, Mary Rowe emerged as a very important mentor. Rowe, a professor of economics at MIT, had served for more than a decade as ombudsperson at MIT and has emerged as one of the leading academic ombudspeople in the world. I had the good fortune to meet her at a workshop, and we talked a lot about our field. As we walked along the beach watching the sunrise, she said to me, "Merle, you have to start writing; you have important ideas." She inspired me, and propelled in part by her enthusiasm, I wrote some of my first papers on conflict resolution and proposed my model, still widely quoted, on how an ombudsperson can contribute to the effectiveness of medical institutions.

My husband was recruited to Yale to be the chair of the Department of Neurology. I loved what I was doing at Stanford, but we knew that Yale would be a good place for him, and we both missed the Northeast. Nonetheless, we were conflicted about leaving California; the lifestyle and weather seemed ideal for raising children. Yale's dean, Leon Rosenberg, was a very persuasive person, and urged me to apply for an opening as the director of the Office for Women in Medicine at Yale Medical School. A few years later, I went from there to become the first ombudsperson at Yale University. I was subsequently also appointed associate dean at Yale Medical School. My jobs are challenging, and I enjoy challenges. **I work sixty to seventy hours a week, and I love it. I feel I've been at the forefront of a field where I can use my natural talent for mediation to solve people's problems and expand a crucial career.**

Universities have been nearly ideal work settings for me, perfect for an individual who likes to interact with challenging people. Yale has been particularly exhilarating. There's an ongoing stream of important and provocative problems to solve. The people, from freshman undergraduate students to high-level administrators and distinguished scholars, have been interesting; and the problems, from complaints by undergraduates about professors who grade papers without reading them carefully to disputes involving distinguished senior faculty who disagree about authorship position, have been challenging. I thrive on that.

Although I'm on the professional fast track, my mother's exhortations about family did sink in. Steve and I continue to be each other's best friends. Our two sons, Matthew and David, are thoughtful, caring, and sensitive people. I've begun to wonder if the need to take on important problems, to challenge oneself, has been passed on to our sons. Matthew wrote his first book while finishing Yale Law School, and David, also a Yale graduate, is launching a career in finance.

It's a turbulent time in academic medicine. Changes in the funding of medicine are triggering profound alternatives in how medicine is practiced, and medical schools are undergoing many stresses, which keeps my job busier than ever. **Life is continuing to present me with challenges, and I like challenges.**

# 4

## The Healers and Discoverers

WOMEN are now prominently involved in many areas of science and medicine, although they continue to be a very small minority group within some specialties. Very few women chair departments at medical schools, preside over medical staffs, or win the most prestigious research awards. Only a generation ago, very few women were part of these scientifically oriented professions at all, and none were considered eligible to be astronauts.

### *Results from the* See Jane Win *Study*

The women in science and medicine share strong common backgrounds in science and mathematics that were, indeed, thresholds to entering their professions. Almost all of the women in this career category have earned advanced degrees, including master's degrees, Ph.D.s, and medical, veterinary, and dentistry doctoral degrees. Although more physicians in our study were involved in the stereotypically "female" fields of pediatrics and obstetrics than in any other specialty, there were also surgeons, orthopedic surgeons, internists, family practitioners, urologists, psychiatrists, cardiologists, radiologists, dermatologists, and medical administrators. Among the researchers in our study were quite a few who are conducting biological, biochemical, or psychological research, and a fair number who were engineers.

Our research for *See Jane Win* found that physicians and scientists tended to be somewhat less social as children than women in other professions, particularly in middle school and high school. They were very active in extracurricular activities and often assumed leadership roles in those activities. Sports and other competitive activities were very important to them. More than one physician commented that sports gave her a group of friends who didn't think of her as a "brain." Sports also taught those girls how to deal with losing. The healers and discoverers tended to be more involved in outdoor activities and Girl Scouts. In fact, many credited camping or family travel for their interest in science. As children, they participated in music more often than the women in most other careers, and quite a few were serious musicians before they became scientists.

Not surprisingly, the physicians and scientists enjoyed and were competent in science and mathematics from elementary school on, much more so than all other groups, and many increased in academic confidence as they moved through adolescence. These career women had the highest average I.Q. They also graduated from their high schools with the highest average class rank (in the top 6 percent). They were less distracted by boys during those crucial teen years and had smoother adolescent relationships with their parents than some of the other career groups. Although more of them identified with their mothers than with their fathers, in comparison to other career groups, larger percentages identified with their fathers than did those in other career categories. Many of their mothers returned to school to continue their education while the daughters were growing up. Specifically, 40 percent of the physicians' mothers returned to school, thus providing role models for an extended education.

The women in this category were frequently considered "brainy" by others although like most of the successful women in our study, they frequently chose words like "smart," "hardworking," and "independent" to describe themselves as girls. Scientists described themselves as "creative" somewhat more frequently than physicians, who were more likely to see themselves as "athletic." More of these women went to parochial, independent, and all-girl schools for elementary, middle, and high school.

These women were mainly happy with their career choices, although more women in medicine expressed mixed feelings about their career than many of the other groups. They spent more time on their job than all other career groups, with more than half working more than fifty hours per week. Both the physicians and the scientists expressed concerns that their careers took too much time from their families. Some of the physicians also expressed concern at how time-consuming their training had been. Some scientists commented that their careers involved too much competition, specifically their need to compete for grants for funding their research. More physicians than scientists indicated that their job was financially satisfying. More scientists than physicians liked the creative involvement in their careers. Both career groups credited their careers as being challenging and making a contribution.

## *How Jane Won*

Thanks to NASA, we were able to include two astronauts in this chapter in special celebration of the fact that only recently have women even been considered eligible. A generation ago, they were simply told they need not apply. The contrast between the two astronauts' childhoods is also interesting. Commander Eileen Collins was lured by the skies as a child but perceived herself as only an average student until young adulthood, when she was motivated to excel. Astronaut Cady Coleman, Ph.D., was an exceptional science student from childhood. Although Cady's was the more typical pattern for scientists, Eileen's history emphasizes that even average students can improve their qualifications when they're motivated to succeed.

Pediatric neurosurgeon Dr. Alexa Canady and plant physiologist Dr. Camellia Okpodu remind us of the racial prejudice that continues to exist among scientists. Alexa considered herself a "twofer," filling a quota as a woman and as a minority, facing prejudice against both groups in the male bastion of neurosurgery. She believes that racial prejudice may have equipped her better to handle the prejudice against women simply because it helped her develop resilience. Both Alexa and Camellia struggled and triumphed and share with us tools they used to persevere. Hopefully, one day racial prejudice will disappear, but many women may still need courage to overcome it.

Lilian Gonsalves, M.D., a psychiatrist, and Sosamma Berger, Ph.D., a biochemical researcher, illustrate the blending of cultural differences. Lilian received her education through medical school in India, and Sosamma was drawn to this country from India to complete her graduate education. They both shared how they managed to raise families and keep high-powered careers growing while their husbands continued their own scientific careers.

Susan Lemagie, M.D., and her husband, John, followed their idealism to Alaska, where they believed they could make a difference together. In a partnership where John initially did most of the home management, Susan could manage a career that required night and weekend calls. The smaller population of Alaska compared to more populous states has allowed Susan to become a community leader and an inspiration to women both locally and nationally.

Environmental engineer Teresa Culver, Ph.D., shares how her family's encouragement of science and the love of environment propelled her toward environmental engineering, a career area made up of less than 15 percent women. All Teresa's siblings have chosen scientific careers and continue to cheer one another on as they did in school sports and musical performances—an inspiring example of how crucial family members can be in motivating one another.

# ℒURED BY THE SKIES

## Eileen Collins
NASA ASTRONAUT AND SPACE SHUTTLE COMMANDER

*As a pilot and NASA astronaut, Eileen Collins has logged approx-*
*imately 5,000 hours in thirty different types of aircraft and 537*
*hours in space over three space flights. When she was inducted into*
*the National Women's Hall of Fame, Eileen stated, "I want to do*
*well because I know that I am representing other women, other pilots,*
*military pilots as well as civilian pilots, who are hoping to come to*
*NASA and be space shuttle pilots themselves."*

*Eileen grew up in Elmira, New York. She completed a master of*
*science degree in operations research from Stanford University and a*
*master of arts degree in space systems management from Webster*
*University. She is married to Pat Youngs and has one child.*

*When, as a girl, Hillary Rodham Clinton wrote to NASA about*
*becoming an astronaut, she was told that women couldn't qualify.*
*She consoled herself by acknowledging that she probably couldn't*
*pass the vision test anyway. That vision test was Eileen's biggest*
*obstacle as well; however, she not only passed the test and became an*
*astronaut, but was the first woman selected to command a space*
*shuttle mission.*

Summer camp provided my first inspiration for becoming a pilot. I
attended summer camp every year between ages seven and twelve,
and it was there that I discovered my love of the outdoors. I gazed at
the stars at night and became passionate about astronomy. I became
interested in early American history by finding Indian arrowheads
and experienced my first attachments to science and adventure. The
camp lasted seven weeks—five weeks of day camp and two weeks of
sleep-away camp. It wasn't an extravagant camp and only had four
activities: crafts, nature, swimming, and recreation. **The getting
along, cooperating, and living with others at camp in combination with the adventurous spirit of those summers were perfect preparations for the military.** Furthermore, there was a
nationally recognized glider airfield near the camp. As I observed

those gliders, they lured me toward the sky. I imagined that someday I, too, would fly.

**My mother was an important role model to me because she
was so independent.** When I was nine, she took a job at the local
prison office, where she would complete the forms for paroles and
probations. **She seemed to like her job and had such a good grip
on how she handled life at work and at home that she instilled
in me confidence in my independence and decision making.**

My dad was a surveyor, and he would let me look at his plans for
roads and buildings. **I was interested in his diagrams and plans,
which led me directly to a fascination with geometry and math.**

Our parents found the means to send all four of us to parochial
schools because they considered the combination of our religion and
general education important. I was the second child and the oldest
daughter. Unfortunately, I was quite shy. I didn't raise my hand
much in school, would freeze up if I had to talk in front of a group,
and considered myself only an average student. I always did my
homework, and I favored math and science over other classes, but I
don't think I studied as hard as I should have. I now regret that I
didn't take more advantage of the academic opportunities.

I enjoyed Girl Scouting for three years, played guitar briefly, was
in cheerleading and drama, but was never overly involved in any of
the activities. Again, I allowed my shyness to overcome me.

Hurricane Agnes stormed through our area when I was in tenth
grade. Our home was damaged, and I knew repair was costly. I volunteered to change to public schools to save my parents the tuition
and convinced them I was interested in comparing the experiences at
the two schools. **I made some new friends and continued some
of my friendships at my previous school, again adjusting well
despite my shyness. I didn't date in high school, wasn't part of
the popular crowd, and was independent, but I didn't feel isolated. I always enjoyed transition and adventure and wasn't at
all fearful of new experiences.**

It was in high school that I began reading books about flying. Almost all the books were about male military pilots in World
War I, World War II, Korea, and Vietnam. **I was disappointed
that all of the pilots were males. Then I read about Amelia
Earhart and Jacqueline Cochran.** Jacqueline's book especially

inspired me because she wrote about how she grew up in poverty and eventually became a famous and talented pilot.

My parents were slightly strict as far as discipline but always encouraging about our education. They told us they would be pleased if we attended college but, of course, they couldn't afford to send us. We'd have to earn our way.

At my high school graduation I suddenly realized I could have done much better at school if I had applied myself more. It was that eye-opening experience that made me determined to change my direction for college. **Because I had to earn my way through college by working thirty to forty hours weekly, I believe I was even more committed to my education. I researched and selected an affordable community college that had the best math and science programs available. I studied constantly, truly applied myself, and thoroughly enjoyed my education in a different way than I had ever before. I joined Toastmasters and overcame my fear of speaking up in front of others.**

After completing my associate degree, I announced to my parents that I planned to join the air force. They were astonished but nevertheless supportive. **I completed my college degree in the Air Force Reserve Officer Training Corp. The air force paid my tuition at Syracuse University, although I continued to work many hours to pay my room and board and keep my grades high as well. My new experiences in college proved to me that I am truly an independent person, an extrovert, and someone who enjoys leadership positions.**

The biggest break in my life was when I was accepted into pilot training. The final test for acceptance was an eye examination. Much to my shock and chagrin, I failed the first eye test. I had learned to study hard for other tests in my life, but when I was told that I would get another chance to take the eye examination, I knew studying wasn't the answer to passing that test. I'd been warned that I'd better rest my eyes and get plenty of sleep. In contrast to all of my past test experiences, I remember promising myself **to stop studying and get that sleep. I ate an optimal diet with lots of vegetables and so many carrots** that my fingertips turned orange. I even did eye exercises! I passed the second test and thus qualified for military pilot school in 1978. That was the initial step to becoming a military pilot that finally led me to acceptance into the astronaut program in 1990. Five years later, I had the inspiring opportunity to pilot the shuttle *Discovery*. I flew again in 1997, and later as a shuttle commander in 1999. **Considering how shy I was as a child, being in command was not a small accomplishment for me.**

I feel fortunate to have become the pilot I dreamed about becoming in childhood. I feel lucky to work with NASA, where men and women are treated equally and where there is respect and professionalism among all involved. About the only difference I've ever seen in the treatment between me and male astronauts is the amount of press and media attention I've received because I was the first woman commander in the space program. I do remember wondering as a child why only men were astronauts. Now that's all changed, and I was fortunate enough to be part of that important change.

# Rowing Crew Taught Her to Excel, One Stroke at a Time

## Cady Coleman, Ph.D.

NASA ASTRONAUT

*Cady Coleman was born in Charleston, South Carolina, and graduated from W. T. Woodson High School in Fairfax, Virginia, in 1978. She received a bachelor of science degree in chemistry from the Massachusetts Institute of Technology in 1983, and a doctorate in polymer science and engineering from the University of Massachusetts in 1991. She is married to glass artist Josh Simpson.*

*Cady was selected by NASA in 1992 while in the air force. A veteran of two space missions, Coleman has logged over 500 hours in space. In completing two flights, Coleman orbited the Earth 335 times, traveled over 8.3 million miles, and logged a total of 20 days, 20 hours, 41 minutes, and 21 seconds in space.*

I had a very special mom. I have never been able to figure out how she did it, but **she brought me up to think that I could be anybody I wanted to be.** My mom orchestrates situations to be sure that everyone is being taken care of. I get a lot of my team-building skills from her.

My father worked in exploration. He was the chief of salvage and diving for the navy. He was in a program where men lived under the sea and went farther and deeper to find out what a wonderful place it was. **It's a natural for me to want to go places I haven't been before because it was important in my childhood.**

I was in gifted-learner programs starting in sixth grade. I liked math and loved science. **My teachers were excellent, and they made it really exciting to learn chemistry and physics.**

**I was known for being nice, and I had a lot of friends, but I wasn't one of the prettiest or most popular girls in school.** I played flute in the concert band and then also in the jazz band, even though it didn't usually include flutes. I convinced the director that I really wanted to play in it, and if it didn't work, then he could kick me out. Playing solos in the jazz band gave me the courage to try out for drama production, and to play for local dinner theaters.

My mom was great at finding cool programs for me to participate in. **An important influence for me was a National Science Foundation fellowship.** I got to work at the Coast Guard Oceanographic Institute. We would collect the data to help understand normal currents in that area. **I worked with a group of adults. Programs that bring kids and adults together are very important.**

**Between high school and college, I was an exchange student in Norway and learned an immense amount about myself.** I was in a language camp, and one of the instructors at the language camp was a guitar player. We were all sitting around one night, and he said, "Cady, why don't you go get your flute, and I can play my guitar?" I said, "Well, I don't know how to play what you're playing." He said, "You'll know what to play," and he was right. We had a great time.

My best friend in Norway was a woman named Xiv who lived near me and was a wonderful guitar player. We actually earned money playing folk songs on the streets in Norway. I've been playing the flute, both in public and in private, ever since.

Even though I was a little shy, **music gave me the confidence to stand out.** Whether you're the only flute player in the jazz band or sitting on the street in Norway, **you realize it might not be so bad to stand out in other situations. These little steps made me realize I have something to say.** It's the way I think of public speaking now. To get up and give a speech in front of people can be challenging, but I realize I have experiences to share that people might like to hear about.

In Norway, I lived with a family where the two boys were national hiking and track champions, and the whole family was athletic and went cross-country skiing several times a week. **I learned that if I wanted to go cross-country skiing, I didn't actually have to be good at it, only enjoy it.** To my surprise, it turned out that I wasn't bad at sports. When I returned from my year in Norway, I went to college and joined the crew team. **I learned a lot about myself by rowing on the crew team, and I valued the opportunity to interact with other women at MIT.**

About 15 to 20 percent of the students at MIT were women. I

lived in a coed dorm that was about 40 percent women, very supportive, almost family-oriented. You could walk in any time and know whoever you met in the hallway. **I made a point of surrounding myself with people like that. I've always wanted help and support from tutors, parents, siblings, and other people. Their words of encouragement are important to me.**

By the end of my freshman year, **I realized that I could major in anything I wanted, which was exciting for me.** I decided I should major in whatever was hardest for me. **After a semester in electrical engineering, I switched back to chemistry and decided it wasn't such a crime to do something that might not be the hardest for me but was a subject that I really liked and had an intuition and passion for.**

I worked through a revelation during sophomore year. MIT is actually a place that can stomp on you. I would take a test and think I'd prepared well, and I would get there and realize that I knew fewer than half the answers. Then I would find out that the actual class average was 30 and that I had a 32. **I'd have to remind myself while I was taking the test that if it's hard for me, it's probably hard for everybody.**

I decided to try to be an astronaut when I was at MIT. Dr. Sally Ride, the first American woman astronaut, came and gave a lecture. I listened to her talk, and I thought, "I want that job!" **I thought, "If she can do this, I can do it." I could identify with who she was because she was a scientist, and it was clear that she used her education. She did some teaching and also flew jets and went to space on the space shuttle.** I somehow knew that a laboratory wasn't enough for me. I needed to do something with people, but I never dreamed I could have a job that would include adventure too. The day Sally came to speak was a memorable day for me. **That's why I think it's so important that accomplished women speak to girls. Seeing a face and feeling like you can touch a person helps girls realize that they can achieve their dreams.**

The crew team turned out to be a unique opportunity for me. **I learned about what I was capable of and how to excel, even when I felt overwhelmed.** For example, when it's 11:00 at night and I'm just beginning an assignment, it gives me the same feeling **as being at the beginning of a race and only being ten strokes** into it and being very tired. The only way to get through the race is not to think 206 strokes ahead because you'll just give up. Instead, you think, "This stroke, and then the next stroke, then the next stroke." It's the same feeling in trying to write a dissertation. If you think about the whole picture, it's really too big and discouraging. What I learned to do is concentrate on the part that I can bite off, and then bite off one piece at a time.

I have often thought that if you have some level of ability, much of the rest is persistence and hard work. That certainly seemed to fit for graduate school. I actually worked on a research project for two and a half years, at which point I was unlucky enough to find out that someone else was working on exactly the same project. They used the same catalyst, same molecules, same everything, and they published it first. After all that time and effort, I had to change my project. It was a tough time.

There are so many discouraging things that can happen. Topics don't work out, you may not be with the right faculty member, things always turn out to be hard in one way or another, and that is what it's all about. You have to have the ability to persevere. When your experiment fails at midnight, and you know you'll lose everything if you go home, you really have to be tough to stay and start again. It's having the perseverance and the belief in yourself to do all that, to stay one more night and not become overwhelmed by the whole battle.

The hardest thing I've ever done in my whole life was work full-time during the day and then try to change gears and work on my dissertation at night.

It was a very challenging time, but I did have support from friends and siblings. I'd always been the sibling that was academically ahead and mature. For those two years, my siblings took care of me. They would call and encourage me, "Just do one more chapter and hang in there, and it'll be done." We have different interests and skills but still have the ability to help each other a lot. It might be easy to resent your sister, the astronaut. Yet my sibs are all neat in their own ways, and they know it. When my astronaut picture had a black electrical tape mustache on it minutes after I brought it home the first time, I knew they'd have no problem handling the whole thing.

I've received many opportunities in my lifetime, but there

were experiences I would have missed if those in charge didn't have the vision or imagination to understand that the job could be done by a woman. As a woman, you have to be persistent in volunteering and making some people understand both your desire and your capability to do the job previously reserved solely for men.

# SHE WAS A "TWOFER"

## Alexa Canady, M.D.

PEDIATRIC NEUROSURGEON, CHILDREN'S HOSPITAL
OF MICHIGAN, DETROIT

*Dr. Alexa Canady ventured into a career where there were few women and very few African-Americans, and it seems as if because of her pioneering work, doors will be a squeak more open in the future. Alexa admits that the unfortunate racial prejudices she experienced in her life may have equipped her to be stronger in the face of rejection than typically successful white women. Those around her consider her a brainiac, and a very compassionate doc.*

My introduction to racism began early. My brother and I were the only black students in a white school. In second grade, I took a reading test as part of the normal school achievement testing. My teacher reported my scores as mediocre. My grandmother, who taught elementary education at Lane College in Tennessee, had come for the summer to take a course in psychometric testing. One of her classmates tested me, and I achieved much better than the school scores, so my grandmother's instructor had me tested before the class at Michigan State University. The results of those scores were compared with my school scores, and it ultimately turned out that the teacher had lied about my scores and had assigned them to someone else. My I.Q. scores were superior. After the new testing, I went from second to fourth grade, and it made my school life more interesting. All I would have learned in third grade was multiplication tables, so I learned those in the summer.

My father is a dentist and my mother was going to go to graduate school in genetics, but it didn't work out because of pressure to stay home with us kids. The women on my mother's side of the family had all finished school early. My mother finished high school at sixteen, and my grandmother was teaching by the time she was eighteen. **My grandmother made a difference for me because when I was a little kid, she treated me like an adult.** She taught me square roots, and when I took the placement test for junior high school, I knew the answers to the square-root questions when no one else did.

**My family gave me lots of cultural exposure.** I had music, ballet, tap dancing, art-enrichment classes, and Saturday mornings at the Y. I played piano, went to national music camp for two summers, danced through junior high school, and was a debater through high school. My friend and I took Saturday courses in Fortran computer programming at Michigan State.

I always read prolifically as a youngster, especially a series of little blue biographies. I would read ten to twelve of those a week, and the stories were inspiring. At first, the librarians at the local library wouldn't let me read the young adult books, so my mother had to go to the library to insist I be allowed to read these more advanced books.

In junior high school, which was racially mixed, I was a cheerleader and busy in school activities. I had my own group of friends. By high school, which was predominantly white, **I was in the "out" crowd, but it was the intelligent "out crowd."** The early sixties was a good time for that. **Some of the teachers were interested in our group and gave us both credibility and support.** We were invited to their homes to discuss interesting issues.

Math was a favorite subject. **I took advanced algebra at the same time as geometry and took trigonometry the second semester. I completed the senior courses my junior year, and in my senior year, my friend and I went to the junior college to take a calculus course.**

My early college years at the University of Michigan were difficult for me. **I had many identities.** I was a debater. I also played baseball, football, basketball, whatever was in season. I joined the same sorority my mother and grandmother had belonged to. The three groups were quite distinctly different experiences. **I could be different in different places and find out who I really wanted to be.** Still, I had trouble finding my identity. I wasn't the scholar I had been in high school. I no longer perceived myself as a mathematician. I felt lost. I stopped going to classes for the first semester of my sophomore year, and despite that, did reasonably well. I went to classes only sixteen hours the second semester, and it was a disaster. I did strange things like appear for the final, only to find it was a take-home test everyone had received two weeks before. After my second year, I was on academic probation.

I spent summers at Ann Arbor, and **my father would come once a week and have dinner with me. That helped, although we didn't talk about my school problems. His being there and the fact that his was not an inquisitive presence made me feel important. I perceived it as a message of absolute support.** I began to turn myself around.

**I went to work for the student newspaper, the *Michigan Daily,*** as a reporter and eventually an editorial-page editor, and **it got me back into an academic culture. I participated in a health-science summer program for minority students** only because it offered payment. I worked during the day for the summer program through the medical school and then went to the *Daily* at 5:00 P.M. and did my job there. It worked out wonderfully.

**My passion for mathematics was replaced by a new passion—** medicine. I changed my major to zoology, and applied to medical school. I was accepted into the University of Michigan Medical School for several reasons: **I had many intellectual pursuits,** including debate and being editor of the newspaper. **I'd been at the medical school program in the summer and earned advocates at the medical school. My MCATs (medical school exams) were good. I had also done some research in the genetics lab and had a mentor there. All of those attributes made it possible for them to tolerate my poor undergraduate grades.**

I shadowed a neurologist at St. Louis University for a month between my second and third years of medical school, and had a first-hand chance to see what neurosurgeons do. In my senior year of medical school, I spent more time in neurology and neurosurgery, and knew that neurosurgery was where my personality fit best.

My parents were fairly cool to the idea because they weren't sure if I could get into neurosurgery or if I could make a career of it because I was both a woman and an African-American. I shared their concern, but **I had to try.**

I was actually accepted into two programs. I'd gone to Yale as a surgical resident, and was slotted to be the neurosurgery resident. I had applied to the University of Minnesota, but they expected two years of general surgery before starting neurosurgery, and I didn't want to do an extra year. The chairman of Minnesota phoned me and said, "Would you be interested in being our neurosurgery resident?" He told me I could be admitted with only one year of general surgery. Then I went to the chairman at Yale and explained, "I've been offered a position in Minnesota. Can you tell me whether I'm going to get Yale's slot?" It was early September, and he wouldn't tell me for sure until October 15, so I took the Minnesota position. I learned later that I was going to get the Yale slot, and the Yale people thought I should have known. In 1976, **they didn't understand that no black woman in her right mind was going to turn down a genuine offer for a "maybe."**

At the University of Minnesota, again, I was a "twofer." They only had to take one person and got credit for two—a woman and a minority. The dean of the medical school came up to me the first day and said, "You must be our new equal-opportunity package." To which I replied, "Yes, I must be." It turned out that he said that kind of thing to everyone. For example, to my friend with a beard, he said, "Do you think you're going to survive this residency with a beard?" **The dean wanted to know how we responded to stress, and whether we would back down. He had nothing else to say, and after that we were great buddies.** I stayed at Minnesota for five years and finished my residency there and did a year of fellowship in pediatric neurosurgery at the children's hospital in Philadelphia.

**Mentors are absolutely critical,** and I have had many. There were only about three or four women neurosurgeons in the country at the time, so I was fortunate to have two supportive women neurosurgeons in my career, one at the University of Michigan and one at Yale. My greatest career mentor was in my fellowship. He taught me everything I know about how the world works in neurosurgery. Every morning, from 7:00 to 7:30, I got a philosophy lecture from him on how to build a career.

I got married after I had been in Detroit four or five years and have no children. **My marriage was very important in that it freed me to let work be less important.** My husband is retired from the military and has a sense of duty and responsibility, so he doesn't hassle me on that, which is not always the case for neurosurgeons.

There is something you know intuitively as an African-American woman that white women just don't seem to know. **I never had the illusion that everybody wanted me to be part of anything, and as a woman and a minority, I had to keep my focus on what I needed, recognizing that I had to have a document at the end of my training**—proof that I'd accomplished what I said I did. I never thought that the neurosurgical world would be hot to have me, so I wasn't surprised when I ran into people who weren't welcoming.

As women, we have to understand that access has been granted to us not because we're any different or any better than women who came before us. **It has been granted by external political forces. We can't expect to be validated as individuals, but we can make the field different for those who come behind us. We must do good work, and eventually the work will speak for itself. If we go to a place that doesn't want us, and we're affected by how they perceive us, it can destroy us.**

**My experience as an African-American girl helped me immeasurably as a woman because I had experienced rejection before.** The average girl who has been intellectually and academically superior entering a male-dominated career may experience her first rejection ever, and it shocks and defeats her. She asks, "Why would they not want me? Everybody else did." It is so strikingly different from the African-American experience, in which I was happy to get in the door. **I learned every day not to count on others' acceptance as a measure of my worth.**

Today I am a professor of neurosurgery and vice chair of my department. I can say that I would make the same choices today that I made before, which is all I can ask at this point in my career.

# Women Physicians Were Her Role Models

## Lilian Gonsalves, M.D.

### PSYCHIATRIST, THE CLEVELAND CLINIC

*Dr. Lilian Gonsalves combines her interest in women's issues with her practice of psychiatry. As an immigrant to this country, she has managed to build an outstanding practice with the prestigious Cleveland Clinic and raise her family. Her well-established reputation has recently earned her election to the Board of Governors of the Cleveland Clinic Foundation.*

I grew up in Bombay, India, the third of five children. My father would say, "**I want all of you to have careers, especially the girls because you really don't know what's going to happen to you later, who you are going to marry, what's going to happen to your marriage, and what destiny has in store for you.**" **I heard this message loud and clear.** My sister is a schoolteacher, and I became a psychiatrist.

**I went to an all-girl school** where every teacher in the school was a woman. I played the piano and took music lessons right through to my first year of medical school. I also swam, played badminton, and did yoga. Health was a big part of our family.

I attended an all-girl college too. My physics professor was a male, but he was the only exception. I was accepted into medical college when I was eighteen years old. I was fortunate because school came easily for me. **I was consistently in the top 1 percent of my class. On one occasion, I slipped from the top 1 percent and was totally traumatized because I thought, "How am I going to face my parents?"** It was no big deal when I went home, but that's how important it was for me to perform.

My family all live in Bombay except me. My parents had a very traditional marriage. My dad is a business school graduate and a self-made businessman. He is outgoing, a risk taker, very bright, and forward-thinking. My mother is a high school graduate who stayed at home, as is traditional in India. She maintained a softer, quieter tone but was really the rock in the marriage.

Indira Gandhi, who was the prime minister of India while I was in high school, college, and medical school, was one of my role models. I admired her courage, her brilliance, her elegance, and the way she stood up for things. In fact, the joke about her was that she was the "only man in the Cabinet." In India's big cities, it's not uncommon to see women in professions.

I'm the only physician in my family. In India, medicine is a noble, prestigious profession. I heard from the family that it would be good to become a doctor. Also, the doctors I saw were women. My mother's gynecologist was a woman. Our family physician was a woman, and I still remember her house calls fondly. I admired her, and although I never really got to know her, at some level she was a role model for me. Before I decided to go into medicine, I met the daughter of my parents' very good friend. She was an obstetrician-gynecologist in London. She told me how wonderful medicine was, how she enjoyed her work, and how she had graduated from the same college I attended. I asked a lot of questions, and she was very helpful. I got into medical school on merit. There was no quota system.

I met my husband in medical school. He had grown up in South Africa and is also of Indian origin. He'd left South Africa because of apartheid. After we got married, we decided to come to the United States, as there were more opportunities here. My brother knew an ear, nose, and throat surgeon who was at the Cleveland Clinic. I sent him my curriculum vitae, and the next thing I knew I had a job at the Cleveland Clinic in psychiatry. Ninety-five percent of my patients are women. Most of them come from ob-gyn and primary-care physicians.

I'd never been to the States, but as a family, we'd traveled to London and Europe. When I came to the Cleveland Clinic to begin my residency training, I was in culture shock. First, I'd moved from hot, tropical Bombay to the Cleveland blizzard of '77. The other shock was that we had only 10 women residents out of 450. I thought I'd come to the developed world, where everyone had equal opportunity. I couldn't believe it! When I became pregnant, it was even worse. People would look at me like I'd fallen from Mars.

Fortunately, it's changed. There are probably hundreds of women medical residents now.

Once I got to the Cleveland Clinic, I made a lot of friends, but I missed my family. Thanksgiving, Christmas, and all the other holidays were so family-oriented. We had many friends who invited us over, but it wasn't quite the same as family.

**Women can have it all, but not at the same time. Our biological clocks and career clocks tick in harmony.** This is a decision that each woman has to resolve in her own heart. I had to make a choice too. I had my first child right after I finished my residency training. I was at home for nine months before returning to work. The chairman created a position for me. That was a hard time, because at nine months, a child's separation anxiety is at its height. Our daughter cried and screamed and had her legs wrapped around me the first day I left for work.

**My husband and I drove to work together that day and talked about our daughter all the time.** That was hard. **What helped is that we had a very good child-care person, Sue.** She was with us for the entire seventeen years, until she died from complications of diabetes. When our children were young, however, my recurring nightmare was that Sue would get sick and not show up for work. Fortunately for us, this didn't happen. Come rain or shine, she was there, sometimes as early as 6:30 A.M. if we both had 7:00 A.M. meetings. **If you want good child care, you must be willing to pay for it.**

Today our daughter is a freshman at the University of Pennsylvania, and our son is a freshman at Hawken High School. We travel to India to see our family almost every year. **We've exposed our kids to both cultures. When we go to India, there's the strong sense of family and love and affection from grandparents, uncles, and aunts.** We have a diverse group of friends and also belong to the Indian Physician Association, which promotes social activities, cultural issues, and philanthropy within the community. Our kids have a diverse group of friends too.

**Having children slows your career down to some degree, but if you put off having children, you have to live with the fact that you might not be able to conceive in your late thirties. It's important how your partner feels,** and I've been very fortunate. I couldn't do this without him. My anesthesiologist husband is someone who supports me not just by his words but also by his actions. It's been a team effort. Organizational skills help. I learned to be organized growing up. **I believe the key is to talk about this with your husband on a daily basis and to keep your good sense of humor.**

# She Wanted to Make a Difference for Women

~

## Susan Lemagie, M.D.

OBSTETRICIAN-GYNECOLOGIST AND WOMEN'S HEALTH ACTIVIST

*Dr. Susan Lemagie lives in rural Alaska, where she maintains a solo medical practice and raises her two daughters, Sarah and Margaret, with her husband, John. She serves on multiple public committees and boards, and enjoys planning conferences for women and health-care providers. She is past chair of the Alaska Section of the American College of Obstetricians and Gynecologists. As an avid rock gardener, exercise enthusiast, and mother, she is constantly re-learning how to balance her time creatively for a fulfilling life.*

As a child, I never would have expected to become a physician. I had never seen a woman doctor and was very squeamish. I hated blood and was very modest.

I grew up in Tacoma, Washington, surrounded by a tight-knit family and lots of friends. In elementary school, I was a good student, and I remember that my teachers wanted me to advance to a higher grade, but my parents decided against that. The teachers gave me lots of encouragement and extra projects to keep me busy in school. I went to an excellent junior high school with accelerated classes in science, math, English, and Spanish. The space race was on, we were encouraged to excel, and I loved the learning. At the end of the year, as a beginning student, I was surprised to be awarded the school English prize, and everyone told me I would grow up to be a journalist.

Then my father accepted a job transfer to manage a larger and better Safeway store on the Olympic Peninsula. I was excited about moving someplace new, and I enjoyed the summer before school started, making new friends and exploring the small town. But I will never forget that first day in a dumpy school, sitting at my old-fashioned desk, complete with runners and inkwells and fifty years of carved initials. The teachers were uninspiring, the classes were boring, and the curriculum was ancient. I remember weeping behind my books.

My new peers were also harder to understand. There was much more flirting, and the girls wore tight, slinky skirts that were totally out of date at my old school. I had just come from a big city where there had been students of many backgrounds and races; here, there were no African-American or Latino kids. **I felt like I had moved to a different planet.**

I was already different—not interested in boys, popular music, or clothes. I'd asked my parents for a chemistry set for ninth-grade Christmas, and I set up my own private lab space with a sink and running water in the former servants' quarters in the attic of our old house. I loved to tinker there and spent my allowance on chemicals and glass beakers.

**My mother, who had been popular as a teenager and married when she was seventeen, just didn't understand why popularity wasn't important to me. She would alternate between being furious with me and proud of what I was doing. I hated the social pressure.**

I don't remember feeling especially nerdy. I was in the "college" track, in the "right crowd," not the superpopular one, but the one with all the bright, clean-cut kids. I was president of clubs, involved in the community, and had lots of friends, including a couple of boyfriends. I was liked and respected, but I was definitely not happy. I knew what I was missing from my old school: the taste of being encouraged, challenged, and having the "cutting edge" of science thrown at me.

I was known for my cynical humor and my emerging activism in political campaigns. There was a lot going on in 1969, and I learned about it in an unusual way—morning debates with my senior calculus teacher. He must have weighed four hundred pounds, was very conservative, and seated me right next to his desk, the better to discuss the news with me. Even if the rest of the class was studying calculus, we'd be discussing Vietnam, the Democratic rally in Chicago, feminism, or abortion rights. His influence was tremendous, but not in the way he expected. I had the opportunity to clearly see what I was up against as a woman in the outside world.

My Washington State Pre-College Test results reinforced this. My scores were among the highest in the class, yet I was rated very likely to succeed as a teacher, secretary, nurse, or librarian, while my lower-scoring male colleagues were rated as engineers, physicians, scientists, and attorneys. I showed the results to all the guys in calculus, and they roared along with me.

With little counseling, my only options for college were in-state, and I chose the University of Washington, partly for the sense of being anonymous after my small-town experience. I signed up for advanced classes, found a mentor in an English teacher, worked hard, and did well, but still felt unsatisfied. I wanted new challenges, and I didn't know what I wanted to do with my life. My high school boyfriend was pressuring me to marry him, and I wanted to escape. My English teacher suggested that instead of ruining my GPA or dropping out, I attend Urban Plunge, an encounter group being held one weekend in January. It changed my life. Through my future husband, John, whom I met there, I found a like-minded, more sophisticated crowd, mostly young college graduates who attended Quaker meetings and were already in professions. My social and political life blossomed. Instead of going home for a summer job, I worked in Seattle and lived in a commune with my new women friends.

School was still a problem. Classes weren't especially challenging, and I lacked a goal. I tried to fit in; I bought penny loafers and a season pass for the football games, and immersed myself in experimental biology, women's studies, and modern dance. Then I got the classic college illness, mono, and ended up in the infirmary on steroids for a week. Lying in the clinic, I read *Of Human Bondage,* and for the first time, realized that I could be a physician. I needed to recover my health, so I dropped out of college at the end of the quarter, volunteered at women's health clinics, worked to raise money, and then traveled around the United States with John for three months.

You can imagine what my parents thought of all this. **My mother almost disowned me, but my younger brother stuck up for me, and over the years Mom and Dad became my supporters.** As I look back, I think they were worried that I was on drugs, when I hadn't even smoked pot. **I didn't realize this at the time or I would have reassured them.** When I started back to summer school, I was on my own financially. **I turned down marriage and/or financial help from John because I didn't want to**

**depend on him at this point in my life. I wanted to secure my own path first.** So I waitressed, washed pots, clerked in the post office, and became an audiovisual tech on campus. With my new focus on premed, I worked from eight in the morning to eleven at night, and loved what I was doing. Chemistry, physics, and calculus were definitely challenging.

I knew I was a shoo-in for medical school, despite the fact that few women were being accepted and my counselor's suggestion that, at twenty, I was too old. When I applied, I had a 3.99 GPA, was Phi Beta Kappa, had lots of volunteer and paid medical experience in clinics and research labs, and had scored in the ninety-ninth percentile on my MCATs. The University of Washington appealed to me: it was a good school with a progressive curriculum, my friends were in the area and could help support my soon-to-be-limited social life, and I didn't want to amass a huge debt. I wanted to "follow my bliss," as it's now called. During a solo weeklong hike in the mountains near Monterey, California, I had written in my journal about how I wanted to feel at age sixty-five. I knew I wanted to be a social activist in a rural medical practice. I wanted to live a "worthwhile" life.

The medical school interview was a shock. I sat at a big table surrounded by men who asked, "Do you think we should admit people just on the basis of their GPA?" "So, you got a B in folk dancing." "I see you took tennis pass/fail. Don't you like tennis?" "Do you have any friends?" I did a good job answering the irrelevant questions, but I was annoyed at the hostility and the feeling that they were really trying to dump my credentials and look for reasons not to accept me. Finally they asked, "What do you think about the recent court case in the newspapers?" Now, this was something I had strong opinions about. Three "older" women in their late twenties and early thirties had sued the medical school after being denied admission, claiming age and sex discrimination. The case had received lots of front-page publicity in the Seattle papers, the women had been admitted and had just started school, but the terms of the final settlement were secret. I knew those women. One worked with me in an immunology lab, another in a clinic, and the third was a friend of a friend. Naively and honestly, I replied, "Gee, that's a really difficult question for me to answer. Those women are my friends. I just hope

I don't have to do what they did." There was a hasty end to the interview. The acceptance letter was in the morning mail.

John and I married the following spring. Immediately after our civil ceremony, I left on a train trip across the country, visiting friends along the way and apologizing to everyone for getting married. I was a feminist, too young, and had never wanted to get married, but I trusted John and was optimistic that we could make new rules. He was always very supportive and proud of me. When I told him I was going to study premed, he enrolled in nursing school so we could work together in the future. He wanted to support me through medical school. **We made up a marriage contract, setting up guidelines on finances and resolving future disagreements within our values that we honor to this day.**

After three months together in Europe, John and I returned for a family wedding ceremony and good-bye party at my parents' house. I completed medical school in Seattle; then we moved to Massachusetts to be near John's elderly parents for the four years of my residency training. **Sarah's birth during my third year of residency was extremely educational for me. I immediately changed what I told my pregnant and laboring patients.** A little empathy really goes a long way!

John's brother was an Episcopal priest in the Alaskan bush, and we'd fallen in love with Alaska on previous visits. After my specialty training, we moved there, and I joined another woman ob-gyn in a small-town practice. I worked with her for a year, and then set up my own practice. Our second daughter, Margaret, was born during our first year in Alaska. The year I studied for boards, nursed an infant, mothered a toddler, set up my own practice, and delivered twenty to thirty babies a month was by far the most stressful year of my life.

I'm still learning to live my life, but I have the courage to put my whole self into it. I may have more problems and experience more risks, but I will never have a boring life. Being open to great sorrow and overcoming fear with God's help is the ticket to great joy! I love my work and feel that this is my calling. I enjoy helping my patients, reading scientific journals, continually learning new techniques, and mentoring young medical students. **It's really important to feel that I can make a difference,** and that I have a role in causing change, in individual patients' lives as well as in a community.

Raising my own daughters helps me understand my life better and the lives of young women in our society. I believe we need to keep challenging girls so they continually connect with the relationship between efforts and results, that we keep encouraging them to take risks, make commitments, and achieve. **We need to teach girls to have the courage to keep trying and to be vital members of our society, and that's an important part of the contribution I want to make.**

# *If* Booker T. Could Do It, So Could She

## Camellia Okpodu, Ph.D.

PLANT PHYSIOLOGIST AND ASSISTANT PROFESSOR

*Dr. Camellia Okpodu is an assistant professor in biological sciences at Hampton University in Virginia. Her area of specialty is plant physiology. Her path to success has involved many struggles related to racial prejudice, none of which have sidetracked her on her continued determination for success. Notice that her love of plants dates back to childhood on her grandfather's farm and winning an award in 4-H.*

I'm at the beginning of my career. I'm trying to establish a lab at Hampton University, and I'm going through the learning process and heartbreaks that go along with writing grants to fund research.

I'm the mother of three daughters, aged thirteen, seven, and five. My husband works in Blacksburg, Virginia, more than two hundred miles away, so we only see each other on weekends. I think all moms are single parents because kids are so dependent on their mothers— especially when they're little. I had my first daughter before I finished undergraduate school and my second and third daughters while I was finishing my doctorate. Our first daughter was planned; our second and third—well, we weren't as organized. They're all vibrant little ladies, we have a lot of fun, and everyone likes to bring their children to our home. My mom lives with us right now, so we have three generations of women in our home.

**I've always liked plants. I grew up on my grandfather's farm. The first ribbon I ever won was for my leaf collection in 4-H.** Since I was interested in biology in high school, my counselors guided me toward medicine. I didn't know about the other things I could do with a biology degree. When I became an undergraduate at North Carolina State, though, I realized I wasn't meant to go to medical school. **One day I heard a professor give a lecture on plants. I was so interested that later she became my adviser.**

I was an undergraduate in the 1980s. The school hadn't done much toward encouraging diversity, and I was one of the few

African-Americans. **I had very little guidance and no real mentors, but I knew I deserved to be at school, and I'd do whatever I needed to in order to pass the courses.** I hit more than one impasse as an undergraduate. There weren't a lot of black men at the school. I met a very nice young man who happened to be Caucasian. We were in classes together, so we studied together. We didn't date, but we were really close friends. I started getting hate messages in my mail, rude comments, even hate messages on my door. **I had never experienced anything like that.**

I received a C in my physical chemistry class. It made no sense—I had come to all the classes and done well on the quizzes and exams. I was the only black person in the class. I had sat in front of the professor four days a week, in the same chair, in the same place, yet on my grade sheet, he'd indicated I hadn't come to class, and that's why I'd received a C. I knew I shouldn't confront him—not only was he the professor, he was also white and older—but I got the courage to challenge him. I brought in my exams, assignments, and quizzes, and showed him my average. He refused to change my grade. I knew I was getting a C for "Colored," and I at least wanted a B for "Black." From then on, when I went to class, I knew what my grade would be no matter what effort I put in. That still didn't keep me from making my best effort. I knew the professor had to live with himself, and it was not my problem. **My goal was to get my degree. I had to get through the small things to get to where I needed to go. My mother used to say to me, "If you want an omelette, you have to break a few eggs."**

Shortly after this incident, I went to the library and up to the eighth floor of the stacks to sit and cry. I felt like dropping out of school. I remember thinking, "If I can't transfer out of this school, I'll just quit." I sat down on one of the little footstools designed to help reach books, and as I sat, a book fell out of the stacks and hit me on the top of the head. I picked it up; it was *Up from Slavery,* Booker T. Washington's autobiography. I had read the book in high school, but I read it again, sitting there in the stacks. I got to the point where Booker T. walked from Richmond to Hampton so he could learn to read. I started thinking, "I have everything I want. I have every modern convenience I can think of. **If this man can walk such a distance to get an education and had to be so** courageous to learn to read, why do I have the right to sit here and complain because a few people don't think I should be here? What's wrong with me?" I took courage from his story. I said, "If Booker T. can do it, I can too." After that, I never earned anything less than a B in any class besides that chemistry class.

I took three graduate courses as an undergraduate, and through my graduate-level biochemistry course, I met my mentor, Wendy. At first, I disliked her. When I started school, we had no money, and I didn't have many clothes. I wore the few dresses I had. I had very long, thick hair and couldn't afford to get it processed. Instead, I had to let it go natural. Wendy criticized my hair and the way I dressed. The other reason why I disliked Wendy was a deflating remark she'd made. We were in the Boston airport with at least five hundred people all coming back from this meeting, sitting around waiting for our planes. I was very excited because a world-renowned woman geneticist who was written up in all my textbooks had just offered me a postdoctoral position in her lab. I told Wendy about the offer, and she said in a voice loud enough for everyone to hear, "The only reason she's interested in you is because she has a quota to fill."

**If it wasn't for Wendy, however, I probably wouldn't be where I am now. From her I learned that appearances do count. I learned to be cognizant that certain attributes may offend other people. Wendy made these comments to motivate me. She had the utmost belief in me. She convinced me I could succeed in graduate school. She has been instrumental in helping me become a better scientist.**

After college graduation I got married and became a full-time parent with my first daughter. I was having fun, but my husband was unemployed at the time. **I decided that I could probably get a better job if I went to graduate school. I didn't ever want to depend on someone taking care of me. I wanted to be able to take care of myself.**

I was going to go to Missouri to do my postdoc, but my husband decided to take a job at Virginia Tech. We had just had our second daughter during my third year of graduate school, and I didn't want to go to Missouri without my husband. The girls would never know their father, and it was too far away. I decided to follow him to

Blacksburg, Virginia, instead. The university gave me some soft money, and they invited me to find a lab to work in. Blacksburg was a big culture shock for me.

I'd grown up in a rural area in North Carolina, and the culture of my community explains why I never made a division between black and white. Because the blacks were children of former slaves, they farmed the land together and operated the farm collectively. The white people around us were no better off economically. **I didn't grow up thinking I wanted to be white.** We made a living on farming and fishing and grew most of our food. I don't remember going to the grocery store until I was in high school. **I grew up with that healthy consciousness of just accepting people as they are.** My best friend, Pauletta, was a little white girl down the street. I didn't care what color she was. The only racism I remember was that her father didn't like me coming to her house. **My mother taught me that people viewed you on the basis of how you act and not what color you are.** In fact, I really didn't think of myself as being black until I got much older. I never had to.

When we moved to Blacksburg, I thought everybody was going to treat me like Pauletta did, but that didn't happen. People made judgments about me based on what I looked like and how I spoke. I realized I had to get out of Blacksburg, or I might end up in jail for protesting so much. For example, I went into a dress shop with a sign that said "All unattended children will be sold as slaves." Something in my belly went into a knot. It made me feel very small. I said to the person at the cash register, "I just noticed this sign. Perhaps this is not what you want to say," and I left the store. **Later, I went back to the store and explained to the proprietor that no oppressed people would find this sign funny.** I threatened to write her up in the newspaper, and she called the police. I don't know where I got the courage to do this. Much later, I returned to the store and saw that the sign was gone. I mentioned it to her, and she said, "I took it down, but it wasn't for you." It didn't matter whether she took it down for me or not, but after that, I packed my bags and got the job at Hampton. I knew that **the choices that my daughters would have in Blacksburg were few.**

Where I live now is easier. It's more like where I grew up. **I've managed to raise our children in an area where our schools are** diverse. I have relatives in the area and it's not such a rarity to be black. When we were in Blacksburg, my two-year-old was aware she was black. I didn't want my daughter to be conscious that she was any race at that age. Now, **my daughters have friends from many ethnic groups to play and socialize with, and I'm much happier about that.**

**My objective now is to do my very best at whatever I do. I'm trying to learn to write competitive grant proposals, and I find this difficult.** I've found the old boys network is alive and kicking, but I feel like John Paul Jones on this one: "**I have not yet begun to fight.**" **I'm learning the politics around getting proposals funded. It's all about persevering.** We have a lot of trees down here and a lot of paper is made. I'll turn the paper into proposals. **I'll not quit trying to write proposals until I get one funded. In other words, "No" is not going to stop me. I have hit a wall with this, but when I come up against a wall, it usually has corners. I just need to turn the corner. I'm still having a lot of fun, and I'm not going to use excuses. I do what I do because this *is* my enjoyment. I'm truly passionate about my work.**

# She Embraced Complexity

## Teresa Culver, Ph.D.

CIVIL ENGINEER AND ASSOCIATE PROFESSOR

*Civil engineering is a career field with very few women, yet Teresa thrives there. Her childhood provided her with experience in equality that helped her and her brothers and sisters feel comfortable in everything from science to music, sports, cooking, cleaning, and household chores. Brought up as cheerleaders for one another, Teresa and her siblings are all highly successful in their careers and root for one another as adults. Teresa is currently associate professor in the Department of Civil Engineering at the University of Virginia in Charlottesville, Virginia.*

As a child, **I spent a lot of my time learning about the natural world.** Now, as an adult, I do research and teach environmental engineering. Although at an early age I loved teaching other children and was always talented in math and science, I never planned on becoming a professor. In fact, I didn't know anyone who had obtained more than a college degree, and I never expected to earn a doctorate.

I have five brothers and sisters, and I was the second youngest. All of my siblings were scientifically and technically trained. One of my sisters is an electrical engineer, and the other is a laboratory manager in a biotechnology firm. One of my brothers is also an electrical engineer, another is an aerospace engineer, and my oldest brother works in the automotive field. Although I had very little one-on-one time with my parents because I had so many siblings, my parents encouraged us all toward careers in science. **They both loved science, and together we worked on science projects, watched television shows about nature, and took outdoor-oriented vacations.** My dad would save his vacation time up for the summer, and **the whole family would pile into our station wagon and camp and hike for five weeks.** My parents combined our hiking trips with naturalist programs that taught us about the environment, so I grew up loving nature. When I was very young, I thought I might be a forest ranger. Later, as my interests became more sophisticated,

I became interested in pollution and contaminants, and by the time I entered college, I knew that I wanted to become an environmental engineer.

My mom, a full-time homemaker, has a nursing degree, and my dad was an aerospace engineer for the government. **They had high expectations for all of us. We were always expected to work hard in school. They were very supportive of our interests, attending any events in which we participated, whether it was a wrestling match or high school band concert. We all learned to cheer for each other. We were lucky kids to have such parents.**

As a child, I spent a lot of time with boys, especially my brothers, because there were few other girls in the neighborhood. I was particularly close to my little brother. An older brother two grades ahead of me had difficulty in elementary school. I used to help him with his homework, and he introduced me to his friends as "the smart one." He'd call himself "the dumb one." It never seemed to bother him to have me help him with his spelling. We spent a lot of time together, he learning and I teaching, and both of us having fun. He seemed so proud that I was a "brain."

**I idolized my older sister because she was a good athlete and musician and had a great sense of humor. I remember my parents treating my sisters and brothers alike. There were no gender-stereotyped roles in chores, expectations, or activities.** Everyone was expected to do everything. The only difference I can recall was in high school when my sisters and I were expected home earlier than my brothers.

Elementary school was easy for me. I was the nerdy little kid that finished the math book early. My teachers would often let me race ahead independently in math. When I finished my textbooks, they would appoint me as the mathematics teacher's aide because I was so far ahead of the other students. I thought that was cool. Teachers asked me to read to younger children. I liked helping other children, and I was happy and hardworking in elementary school. In addition to my schoolwork and musical activities, I read voraciously, watched TV, and **participated actively in Girl Scouts for eight years. I loved backpacking** and sometimes brought my younger brother with me.

**I've always enjoyed complexity. Even at an early age, I would**

combine and create complex systems. It was almost as if my work as a systems analyst began in my childhood. I used to take out five board games at once, create ways to connect them all, and teach these complex rules to my brother and his friend.

I found the logical structure of science appealing and liked dichotomous, right-or-wrong answers. I loved working toward receiving 100 percent on homework and enjoyed feedback that said, "Yes, that's exactly right." Even when my answers were wrong, I felt more comfortable with the type of disappointment that could be quantified. In comparison, I found creative writing and language arts less satisfying. There is no such thing as "perfect" writing; it can always be improved. I never liked reading poetry; I just didn't get the point.

I learned the value of hard work from my music instruction. I played the oboe. Although I wasn't naturally gifted in music, I still wanted to do well. My band director was a great mentor. He encouraged me to try out for orchestras that I thought were out of my reach. I eventually played in those higher-level orchestras, and meeting the challenge strengthened my confidence. In high school, I remember practicing the oboe for two or three hours to master a difficult part. Later, I translated this approach into an academic context. When my college work was challenging, I knew that I could master it with a few hours of careful work, just as I had my difficult music as a child.

Competition always motivated me. I can't imagine playing volleyball without keeping score. I was on the field hockey team even though I wasn't the greatest athlete. I was never a starter on the team, but I was thrilled and motivated just to help the team win. Their victories were mine even if I sat on the bench, and the losses were only temporarily disappointing and never discouraged me from playing at my best. In instrumental tryouts, I liked seeing who was best. It motivated me to try harder even if I wasn't best. The competition built my confidence and taught me to focus. Although I knew I was better in academics than music or sports, I participated in all three. I learned important lessons by participating in activities that weren't all that strong for me.

I was the valedictorian of my high school class and a National

Merit scholar. At graduation, I received the highest-performance medallions in four areas: music, math, science, and English. I received scholarships and went off to engineering school at Cornell University. I was excited about the variety of course offerings, so I overloaded my schedule, taking twenty-one credits per semester. I took biology courses and even organic chemistry as electives. I worked intensely on my schoolwork, getting only five hours of sleep a night.

**After the first semester of my sophomore year, I burned out and needed a break. Although I was afraid that my parents might not approve, I decided to take the next semester off. When I returned, I felt refreshed, and I had a more clear view of my own objectives and values.** I transferred to a major that more directly prepared me for a career in environmental engineering, and **I also allocated more time for relaxation and enjoying the outdoors.**

There was one professor I really admired who taught environmental systems. Considering that he was at a large, powerful research institution, with seventy or more students in his class, I was surprised when within a couple of weeks he learned everyone's name. He showed such an interest in teaching his students; furthermore, I loved the subject. Another professor, whom I respected, would leave every day at five o'clock and spend the evenings and weekends with his family. **I decided that was "cool" and liked that his family was important to him because family was always so important to me.**

Only one professor ever encouraged me to attend graduate school. I was taking a graduate level class as an undergraduate when this very aloof professor asked me about my future plans. When I told him I was not planning to go to graduate school, he responded, "You've got to be kidding!" However, in spite of this less than effective advising, after working as a technician for a year, I began considering grad school. **Although I was ready to end my graduate career with a master's, in my final semester of my master's program, my major professor convinced me to stay on for a Ph.D., suggesting a plan that allowed me to complete my doctorate in only three additional semesters. Because of her guidance, I finished my doctorate.**

Now I have marriage, parenthood, and career to balance. My husband and I do a lot of compromising. Both of us have made decisions to accommodate the other. At one point, I turned down a very promising tenure-track position to take a less prestigious post-doctoral position so we could continue to live in the same city. Like-wise, my husband has stepped away from his career to provide primary child care. During the ten years following graduate school, my husband and I worked twelve different jobs combined. **We have taken turns being the family "breadwinner," returning to school for more training, and taking care of our children.**

Now, as an associate professor, I'm well aware that my job could consume all of my time. I often notice my colleagues taking this route. **I'm reminded of my childhood fun in combining complex games. I'll try to continue the work and family balance in the same spirit as I did those games.**

# Making a Medical Discovery Was Her Goal

## Sosamma Berger, Ph.D.

ASSISTANT PROFESSOR OF MEDICINE, BIOCHEMISTRY, AND
ONCOLOGY, CASE WESTERN RESERVE UNIVERSITY

*Dr. Sosamma (Suzie) Berger earned her Ph.D. in biochemistry from Hahnemann University. She has held postdoctoral fellowship positions at the University of Miami and at the National Institutes of Health. She is currently assistant professor of medicine, biochemistry, and oncology at Case Western Reserve University in Cleveland, Ohio. Her research focuses on enhancing the effectiveness of chemotherapy. Suzie and her husband, Nate, have three successful, happy, young-adult children. Her story provides an inspiring blueprint for immigrants who decide to make the United States their new home, blending their own culture with American culture.*

When I was a child in India, I always wanted to be a doctor. It was not unusual for women in India to become doctors, because females did not want male doctors to examine or touch them; so women went to medical school. One of the finest medical schools in India was founded by a British woman doctor who began it as a school for women physicians. She saw that many women were dying because they wouldn't allow male doctors to help them. **I wanted to make a medical discovery, and our parents encouraged us toward whatever we wanted to do.**

I'm the youngest of six children, and all of us became professionals. Two of my brothers are in engineering fields, one brother has a Ph.D. in theology, and one is a physician. My sister also completed college, but she got married and became a housewife. All my siblings, except for one brother, now live in India.

My father was a farmer, and I was most like him. I would cling to him whenever I could. My sister would be in the kitchen doing things with Mother. I wasn't a kitchen person; I was an outside person.

**Many of my older cousins were in science, so ever since I can remember, I wanted to be in science.** My grades were always high. **Boys didn't distract me because we weren't allowed to be with them in India. We were taught that we were not supposed to be interested in boys.**

A couple of my cousins were the first female doctors who helped underprivileged people who could not go to the hospital. **I used to go with them and watch them, and I really wanted to be like them.**

Our schools in India did not have extracurricular activities. I went to school, studied hard, and did what needed to be done at home. We were required to take difficult national exams, competing with thousands of students to get into high school, and then again into college. Most of my grades were A's, but one or two were B's because I was not as good in writing and liberal arts as in science and math.

I went to a small girls' college when I was fifteen. My parents were very strict and didn't want me to go to a mixed college. My brother and my cousins were in medical school in the same place, so they always kept an eye on me and took care of me. We weren't allowed to even see men. I had to have permission from my parents for my brother and cousins to visit me. After my first two years, I moved to a mixed-gender college in Bombay to do my remaining work. I had cousins there to help me, and I lived in the dorm. I considered going into physics, which was my favorite subject, but I decided to major in chemistry and minor in biology and physics.

I was very young, nineteen, when I finished undergraduate school. I wanted to come to the United States to further my education, but my parents didn't want me to leave India. I had many cousins who had come to the States, and three of my brothers were here. One was in Portland, Oregon. He said to my parents, "Why don't you send her over here? I have a family who would be very much interested in having her stay with them." My parents knew this family through a missionary and consented, so I came to Oregon and went to Portland State College for one year. Then I was admitted to the University of Washington in Seattle to finish my master's degree. **I stayed in an international house, so there were students there from many countries. That made my adjustment easier, and people were surprised I could speak English so well.** I made friends easily, although I felt different and wore a sari.

I had planned to go to medical school, but I became so interested in research that I chose that direction instead. I finished my master's degree in one year and then went to Philadelphia to do my Ph.D. in biochemistry. That's where I met my husband, Nate. I was working in white-blood-cell research in the biochemistry department, and he was interested in doing similar research, so we worked together. After Nate finished medical school and did his residency, we were married.

At first my parents didn't approve of my marrying Nate because he was Jewish, but then they changed their minds. My minister brother had met Nate and liked him very much. He worked on my parents, telling them that Nate was a good guy. My father rationalized very well by saying that Christianity came from the Jewish religion, and so the religions are all one. My parents seemed satisfied with our decision.

Nate took me to visit his family as a friend, and they liked me very much. He didn't tell them we were seeing each other personally. When Nate did his internship in Chicago, I continued to visit them. After a year or two, he told them he was going to marry me, and they were not very happy about that. I decided to convert to Judaism. A rabbi married us, and it was no longer a problem for Nate's family.

We had our first child when we were working at the National Institutes of Health. When our son was three months old, we moved to Washington University. Nate was doing a fellowship in hematology, and I had a position there as an assistant professor in the pharmacology department.

When the children were young, I stayed home for a few months. **I would then work three days a week. On Wednesdays and Fridays I'd be home with the children. Then I'd go to work on Sunday when Nate was at home. At least one parent was with them all the time.** Washington University had a wonderful nursery school, but I didn't want our kids to go full-time. I would send them there half a day so they could play with other children. Then I had a baby-sitter who came into our house for the other half day. One baby-sitter said to me, "If you want to raise the children your way, you should stay home," and I said, "That is exactly what I'm going to do." I stayed home until I hired someone else. **I worked part-time so I could keep my feet in the profession. In my research career, I really have to. Once all three of the children were in** school, I worked full-time. I had a very strict policy that I must not be more than a ten-minute drive from the university, so if anything happened I could drive home quickly.

I continue to wear a sari as a way of preserving my Indian culture. Many times I have felt funny when people stare at me because I look different, but it doesn't really bother me because I'm proud of being an Indian person. We have been back to India with our children several times. The children all know our families and talk to them on the phone regularly. We hope to visit them again soon.

# 5

# The Nurturers

W E'VE grouped educators, allied health professionals, and home-makers together not only because they establish nurturing others as a priority, but also because those careers more readily allow sufficient time for family and other relationships. They are indeed the most traditional careers selected by women—the careers that, from the start, have allowed and invited women to join. Today they remain careers that are primarily filled by women.

## *Results from the* See Jane Win *Study*

One of the criteria for inclusion in our study was satisfaction in one's career of choice, so we haven't profiled women who were unhappy in their choice of a traditional career. Perhaps to no one's surprise, more of the women in these three groups were married; fewer were single or divorced. More of them described their family lives as very happy, the homemakers most of all. The birth-order distribution was somewhat different for the three groups. Among the educators, considerably more were oldest children in the family and fewer were youngest, compared to the total group. More of the allied health professionals and homemakers were middle children, and more came from larger families. The large size of their families could explain the large number of middle children and might explain why they made

those family-friendly choices. Women who chose homemaking typically credited their own parents for providing role models of quality parenting.

This group was most likely to say that others perceived them as
"smart," "hardworking," or "good little girls," but they also listed
"happy" and "kind." (They described themselves as "independent"
girls less often than those in other careers.) These women tended
to have good relationships with their parents, but better relationships with their mothers than their fathers. More of them identified
with their mothers than did women in other career groups, and
fewer of their mothers returned to school or careers while they were
growing up.

Although just as many began as excellent students in elementary
school, in describing their middle school performance, more of them
downgraded their ranking to only "good students." They tended not
to study as much by middle and high school and didn't rank as high
at graduation. Their grades in general, particularly in math and science, fell during middle and high school. The exception was the allied health professionals, who struggled more in math but not in
science; they continued to find it a strong subject throughout high
school. The best subjects for the educators tended to be reading,
English, and writing. English and writing ranked first for the homemakers. Fewer women in all three groups took accelerated or
advanced-placement courses in high school, and fewer of them
skipped grades or subjects. While fewer of the homemakers and
teachers attended independent and all-girl schools, the nurses attended just as many independent schools as the total group, and a
higher percentage than typical, 18 percent, attended all-girl high
schools, perhaps a credit to science programs at those schools.

Slightly fewer women in all three categories were involved in
music, but more of the educators and allied health professionals were
involved with sports. The homemakers watched considerably more
television than the other two groups and, for that matter, any other
career category. All three of these career categories tended to be more
social than many of the other career groups.

When we asked the nurturers why they recommended their careers, the allied health professionals and educators most often said it
was because they "made a contribution" and found their career

"challenging." One hundred percent of the homemakers indicated they thought what they were doing was worthwhile; almost as many also said it was "fulfilling." Educators also frequently indicated that they considered their careers to be "creative."

Among the allied health professionals, respondents were typically registered nurses who worked in nursing or nursing administration. There were also some physical and occupational therapists. No practical nurses or nursing aides were included in this study. Most of the nurses had bachelor's degrees, and some had master's and doctoral degrees as well.

Although a few homemakers had grown children, most respondents had very young children at home. A few also held part-time jobs outside the home, but they considered their homemaking and child-rearing responsibilities primary by far and expected that to continue despite their earlier career training. Some acknowledged that they had little commitment to the career for which they were trained and expected to change their career direction after their children were grown. Others, particularly those trained as educators, expected to return to that career after their children were grown.

## How Jane Won

We interviewed educators at all levels—elementary, middle, and high school and even a teacher of teachers. Lisa Hayes-Taylor is a nationally certified elementary school teacher who wanted very much to be a role model for her daughter. Her daughter's words confirm that success. Elizabeth Dabrowski, who praised her own single-gender Catholic education, has had the opportunity to pass that tradition on to other girls in the fine Magnificat Catholic Girls' High School, where she teaches. Dr. Frances Karnes, who now influences so many educators, had the wisdom and foresight to value individualization for all children long before it was in vogue. She was a pioneer in a traditional career.

The two nurses we interviewed were indeed both social and caring, but beyond that, they were excellent students and showed leadership early in their childhood. Although nursing is at the core of their careers, both are managers, and Pauline Robitaille is a nurse-manager award winner, while Jeanette Ives Erickson rose to become senior vice president of Patient Care Services and chief of nursing at the prestigious Massachusetts General Hospital in Boston.

The two homemakers are from different generations, but both are devoted mothers and community leaders with extraordinary managerial skills. Roberta Baldwin, the older of the two, admits that although she loves what she does, had she been born at a different time, she would have also developed a career. While Jan Dorman describes herself as mainly a home manager and a community leader, she keeps a part-time consulting business going as a sideline and acknowledges that she'd miss it if she had to give it up. These two homemakers were both social and excellent students in childhood, so they had many choices available to them, but similar to the homemakers in *See Jane Win,* these women remembered the wonderful home lives of their childhood and wanted to make that possible for their own children.

# $\mathscr{F}$ROM BUSINESS MANAGEMENT TO FAMILY MANAGEMENT

## Jan Dorman

HOMEMAKER AND COMMUNITY LEADER

*Jan Dorman is a part-time community volunteer, part-time business consultant, and full-time mom. She is a graduate of the University of Delaware and received her M.B.A. from the Wharton School at the University of Pennsylvania. After working in management for years, she decided to redirect her energy toward family management and community work. At forty-three, she is married and the mother of three children, aged seventeen, thirteen, and eight, with a fourth child on the way. We selected Jan for our book because of her visible contribution to her community.*

After years of working in business management, I have a small, part-time consulting practice out of my home. I work with companies and individuals, helping them make decisions through strategic and operational planning. That's my career, but **my day-to-day life has little to do with my career.** A few years ago I moved from business management to family management and **find myself using a lot of the same tools and techniques I applied in business.** Now I manage our kids, the house, our family activities and schedules, as well as help our three kids learn to manage their homework. While our children are at school, I attend business meetings and do my consulting.

**I also volunteer in the community;** for example, I chair the religious school committee at our synagogue and am a member of the board of a local bank. I'm identified within the community for my business skills and often serve as treasurer or president of organizations. Fortunately, I'm in a situation where I don't have to pursue a career for financial means.

**What I really love about my day-to-day life is organizing everything.** It can make me pull my hair out, but it's also very satisfying. I don't like running all over the house trying to find someone's algebra book. **I'm constantly designing systems to make**

our chaotic home life more manageable. Each kid now has a shelf in the family room where they keep their textbooks when they're not in their backpacks. Each kid has a bin for their papers hanging on our porch. Even dealing with financial matters, like balancing the checkbooks and working on budgets and financial statements, is really gratifying. This may sound weird, but I like this stuff. **I like the very orderly things in life,** and I shouldn't admit this as a career woman, but I even like cleaning house sometimes. **It brings a sense of order to my world. Putting a meal together and gardening are also very satisfying. I like to see the results of my labors.**

Another role I often play is that of the mediator. Perhaps I excel at mediation because I was the middle child of three girls. As a child, **I did some things that seemed to forecast my role as a decision maker and leader.** In grade school, I always wanted to be a nursery school teacher when I grew up; as an adult I've cofounded a preschool at our synagogue. When a group of colleagues or friends comes together to address a problem, **the solution is often obvious to me.** I patiently let the discussion take its course, but if I see other group members meandering and losing focus, **I "cut to the quick" and find myself speaking up, guiding, and directing the group.**

Girl Scouts played a significant role in my life. I started with Brownies and went all the way through Seniors. **Earning merit badges was satisfying to me—having achievements and expectations laid out in an orderly manner, and then seeing the fruits of my labor with the award of badges and pins. My Girl Scout leaders were first-rate, and I learned a lot from them. Also, safety patrol was a formative experience in fifth and sixth grades.** I ran for office and became the safety patrol captain. I can remember standing "at ease" down in the field during my first day of safety patrol training and being stung by a bee. I didn't say a word. This was patrol! **This is what I was supposed to do!** The teacher kept talking, and tears were streaming down my face. Finally, the teacher came over and asked if I was okay. At that point, I pulled my arm around, and there was this bee sticking out of it!

Growing up, we attended a small synagogue where there were very few kids. The synagogue decided to start a youth group, and of course, **I became president.** There were only about four of us in the group, but we went to big regional conventions. This kind of exposure was new to me. I had always assumed that all families were just like my family, and what I learned through these experiences was that our family was unusual, and we were pretty insulated from the rest of the world.

There were certain, very important values in our family that have shaped my adult decisions. First, the members of our family get along with one another. We were and still are a very close family. Also, our family values honesty. Both of my parents came from working families, and we learned to work for what we have. We were taught to be frugal. My parents were savers, always putting money away for college and retirement. I never felt I had to do without, but we were always careful with money. We were expected to do well in school and go to college. We'd bring home a math test with a 98, and my dad would say, "Why didn't you get 100?" It was in jest, but there was a message that our parents had high expectations for us.

Community service was another important part of my parents' lives that has influenced my life, and now, hopefully, I am passing that on to my children. When I was eight, my dad was appointed to the House of Delegates in Maryland, in part reflecting his community involvement. He's been in politics since I was a child and is still a state senator today. His political involvement shaped our family life because we were put in fairly public situations. We were told what behavior was expected of us as five-, eight-, and ten-year-olds, and we all tried to meet those expectations. In retrospect, this was a good experience for me. As one of the "smiling" Dorman children, I learned to shake hands, go to the parades, campaign at the polls, hand out campaign literature, relate to adults, and listen to my dad give speeches. By nature, I was introverted, but since it was expected of me, I stepped outside of myself and performed those activities, and it built my social confidence.

My self-confidence was also bolstered by being Jewish in a predominantly non-Jewish environment. I remember feeling special and different because of our Jewish faith and religious practice. Having to stand up and explain who I was, what I was doing, and why I was different made me feel strong.

I also gained confidence through those awkward teenage

**years by going to a finishing school.** One day a week we'd drive to downtown Washington and be trained in "how to be a lady." **We were taught how to apply makeup, move with good posture, stand properly while waiting for someone, shake hands appropriately, and walk a runway.** I even remember practicing getting in and out of different cars, stepping up to get into trucks or gracefully lowering into a sports car. To this day, I still get comments on my strong handshake, which I learned as a teenager in finishing school.

When I started college, I learned about introversion and extroversion in my psychology courses. School environments and society in general are geared toward extroverts, since the majority of the world's population is extroverted. **I realized I was introverted, and finally understood why I was so uncomfortable in social situations throughout my life. I had always preferred one-to-one interactions. Once I understood this about myself, I felt better about myself.**

I started off in college thinking I'd like to be a psychologist. As a junior, I became a resident adviser in a freshman women's dorm. **That experience taught me I didn't want to practice psychology because dealing with the students' problems was too emotionally draining for me. I did some self-examination and career testing to help determine my strengths.** I enjoyed numbers. Even if I couldn't care for people directly, as in counseling, I figured I could at least support the business side of health care. I decided to pursue graduate study in business and focus on working in a health-care setting. I had grand ideas about **improving the world through the business side of health care. My goal was to enable others to provide the direct patient care.**

I went to the Wharton School for my M.B.A. and majored in health administration. The program was a good fit with my interests and provided a good foundation for my career in health administration. I met my husband, Elliot, in the summer between my two years at Wharton, and we were engaged by December. Elliot had just finished his Ph.D. and had moved to Ithaca to teach at Cornell. By the time I was starting my job search, I was twenty-four and faced with some interesting decisions. I could either take a high-paying, prestigious job in Atlanta with Booz-Allen, the high-powered consulting

firm, and pursue my career with a crème de la crème consulting position, or I could get married and move to Ithaca, New York, not exactly the health-care-management capital of the world. **To make my
decision, I used a decision tree, just as I had learned in business school. I wrote out all the options, estimated their relative
merits, considered their possible consequences, and picked the
choice with the best expected outcome.** I decided to move to
Ithaca and marry Elliot, a reflection of the importance of family and
personal happiness in my life.

I found a job outside of Ithaca in a small health-planning organization. Seven small hospitals had formed a consortium, and I did
health-planning work with them. I did that for two years, until we
decided to start a family. I searched for a new job that didn't require
a commute. Finding a job at Cornell, I became business manager for
the Department of Student Unions and Activities. I did that for another two years and learned about the business of higher education.
When an opportunity came to work at the Cornell Book Store, I
moved to that position. It was the best job I've held. **I worked for
an incredible person, a leader and a role model. It dramatically
changed my business focus from one of managing resources to
focusing on the customers' needs.**

When Elliot was offered a position at the University of Virginia,
we moved to Charlottesville. **Early in our marriage, we tended to
follow a two-year pattern, focusing first on Elliot's career, then
mine, then Elliot's again.** Initially, we both focused on Elliot's career. Then Elliot's contract was renewed, our first child, David, was
born, and **our orientation shifted. My work became more important for a while, with Elliot helping out a lot at home to enable me to advance my career.** This seemed to be the pattern until
Elliot was offered the position at the University of Virginia, and we
had our second son, Zach. It became very clear that **Elliot's was the
primary career of the family.** At that time, **our earning potential
was quite similar,** but his job was so specialized, we had to go
where his job would take him. **I could do business management
anywhere.**

When we moved to Charlottesville, I saw it as an opportunity to
back off the so-called fast-track business mentality that I'd adopted
at Wharton. **I looked around at my ten or so female peers in**

health care at Wharton and realized I was the only one working full-time with kids. That was a bit of a shock! With our move, I decided to try staying home full-time. Zach was under a year old, and David was three. I thought it would be like Ozzie and Harriet, and I'd be happy being home with the little guys. We'd play together all day, I'd keep our house clean, get dinner made and on the table, keep the family business straight, and mow the lawn in my spare time.

As it turned out, **I had no clue as to how to stay home! Within three months, I was sending out résumés and looking for a job.** I found a challenging senior management position in health care and higher education and stayed for five invigorating years. During that time, we had our third child, Anna, and I continued to work full-time. Within a couple years of her birth and when David began elementary school, **the balance between work and family management became increasingly challenging. Because of the multiple demands on my time, I was frustrated both at work and at home.** At home, I couldn't keep up with daily life. We had mail and doctors' appointments, and even with a full-time nanny, home life was hectic and not the environment I wanted to raise our children in. At the same time, I was becoming increasingly unhappy in my job. I didn't like the politics at work. **With Elliot's support, I decided to leave full-time employment and start a part-time consulting practice from home.**

It's been eight years since I left the corporate world, shifting my focus from business management to family management. **I still do what I like to do: organize, work with numbers, and help people.** I do these things as a parent, a spouse, a volunteer, and a consultant.

# An Achiever with Old-Fashioned Values and a Generous Heart

## Roberta Baldwin

HOMEMAKER AND COMMUNITY VOLUNTEER

*Roberta Baldwin takes deep satisfaction in being a great wife, mother, and community leader, and her community and state have benefited from her contributions. Despite her sense of fulfillment, she does want other young women to know that if she had it to do over in our time, she would have chosen a career as well, probably law, and would have also managed to find time to be a terrific wife, mother, and volunteer.*

When I was growing up in the 1940s and 1950s, I was expected to go to college, get married, and perhaps work for a few years. A husband who was successful expected his wife to be a homemaker to care for their children and be supportive to him. My parents expected me to become a nurse. Even the children I played with in the neighborhood expected me to be a nurse. There were seventeen boys in my neighborhood, and although I considered myself to be a tomboy and an athlete, when we played "war" (World War II), the boys would insist that I and the other girl in the neighborhood be the nurses while they, of course, were the soldiers.

My dad was a district manager for a major oil company and my mom a full-time homemaker. I perceived they were always happy in their work.

Both of my parents were firm and supportive and both had high expectations of me. I identified with my dad because I was more assertive than my mom. **My parents did volunteer work in their community, mainly related to church, school, and Scouts. As a result, I saw volunteer work as important.**

I was always an excellent student and felt smart, confident, creative, and happy throughout my urban public school education. I was independent, outgoing, a hard worker, and popular. I think of myself as being both compliant and a risk taker, which may seem like an oxymoron. Although I complied with the standards expected by my parents and teachers, I was sufficiently confident to take the risks of leadership. I remember being told that my I.Q. was 145. My grades in junior and senior high school were consistently high, and I took all the advanced math and science courses that were available because I enjoyed the challenge, was interested, and was encouraged by both my parents and my teachers. I especially appreciated several inspiring teachers who told me that if I worked hard and persevered, I could do anything I chose.

I was always an avid reader and very involved in extracurricular activities, including being a student government officer and editor of my yearbook. I played the piano and sang in the choir. In high school, I decided I would major in medical technology because of my love of science. I actually majored in botany and bacteriology, which were very unusual and pioneering majors for young women of that time.

I married my husband right after college graduation (which was traditional for that time) and worked to put him through medical school. Most wives discontinued their education when they were married to prioritize their husbands' success. **There were almost no female medical students when my husband was in medical school, and the only two female students I knew who lived in our apartment complex worked especially hard because they faced a great deal of discrimination by the faculty. I admired them for just surviving. It wouldn't have occurred to me to go to medical school at the time. It just wasn't what society expected of its smart and confident young women.**

My first and only paying job outside our home was with the American Medical Association, and it was pleasant, social, and not too demanding. As soon as our children came along, we decided that I would stay at home to raise them. We were in a comfortable financial position, and men of that generation took pride in being the sole providers. **From the start, I was not only a devoted mother and wife, but I was actively involved as a volunteer in the community.** I assisted at a nursery school and kindergarten for many years and tutored children at the junior high school. I received an award for being the longest-term Boy Scout den mother. I did the den mother activity for all three of my sons. I was involved at the local, state, and national levels of our hospital auxiliary, American

Association of University Women, Community Day Care Association, community church activities, and was selected president of almost every organization in which I participated. Recently, I've become very involved in legislative lobbying for health care in our state and have "wined and dined" legislators to convince them to support important health issues. I'm also on the board of our community's local women's center, and I advise troubled teenage girls in teen-talk programs. **I've encouraged many to go on to college to find good careers instead of just settling for jobs out of high school, and I find I've been able to help many of the girls.** Perhaps one of the reasons I enjoy volunteerism so much is that as an only child, I was motivated to leave our home to develop relationships with other people. I was always a "joiner," a "mover and shaker" as a child, always busy with school activities, and I continue to be all three in my volunteer work. **Although I don't earn a single dollar for my voluntary contributions, I work more than twenty hours a week at giving because I just love it. I may have personally influenced many hundreds of young people, and it makes me feel good when a young person comes up to me and tells me they remember me from school. It's a great feeling to know I've touched someone's life and helped them.**

I believe we face some problems with volunteerism. People today are too busy in pursuit of material things to find time for volunteering, or because of time constraints, choose short-term or family-related causes. **I feel fortunate that I've had the opportunity to contribute to my community in a way that young people today may not have the luxury to afford.**

**Volunteering has provided me the best that life can provide—the valuable self-esteem that comes from achievement, the rewards of companionship of other volunteers, and the appreciation of those to whom I contributed.** I realize I couldn't do this without my husband's support. His earnings as a family doctor aren't extraordinary, but they're sufficient, and neither he nor I demand an elaborate lifestyle. I would encourage other women to volunteer for a creative, fulfilling, and worthwhile lifestyle. At age sixty-three, I admit that if I had the chance to do it all over, I would have gone to law school; nevertheless, I'd encourage women to become homemakers and volunteers. Perhaps my values are "old-fashioned," but I think **the leadership of our country recognizes how critical volunteerism is to so many children and families, and are in search of hundreds of thousands of people with generous hearts who can give of their time.** As for me, I'll continue to do my share, and I'm proud to say that my three young-adult sons are active in volunteering as well.

# SURROUNDED BY STRONG WOMEN

## Jeanette Ives Erickson

SENIOR VICE PRESIDENT OF PATIENT CARE SERVICES AND CHIEF
OF NURSING, MASSACHUSETTS GENERAL HOSPITAL

*Jeanette Ives Erickson, R.N., M.S., as senior vice president for Patient Care Services and chief of nursing at one of the country's most prestigious hospitals, has taken nursing to a new level of status, power, and excellence. In 1998, she became a Robert Wood Johnson Executive Nurse fellow. In addition to keeping her entire staff centered on the patient, Jeanette has organized Women in Leadership forums to give women a vehicle for networking and learning from one another to balance career and family needs.*

I was always surrounded by strong, determined, hardworking women. My mother encouraged me to either walk past obstacles or to push through them, and to this day I call her for advice. **She worked and was able to balance her work life** and five children, although my dad was away with his own work.

My uncle Tony, my mother's brother, owned a very large restaurant and was also an influential person. I learned from my uncle how to treat people well. **He created a sense of loyalty and a participatory management style without realizing there was a name for his leadership style.** The entire family—my mother, my aunt, my cousins, and even my grandmother—worked in his restaurant. They worked together to take this small neighborhood restaurant and make it a major floating restaurant in Portland, Maine. **I saw my mother not only being a supporter to her brother but also making a creative contribution to his business strategy.**

I was brought up in Maine, a state where the majority of people have a strong work ethic and a sense of community. I was number two of five children, behind an older sister, who, as a child, was accident-prone and sickly with rheumatic fever. My mother delegated some of her care to me, so **I played nurse to my older sister. Maybe that's where I learned my caretaker role.** Following me are two brothers and a sister. **We looked out for each other** and remain very close.

Most of the other people in my life were women, teachers and aunts who also worked. **Two of my aunts influenced my direction into the business side of who I am.** One aunt was an executive with Mutual of New York and shared her business life in discussions with me. She stood tall in a male organization. A second aunt was an executive in the hotel business, which was also a male-dominated business, and planned conventions.

My dad was in the merchant marines and in and out of our lives. I knew he was providing for us, but early on, his influence came through my mother and her stories about him. They are happily married, and my relationship with my father has grown since his retirement. He looks back on his life and realizes what he missed and has instilled in me, **"You need to spend time with family."** He is very different with his grandchildren. I'm forty-nine and four years ago married a wonderful partner, Paul, who supports me in my work. We don't have children, but we stay close to our siblings and nieces and nephews.

I was very active in Girl Scouts and learned a lot of science and took field trips into the woods and the local parks looking at plant life and birds. I always had books about birds. **That was part of my intrigue about life and wanting to be in health care.**

I was very social, participated in reading groups and clubs, and **in high school joined the Red Cross and volunteered to read to children.** As a child, I spent a lot of time reading the typical girl books, the Nancy Drew mystery series, and to this day, I read a lot. My father reads a book a day in his retirement, and I learned that from him.

I was the head cheerleader in junior high school and the subhead cheerleader in high school, **another leadership position, which required a lot of work with groups and strong relationships.** In those days as a cheerleader, you represented your high school.

I thought I was going to be a psychiatrist. I did well in science and loved the science labs, other than dissecting frogs. It wasn't until I was ready to apply to colleges that I made the decision, out of the clear blue sky, to be a nurse. **I talked to a Sister of Mercy, who then became influential in my life.** This wonderful nun, Sister Consuela, at the local nursing school at Mercy Hospital in Portland, Maine, not only was the head of the nursing department at the hospital but directed a nursing school and taught the values of nursing in my classes. **She convinced me to go to nursing school initially and then get my master's degree in administration from Boston University.** I maintain a relationship with her to this day.

Nursing school was very hard. It wasn't like a university atmosphere, where we could come and go as we wanted. There were restrictions about how we could dress and what days we could go out. We had curfews and study hours, and there was a part of that experience that made me rebellious because I hated having all of those rules and boundaries. It was during the Vietnam War, a time when people my age were developing a sense of self through being free spirits. I broke the rules on several occasions, such as going to a peace protest that we were told was off-limits. I felt that our nursing program was ignoring what was happening to people my age. It was as if the Vietnam War didn't exist, and I influenced the school by bringing discussions of Vietnam into the classroom.

**My life was deeply affected by the Vietnam War.** I had a cousin, a boyfriend from high school, and a next-door neighbor who were all killed in the war at the age of eighteen or nineteen. My friend Mary and I recently chatted about our lives and turning fifty together next year. The dominant reflections we had, looking back on our life, were Vietnam and the image of body bags. I became active in the prisoner-of-war effort. I spent many of my nights wrapping POW bracelets and sending them out to people around the country.

There were about forty women in my nursing class. About a dozen of us were really close and remain friends to this day. I worked at Mercy Hospital for fifteen years and was a critical-care nurse for the first three. My preceptor, Barbara Sheehan, remains my best friend after thirty years. Then Sister Consuela tapped me to leave my staff nurse position to take a head nurse position. I resisted at first, but she convinced me I was the person she wanted, and she worked with me to develop my management skills. **I loved taking care of patients** and wasn't sure why I would want to be a manager, but I thrived. I worked on a very large surgical unit with a great staff. I was groomed by Eloise Paulin, my first mentor, to spend time developing my business skills. **She taught me budgeting and how to write a strategic plan.** Both Sister Consuela and Eloise Paulin influenced my ability to be an executive in the core values of the business of nursing. They emphasized, "**If you keep your eye on the patient, you will always be headed in the right direction.**"

While they were teaching me business leadership, something very interesting was happening to me personally. Throughout my junior and senior years of high school and throughout nursing school, I'd had the same boyfriend. We were planning to be married, but **my sense of wanting to be a woman who had a career was beginning to emerge.** I began to realize that my boyfriend, who had actually been a wonderful supporter of mine throughout nursing school, wanted a stay-at-home wife, which was not who I was. **I realized he was not going to allow my best to come forth.** To his shock and that of my family, I broke off our engagement. I loved what I was doing.

All of the women I admired were very successful working women. **My definition of a woman was one who could balance work, home, friends, and family. I never thought of myself as competitive as a kid, but in any job I have taken, I always had to compete.** I always want what is best for the people I work with. People today would tell you that **I constantly say, "This is the best department of nursing in the country,"** and that's a competitive statement.

I continued to take on more responsibility at Mercy Hospital. I worked full-time and went to school full-time for my master's degree, traveling back and forth between Maine and Boston. I was driven to finish the master's program at B.U. The master's program was headed by another strong, influential woman, Muriel Poulin. **She was highly competitive and taught me that if I was going to be the number one nurse, the nurse executive in any organization, I would have to put forth my ideas and be very clear about my objectives. She said I needed to learn to deal with male-dominated health-care institutions and have the same business skills the rest of the executive team had. She advised me to negotiate the size of my office, where my office would be, and warned me if I didn't negotiate that up front, I wouldn't be in the executive suite.** She, too, was very connected to the values of the profession of nursing, always keeping her eye on the integrity of the nurse-patient relationship. She focused on the role of the executive to create an environment where nurses could be successful with patients.

Today I'm chief nurse and senior vice president for patient care at Mass General. The "chief nurse" title was actually something I negotiated for because male physicians who were clinical leaders all had the title "chief." If I was going to position nursing as an important clinical discipline in my hospital, I needed to ask for the same title. I've balanced the patient-care side of nursing with the business side, and I've learned to do that from the strong women who were my role models.

I am now responsible for approximately three thousand employees at Massachusetts General Hospital. Ninety-five percent of them are women. I hope my relationship with them allows them to feel strong and determined in their work.

# STILL ASKING, "WHY? WHY? WHY?"

## Pauline Robitaille

NURSE AND DIRECTOR OF SURGICAL SERVICES AND WINNER OF THE
1997 OUTSTANDING ACHIEVEMENT IN PERIOPERATIVE NURSING
MANAGEMENT AWARD

*In 1995, Pauline Robitaille was the recipient of the Award for Excellence in Perioperative Nursing from the Association of Operating Room Nurses, Massachusetts Chapter 1; in 1997, she won the Outstanding Achievement in Perioperative Nursing Management Award from the Association of Operating Room Nurses. Her awards recognize her accomplishments in perioperative nursing practice and excellence in patient care. Pauline has been employed at New England Baptist Hospital in Boston, Massachusetts, for many years. She is married to her high school sweetheart and has been victorious in her struggle against uterine cancer.*

I've always asked, "Why?" As a kid, I drove my mother crazy because I'd ask her so many questions. She'd give me answers, and I'd ask, "Why?" She'd give me more answers, and I'd say, "But Mom, why?" I told her recently, "Mom, I'm still asking why." In this way, I haven't changed. I'm still curious, I'm still learning, I'm still asking, "Why?"

I am a nurse and director of surgical services at New England Baptist Hospital in Boston. Three hospital units report to me: an ambulatory-surgery unit, the operating room, and the postanesthesia care unit. I've been married for sixteen years. My husband and I were high school sweethearts. I met him when I was fifteen and he was seventeen, right before we went off to college. Although we dated others, we always got back together.

I grew up the oldest of six. My parents divorced when I was twelve, and my mother remarried later and had another child. My mother worked and took care of the family financially. Yet, because of her background, she told me she thought it was a waste of time for women to go to college. She thought they should have children and stay home. **I was very determined to go to college anyway. I** knew I wanted a career, and my mother's advice didn't discourage me. If anything, it made me even more determined.

My father worked a lot when I was young, and I didn't see him much because we all lived with my mother, but when I was a young adult, **I knew he was looking out for me because if there were cars at the house, he would call and make sure I was okay and wanted to know what was going on.** When I was in high school, I lived with him for a little while because when my mom remarried, things were tense at home. I've always felt my dad was cheering me and my siblings on.

My parents instilled good values in us. **I always remember my dad saying to me, "If you are going to do anything, do it well." All my life I'd wanted to be a nurse.** There wasn't one event, or one person, that steered me that way; it was just a mission. I knew I could be a successful nurse. **I knew if I worked hard, I was going to find a way. I was very determined.**

**I started out in parochial school in our small town and earned the highest grades possible and enjoyed studying and learning.** In seventh grade, my school closed, and I had to transfer to the elementary school in my hometown. **That was a bit of an adjustment for me, and my grades dropped temporarily. I remember the thrill of writing papers for the first time—one about love, another about abstract art. I got A's on those papers and remember being surprised.** My favorite subjects were math and science. I was quiet in school and certainly wasn't as outgoing as I am now.

I didn't participate in many extracurricular activities in high school. **My goal was to save money for college, since I knew my parents couldn't support me financially.** Around town, a number of people used to call me "the Little Mother" because I was the oldest and my mom worked, so I had a lot of responsibilities. I remember cooking dinner, helping with the younger children, getting things ready, cleaning, and working. **I've always enjoyed a lot of responsibilities—even now.**

When I graduated from high school, I won some scholarships. First, I went to a three-year diploma program in nursing. I worked eight-hour shifts on the weekends during those years. Then, when I was working on my B.S.N. and my master's in nursing, I worked full-time and went to school part-time. I always made the dean's list because I loved to study and learn.

Once I finished nursing school, I accepted a job as the night-shift charge nurse on a pediatrics unit. **I took the job because I thought it would be a great place for me to develop the skills I'd learned in nursing school.** When I think about it now, I realize I went right from nursing school to a position with a lot of responsibilities. I was in charge of the unit, had a licensed practical nurse and two nursing assistants that worked with me, and we were responsible for the whole floor. When I think about the responsibility I had then and consider how little I knew, I think, "Wow," but at the time, it seemed okay. **I was energetic and thought I could do it, so I did. If there was anything I needed to know, I read and learned it.**

Later, as an operating-room nurse at St. Mary's Hospital, I was asked to teach new trainees. I became a preceptor and honed my interest in educating. I moved back to the hospital I'd worked in after graduating from nursing school and became a nurse educator, the formal beginning of my leadership positions.

At that point, I decided to move to Massachusetts to get my graduate degree so I could become a nurse manager. I eventually got promoted to a nurse-management position in the main operating room and was there for a couple of years when I hit a roadblock. I was working fifty hours a week and trying to finish graduate school. I was burned out but determined to finish my degree, so I interviewed for a position with less responsibility at a different institution and got it. **I wasn't sure how this "demotion" would be perceived later. I knew I wanted to get my master's degree, though, so I just decided this is what I needed to do.**

I was all ready to make another move a couple weeks after I accepted the position when I got a call from my doctor telling me I had uterine cancer. I didn't know what to do, so I called my new boss and told her the whole story, and she was great. She held the position for me while I recovered from surgery, and I was so relieved. Sadly, however, it meant my husband and I couldn't have children.

Now I'm the director of surgical services, and **what I like most about my job is the impact I can have in helping nurses who work with me. I enjoy helping my staff grow both profession-**

ally and personally. I really believe in our goal: to work together to take care of patients and do the best we can.

Many nurses have come to me and said, "Pauline, you're my mentor," and I think, "What? Me?" My goal now is to share and teach. When my staff does well, I feel proud.

I've encouraged many nurses in my group to obtain double certifications, to go on to get their degrees, become committee chairs, become officers, or join the board of directors of their nursing association. I don't feel responsible for their successes, but I see the ways I have facilitated their continued education and their leadership roles in our national organization. Because of this, I love my career.

# A Role Model for Her Daughter

## Lisa Hayes-Taylor

NATIONALLY CERTIFIED ELEMENTARY SCHOOLTEACHER

*Lisa Hayes-Taylor is a third-grade teacher at Key Largo Elementary School in Florida. Her first daughter, Sarah, inspired Lisa to develop a career she had never realistically considered before. She wanted to be the kind of role model for Sarah that she'd had in her own classrooms while growing up. She has recently received recognition as a nationally certified teacher, an honor that has inspired Sarah as well.*

**I loved my teachers.** One day when I was in kindergarten I realized I'd forgotten to wear my underwear, and I wouldn't take my snow pants off. My teacher asked, "What's wrong?" and I explained, with great embarrassment. She was so kind and made everything all right so no one would make fun of me or ask questions. **I thought teachers were wonderful people. I played school a lot, and wanted to be like them.**

I did very well in elementary school academically and socially, and I was chosen to be in plays and special activities. But Franklin Junior High was a social challenge for me. I was torn between being socially accepted by the "wrong," cool crowd and being a good girl. I found math extremely frustrating. **Algebra was the worst experience I had ever had, and I couldn't make anyone understand how overwhelmed and filled with dread it made me. Although I was trying my best, my parents were convinced that I wasn't.** I continued to love language arts, reading, and art classes, and had good grades in most subjects, but in math and science, I struggled just to get C's.

My mom always kept me on a very tight rein, and I found myself wanting to go to the kids' houses where parents didn't hover over you. My mother and I were in constant conflict. **I look back at it now and am really glad she never let up because I was walking that line of deciding which way I was going to go in life. Because she kept such close tabs on me, I don't think I was able** to skew as far off as I would have if she hadn't really stuck to her guns. At the time, I thought I was truly being tortured. I had curfews, and I was expected to do my chores. If I didn't come home on time, there was a consequence, and my mother always made sure I got it. Dad wasn't home a lot. He had started a pool business and was opening up several area branches. He'd come home if my mom said she needed help. **It was always scary when Dad talked to us, but he didn't have the impact Mom did because she would follow through on everything.**

I went to a huge high school in New York with three thousand students. I felt overwhelmed in my first year. However, the school had interesting electives, and I liked having so many options. I took photography and journalism along with my four regular classes, and there was finally something in school that I could relate to.

Overall, I was average, but I continued to be frustrated in math and science. **If some of what we know about learning now had been available then, I might have been more successful. I thought I was the only one who didn't understand.**

**I was better at choosing friends by high school and found I could have fun and didn't have to rebel to have a good time. I** ice-skated and went to the local community park. I had a huge family of cousins, so we did a lot together. There was always something happening on the weekends.

After my sophomore year, we moved to Florida. My parents were having some marriage and financial problems, and they decided to move in hopes of improving their lifestyle. That never came about. My mom was in Florida, and my dad was supposed to travel between the cities. He really never came back. My mom raised four kids and worked full-time.

**The move to Florida was absolutely the most devastating thing I can remember. I felt my parents had ripped the rug out from underneath me.** In Florida I entered school as a junior, and the only thing that I lacked for graduation credits was physical education. The New York requirements were much more stringent than the Florida requirements.

I was a big pain in the butt. Everyone probably wanted to stick a bumper sticker on my back that said, "We don't care how you did up North." I was so mad about being in Florida that I was hard on everybody. I put an editorial in the school newspaper about why we were having hot dogs with red dye No. 5 in the cafeteria and accused the school of "trying to poison us." After the first six months, I settled down. I realized, **"Okay, I'm going to make the best of this; I can't be miserable."**

My algebra teacher was great, and he made me statistician for the wrestling team. I got very involved in school, had a very traditional senior year, went to the prom, and was active in homecoming. I was awarded the "Most School Spirit" award. **What turned me around in Florida was that nobody gave up on me.**

After I graduated, I moved to California. I thought I never wanted to see the Florida Keys again. I went to stay with my uncle and became a PBX switchboard operator. **Moving away wasn't really the answer.** I missed my family and moved back home.

I took a waitress job and started the procedure for going to Florida Community College. I decided to move to Gainesville, Florida, with a boyfriend. I took graphic design classes there at a small community college. I won some awards for a charcoal and a watercolor. My instructor gave me the confidence to try different approaches, and I was very successful in college, but I missed my family.

We moved back to the Keys. I started waitressing again, and I didn't go back to college for about nine years. I liked going to work every day because everyone was usually happy, and I made a good salary. A friend of mine introduced me to my husband when I visited her in Kentucky. We visited each other there a couple times, and then he moved to the Keys. We fell in love, we married, and he never went home.

My daughter, Sarah, was my incentive for going back to college. I didn't want her to grow up with a mom that was a waitress that couldn't go to Girl Scout meetings and couldn't do all the after-school activities because I had to be at work at four. I wanted more for myself. I felt stagnant. **I decided to go back to school and see what I really wanted to do.**

I went to two community colleges to take the preeducation courses that I needed to get into a university. At one time, I was at both schools at once, and **I was so happy. I remember wondering how I could have done nothing for so long. It really was a** revelation to me that being challenged mentally was something I had missed. I had a goal.

I was glad I'd started out at the small community college because I needed the support. The classes were small, the professors knew our names, and the math help I needed was there. I had success in algebra classes because we worked in small groups. I think I got more out of those two years in algebra than I'd ever done before.

I made my sister drive me to the post office to get the results of the CLAST math test because everyone had received theirs. I needed to pass it to be considered at a four-year university. I said, "I can't drive there. I'll just die if I didn't pass." My sister opened up the envelope, looked at it, and told me I had passed.

My husband, my mom, my sister, my brothers, everybody who was in Florida, and my family up north were all very supportive. **They were very excited about my going to school.** If I hadn't had that support, it would have been a whole different picture. I had a really good baby-sitter with whom I could drop Sarah off at six in the morning so I could be in class by eight. She would keep Sarah even after she closed, and she didn't charge the extra twenty-dollars-a-minute fee. I raced down the turnpike to get Sarah after my long day at school.

I was on a mission and was done in less than four years. I was in the Keys, and Florida International University was a major commute, so I was either going to do this a little at a time or just do it. I went to school from eight in the morning until seven at night sometimes. **I'd go to the library between classes or try to work at home,** which was hard with a small child.

I was driven for A's. I stayed up and studied or typed extra. I had nothing to prove to anybody except myself. I graduated summa cum laude.

I was a special-education major, drawn to it by the critical teaching shortage forgiveness loan. After doing my fieldwork, I decided I wasn't a good fit for special education. I liked working with the kids, but I liked to see more progress. Many of the placements in special education were with profoundly handicapped children. **I decided that if I wasn't sure, those kids deserved someone else.** I went into elementary education, which was the best thing that has happened to me. **I was very grateful when I got into the classroom that I had had all that training in special education because I quickly realized that all kids are special. It made a difference in my teaching regular kids.** I student-taught in September, and when an emergency teacher position opened in January, I was hired right away. I got my start in third grade and just love third graders. They're starting to find out about their independence but are still intimidated by the principal. For so many kids, the lightbulb goes on in third grade. They start to have opinions and no longer say only what they think you want to hear.

**I went to an orientation about applying for national board certification because it was a challenge.** Only 33 percent of people pass it, and I bet myself I could do it. The application fee for certification was $2,000, and as an incentive the state of Florida offered to pay it. I thought, "Someone is going to add this up soon, and they're not going to offer it for long." **I wanted to pioneer.** Two other friends decided they wanted to do it, too, and together we decided to go for it. There were twelve of us that started, and four received certification.

First, I had to videotape two sections of my teaching. **Videotaping yourself makes you realize the little mannerisms you have.** One of the things I said all the time was, "Shh, shh, shh." I used to tell my students that on days they were really noisy, their moms and dads could tell because they'd get off the bus and they would have a coat of spit on their heads from my going "Shh, shh" all day long. **After the videotaping, I don't do that anymore.** I use the school signal. We hold up one finger. That means that everyone needs to listen and be quiet.

There was a four-part test we took in July. On the way to the test, the tire flew off my car. We had to pull over to the side of the road, call a tow truck, and be driven to the testing site, but we made it through.

The whole process was unbelievably challenging. **I actually had my in-laws move into my house for three weeks. They took care of my family,** cooked, cleaned, and did the wash, and I typed. I wouldn't have passed if it weren't for their help and support. I went to school at six in the morning, and there were nights I didn't get home until midnight. I wrote professional and personal plans.

I couldn't be happier now, I love my job; I love what I do **every single day.** I try to find gender balance in the classroom. I found myself calling on boys all the time, so **I make index cards and pull a card out to make sure I get to everybody.** As a beginning teacher, I had to work on being fair. When I needed an errand run, I'd automatically ask the girls. In science I would automatically key in on the boys during the experiments. I had to really make an effort to encourage the girls and boys equally. I have worked on gender fairness, and I think now that's second nature.

I am a co-op leader for Sarah's Girl Scout troop, and that's really important. Sarah likes Girl Scouts, and it's something I like doing with her. When my son was born, I considered not teaching even though I loved it. I wanted to be home with my baby during the day when he was an infant. It was a huge worry. When I was pregnant, I kept having dreams that I would drop my baby off at day care, and when I picked him up at night, I couldn't remember who he was. I went to my principal and told her I didn't want to sign a contract for the next year because there were only a limited number of spaces in our day care. She was supportive, and she said whatever it takes, we'd work it out.

My son actually went back to school with me when he was seven weeks old. He is two now and I see him all the time. **My kids are both with me in school. For a woman and a mom, that is a gift.**

## What Lisa's Eight-Year-Old Daughter, Sarah, Learned

My mom worked real hard. She was up all night typing and gone at school a lot. It was a hard time. I learned from her that when you really want to do something, you have to work hard for it.

Because my mom talks about having so much fun teaching her kids, I want to be a teacher. I've had that same feeling ever since I was little, and I've never changed my mind. I have always also liked singing, animals, and I'm not afraid to touch bugs, so maybe I could be a veterinarian, singer, and teacher. I could teach people about animals by singing to them.

# *H*ER LOVE OF SCIENCE INSPIRES THE GIRLS SHE TEACHES

### Elizabeth Dabrowski

CHEMISTRY TEACHER AT MAGNIFICAT
CATHOLIC GIRLS HIGH SCHOOL

*Elizabeth Dabrowski could have been a chemist and conducted her own research, but she doesn't feel that by teaching she's doing something that's second best. Inspiring thousands of young women over the years to love science multiplies by many what she could have accomplished. Her students are the eager beneficiaries, and we want teachers to know they make a difference forever.*

I was brought up in a world where I believed women could do everything, and I planned a future as an astronaut, physicist, or major league baseball pitcher. I don't recall any of my friends being shy, reticent, or wilting violets either. We were kids from blue-collar families who were on the way up. Our dads worked in steel mills and auto plants. We wanted to do more. We were going to play baseball, join the navy, and go on submarines. We liked cars and mechanical things.

I remember my I.Q. was 156, and I graduated as valedictorian of my high school class and with honors in college, but I never reached my original goal of obtaining a physics Ph.D. I completed my master's degree in chemistry but decided not to go on with the doctoral program because I wasn't confident I could handle it successfully. **I wonder if my perfectionism prevented me from following through.**

Laboratories were too silent for me. I love to talk and have always thoroughly enjoyed people. **Teaching girls to enjoy science is challenging and fun, and combines both my love of science with my love of kids.**

At the academic Catholic all-girls high school where I teach, I'm delighted that most girls take advanced physics and chemistry. Yet I worry about girls' fear of making mistakes. The symptoms are all too familiar to me. **I think it takes a certain risk to get involved in difficult sciences. I'm hoping girls won't give up, and I'm delighted to be busy inspiring them.** Many of them want to become doctors, so maybe they'll be perfect doctors, unless their perfectionism prevents them from following through.

I think a lot about the issue of teaching girls. Before I taught at the girls' high school, I taught at a boys' Catholic high school. I recall discussing with parents their sons' discipline problems and remember hearing all too often that "boys will be boys." About five years later, I taught the daughter of some parents that had made that remark about their son. The girl was a wonderful student and well behaved, but before I had said anything to the parents, they said, "Be sure to discipline her. Girls need a firm hand." I wonder why these attitudes continue, why girls aren't given the freedom to make mistakes, and why such perfection is expected of them.

The nuns who taught me and my friends at the Catholic grade school I attended were pretty rough and tough, too, and they also all loved baseball. They were strict when it came to discipline, but at the same time, they were fun and challenging. **Even when we didn't like their strict teaching methods, we realized we were learning much from them. For the most part, they were take-charge nuns and good role models for assertiveness.**

One thing I didn't like about my Catholic school was that we were always being told that our parents would go to hell if they were divorced. In no way did I believe that my smart, hardworking, divorced mother would ever deserve to go to hell. It just made me angry because I was always required to make Mother's and Father's Day cards, and I had no father, so I would cross out "father" and write in "uncle." I remember hearing the priest say, "Kids who are troublemakers come from broken homes." I knew the priests were wrong because my mother was so good, and I was trying to be good too.

**Not only did my mother work hard to inspire me with optimism, she was a totally interesting person.** She encouraged me to be a good student and expected me to go to college, although she didn't have the opportunity to get a higher education herself. My mother never seemed angry or felt sorry for herself. She worked very hard, first as a seamstress, then as a saleswoman in a department store.

**I also had lots of loving parenting because of my two uncles, my mother's younger brothers, who lived downstairs from us, and who adored me.** They had both attended college on the G.I. Bill and graduated, which was pretty unusual in our neighborhood, where almost no one had a college education. Surprising for the time, my chemist uncle worked in a laboratory with almost all women, and I remember his taking me there and letting me look through an electronic microscope. **I was excited about science, and my uncle's colleagues (all women) were always willing to take time to answer my questions or explain what they were working on.** My other uncle was an attorney and worked for a woman bank president, again unusual for the time. I didn't even realize that women scientists and bank presidents were the exception, and my uncles always expected me to go to college.

After eight grades in one neighborhood school, I wanted a change. I wanted to go to a high school outside of our neighborhood, and I wanted to choose the school. I selected an all-girls Catholic high school that was very academic and where the students were really encouraged to think and question. It was a brand-new school, and I was in its second graduating class. The atmosphere around the school was vibrant as the school tried to establish itself. The teachers were all returning to college for their master's and doctoral degrees, and the mother superior of the order, although she walked with a cane, would throw that cane into her luxury car and go tooling around. The nuns actually helped build the mother superior's house; even the sweet old ladies were putting in sidewalks and laying bricks. The sense of newness was energizing and exciting. Our class started their first National Honor Society and initiated traditions that have been perpetuated ever since.

**One of the nuns was really special to me.** She was young, the only Irish nun in the school. She taught English and had us read Irish plays the entire semester. She also required us to read literature of many other cultures. She told us it was to get us ready to meet the many different people we would meet in college. She was a baseball fan and a newspaper journalist, and my friends and I sat around after school and talked to her. If we missed the bus, we didn't care. We just admired her and liked to sit and talk.

Talking was one of my favorite sports. No sooner was I home when I was on the telephone, talking to my friends I had only just left after school. My mother would ask me why in the world I was talking again when I had just left my friends. I would explain that we could talk about the secret stuff on the phone that we couldn't talk about when others were there. My mother would ask me to hang up the phone, and I would grudgingly oblige and get to my homework. I delivered the best grades, although I admit I found my schoolwork to be fairly easy. After the homework, I was back on the telephone talking to my friends until bedtime.

When it was time for me to decide about college, my uncles helped me assemble information on colleges, majors, and, of course, scholarships. I was looking forward to change, and the formerly all-male college that my uncles had attended was admitting its first women. I felt it was my duty to attend.

I loved college and enjoyed having men in my classes. I also liked the many young professors in the school who seemed to take such an interest in what they were teaching. Furthermore, it was fun breaking with tradition and pioneering new language usages. For example, the glee club would change the words of the songs from "sons" to "sons and daughters."

**I hit my first wall at college. I had planned to major in physics but I simply found the first course too difficult. My B grade made me feel inadequate, so I decided I didn't like physics. My chemistry professor was inspiring, and he convinced me to change my major to chemistry.** I decided to become a chemistry researcher like the women I remembered from my uncle's laboratory. My grades were spectacular, and my plans were to enter graduate school.

**Graduate school was a second disappointment. My grades were fine, but the professors' attitude toward me was as if I had just graduated from high school. I felt put down and decided maybe I'd had enough of school.** Maybe I just didn't like the hostile environment enough to continue for a Ph.D., or **maybe I was just accustomed to being at the top, and at graduate school**

there was no top. All the students felt a little like peons. **I simply lost confidence in myself, but I did persevere sufficiently to complete my master's degree.**

Right now I'm contented inspiring girls to love science because I've always loved it. That's a reasonable goal for me. **The girls in my classes will hopefully find in me a role model who will encourage their interest and confidence and open the world of chemistry and its possibilities to them.**

# $\mathscr{A}$ Teacher for Each Child's Unique Gifts

### Frances A. Karnes, Ph.D.

PROFESSOR OF SPECIAL EDUCATION AND DIRECTOR OF
THE FRANCES A. KARNES CENTER FOR GIFTED STUDIES,
UNIVERSITY OF SOUTHERN MISSISSIPPI

*Dr. Frances Karnes has become widely known for her research, scholarly publications, innovative program developments, and advances in gifted education. She is the coauthor of fifteen books and the author or coauthor of more than two hundred journal articles.*

*Frances started as a first-grade teacher and became a teacher of teachers. At a time when most educators emphasized the importance of marching children in lockstep through the identical curriculum, Dr. Karnes pioneered the idea that you could create practical educational programs that allowed each child to move at his or her own pace. The education of gifted children and the development of the leadership potential of youth are the primary focus of her teaching, research, and service activities. Her intense interest in the leadership development of youth is expressed in her recent books:* Girls and Young Women Leading the Way, Girls and Young Women Inventing, Girls and Young Women Entrepreneurs, Competitions: Maximizing Your Abilities, The Leadership Skills Inventory, The Leadership Development Program, *and her latest,* Adventures and Challenges: Real Life Stories by Girls and Young Women.

*In addition to Dr. Karnes's many state and national awards and the honorary doctorate awarded her in 1990 by her alma mater, Quincy University, the Board of Trustees of Mississippi Institutions of Higher Learning honored her by naming the research, instructional, and service center she founded in 1979 for her.*

I was the elder child, brought up in a traditional Catholic family. My mother graduated from Mount Mary College in Milwaukee with a major in English and journalism and worked as a reporter for the *Chicago Sun-Times* during an era when very few women were reporters. She stayed home to raise my sister and me, but was very active as a community leader in our hometown of Quincy, Illinois. My father was department manager for a large pump and compressor manufacturing company, was the breadwinner, and was clearly the head of the household.

**I was goal-directed at an early age.** In an effort to contribute to the war effort during World War II, I'd go from house to house with my red wagon and collect old papers and magazines, scrap metal, and all kinds of items people had put aside for me, **always trying to surpass what I had previously collected.**

Between ages eight and ten, I ran a "sand" store. I'd color white sand with melted lipstick and put it in little perfume bottles, then make designs by maneuvering a pencil inside. I'd sell or barter these unusual bottles of colored sand. Once I wanted a particular button that my friend had, so I came up with a very unique sand bottle to trade for that button. **Even then I was learning entrepreneurial and negotiating skills that would help me in my future career.**

We had a wonderful sense of family. My younger sister and I felt secure, treasured, and special. **Our parents always expected us to do chores.** In addition to doing dishes, we helped with the laundry and housekeeping. One of my regular winter duties was stoking the hopper of the coal-burning furnace and removing ashes and clinkers. **All of us would join what became a family ritual at the end of each school year: cleaning the wallpaper and windows throughout our modest but tidy home. Our parents regularly assigned tasks without providing us with detailed directions and frequently bombarded us with questions and posed problems for their expressed purpose of encouraging us to be independent and self-reliant.**

Girl Scouts was very important in shaping my life. My mother was active and proactive in the scouting movement. She founded and was the leader of two Girl Scout troops of disabled girls at a time when these children were rarely afforded the special attention they needed in school and were generally excluded from scouting. Some of the girls in her troops were mentally retarded, some were physically handicapped, and I recall vividly that one little girl was blind. My mother loved working with these girls. **When she observed something was needed, she'd find a way to meet that need.** When she needed more Girl Scout camping space, she found a parcel of vacant land and persuaded the owners to donate the land. **I observed her strategies and applied them throughout my own career. With her as role model, I became active in scouting at an early age.** While an undergraduate in college, I served as a Girl Scout leader and began my first forays into individualizing instruction when I was teaching the girls knot tying.

I learned to read early, which I always preferred to sports. Growing up on the Illinois side of the Mississippi River just a few miles upstream from Hannibal, Missouri, may **explain why I was enthralled by adventure stories.** I dreamed that Mark Twain's characters were my personal friends and yearned for the day that I could accompany them as I watched barges traverse the river.

**Attendance in Catholic schools from kindergarten through the baccalaureate degree left me with a lifelong interest in rigorous academic subjects but with lingering questions pertaining to the disciplinary tactics in our all-girl school.** My father insisted I take shorthand, typing, and business classes, along with Latin, but my favorites were the college-prep courses in which I excelled. **I'm grateful that my father's preference prevailed, since the skills I learned in business classes have served me well through the years.**

My friend Kathleen and I wanted to take trigonometry and solid geometry, but were informed emphatically that girls were not permitted to pursue such subjects. **We promptly challenged that ruling by signing up for the football team,** and our principal said, "You've made your point." **For the first time, and from that day forward, girls in our school were permitted to enroll in advanced math and science classes.**

My parents had lots of wonderful friends. They were always open to a variety of people, and they encouraged us to be too. **People of different ages and religions were typical visitors.** I often preferred being with and talking to my parents' adult friends to going out with high school friends.

**Music has influenced my life by affording me opportunities for travel and for new and exciting experiences.** I took piano lessons in elementary school and played the violin, string bass, and snare drums well enough in high school to be selected for the all-state band and orchestra program at the University of Illinois. **I**

treasured the friendships I made there and admired and respected the music teachers. I even dared to hope that the orchestra and band experiences would lead to my going to college there.

My parents' preference for the Catholic institution in our hometown prevailed when I enrolled in Quincy College. I studied diligently and did well in this small liberal arts college that offered excellent educational opportunities. However, by the middle of my sophomore year, I'd become impatient. At Christmas that year, **I came home from college and told my father I wasn't going back. My father's response was, "You will finish even if I have to take you back."** Several days later, a friend of mine came to me and said there was going to be an opening for a first-grade teacher at an elementary school. **I was elated about that because I'd always wanted to be an elementary school teacher.** Even as a child, I would have chalk and chalkboard, and I would always find kids in the neighborhood to teach. **That hope of a position (and perhaps my father's threats too) motivated me to finish that year of college for my two-year teaching certificate.**

At age nineteen, with high hopes and much zeal, I launched my teaching career in a parochial school in East St. Louis, Illinois, with forty-seven first-grade children in a classroom hardly adequate for half that number. **Through simple testing, asking questions, and posing problems, I learned as much as possible about each child's level of educational development and readiness for school. My experiences as a Girl Scout leader had made me sensitive to the drastic differences in the rates at which children learn.** I was, therefore, not surprised to find that three among my first graders were already reading above the third-grade level and could also spell, write, and perform math computations at or above that level. Nor was I shocked upon learning that several children at the other end of the continuum could not count to ten and didn't recognize more than a few of the letters of the alphabet.

**I spent many long hours at night preparing lesson plans, selecting instructional materials, and planning teaching strategies that would challenge and provide each child with opportunities to learn at his or her own rate.** I was surprised, dismayed, and shocked when the principal insisted that all children must do precisely the same assignments and should be kept on the same page! I let her think I was teaching that way. In one drawer, I had plans for the whole class working together, but in the other drawer, I had a file of where each student was. The parents found out I was individualizing and wanted the other teachers to individualize as well. The principal wasn't happy. I decided I had to leave, but I knew I needed to earn my bachelor's degree to be able to convince teachers that children should be taught at their individual instructional level and not all in the same way.

I accepted a position in Quincy and gained one additional year of rather frustrating experience, this time as a third-grade teacher. The children in my Quincy classroom were also highly diverse, but again there was persistent pressure from superiors to teach everyone at the same level. By taking evening and summer-session courses at Quincy College, I was able to complete my baccalaureate degree with two years of teaching experience to my credit.

I was determined to teach where I could individualize, so I accepted a position as a teacher of retarded children in the Quincy public schools that provided me with two more years of some of the most memorable and rewarding experiences of my career. My Quincy classroom immediately became an exciting laboratory in which to explore in a practical setting the theories, concepts, and strategies I was learning about in the University of Illinois extension courses. I took courses in learning disabilities and those related to individual differences. It was a joy to teach my mentally retarded students. I could assess exactly where they were and work with each of them at their respective levels.

I continued with graduate study toward a doctorate at the University of Illinois, taught undergraduate courses, and gained extensive research experience. However, marriage, family, and a whole series of other exciting events brought about major and rather abrupt changes in my career plans. Prior to our marriage, my husband, Ray, who was a professor and department chair at Illinois, had been involved in the establishment of Njala University College in Sierra Leone in 1963–64. When our son Chris was about ten months old, I received an exciting call from Ray announcing that we'd been invited to go to Africa. I'd been about to get on the phone to enthusiastically share news with him of my pregnancy with our second son,

John. I was worried about how I could manage our toddler and a new baby in Africa, but there never seemed to be anything that Ray couldn't do. **He wasn't worried, and he was confident we could manage it all. His confidence encouraged me.** We went to Africa in 1967, when Christopher was a toddler and I was five months pregnant. I came home briefly to give birth to John, stayed home for six weeks, and flew back to Africa. We were in Africa for three years, lived out in the bush in an old British plantation house with a big veranda, and **met many interesting people, including ambassadors and heads of state.** There were no restaurants, so we would entertain and have dinner parties.

The Njala University College was rewarding personally as well as professionally. Especially exciting and valuable to me in the context of my subsequent work in the field of gifted education were my many hours of volunteer service to the small international school developed on campus to provide nursery, infant, and elementary schooling for faculty and staff children. **I had the privilege of working with exceptionally ingenious, creative, and imaginative teachers of several different nationalities. We sought to meet the unique needs of every child and provide each with the optimum opportunity to learn at his or her own rate.** I also had the pleasure of observing my elder son get his early schooling in that rich environment.

**Being immersed in so different a culture changed my perspective.** I knew that when I came back, I wanted to earn a Ph.D. and use it to make a difference in education.

Upon returning to the United States, I earned my doctorate. Soon thereafter, my husband retired from Illinois and accepted a professorship at the University of Southern Mississippi, where I also joined the faculty. There was not at that time a single gifted education program in the public or private schools of the state of Mississippi. Before the end of 1973, more than four hundred educators, parents, and other advocates had formed the very active Mississippi Association for Gifted Children and elected me its first president. **The state legislature in 1974 amended the Mississippi School Code to include the gifted and talented in the definition of exceptional children and thus permit the legal expenditure of public funds in support of special programs for the gifted on the same basis**

**as for the disabled.** A program for the gifted was initiated immediately in the Hattiesburg public schools and spread rapidly across the state on a voluntary basis until the early 1990s, when **legislative action made it mandatory on the part of every school district. I felt I'd really contributed to so many children's lives.**

Our new state mandate and the University of Southern Mississippi provided a rich and supportive environment in which I could pursue my compelling interests in gifted education. It was completely overwhelming to me when on September 16, 1999, the Board of Trustees of Mississippi Institutions of Higher Learning named the research, instructional, and service center I'd founded at USM two decades ago the Frances A. Karnes Center for Gifted Studies. I enter the new millennium with high hopes that my association with this center and this university will continue to provide me with the highest order of personal and professional gratification for several more challenging years.

# 6

# The Artists and Musicians

*A*RTISTIC careers are indeed pioneering professions for women. There were almost no women to be found in symphony orchestras a generation ago; the very few usually sat behind a harp or piano. Many more men than women hold the coveted first or second chair in orchestras. There continue to be far fewer women than men in the visual and graphic arts as well, and it can be difficult to earn a living through the arts; the "starving artist" cliché has a ring of truth.

## Results from the See Jane Win Study

We've grouped visual artists and orchestral musicians together because our *See Jane Win* study shows that from early in their childhood onward, they were recognized by others mainly for their talents and their creativity. As they matured, many of them formed their identity around their musical or artistic talent.

Some of the women in our *See Jane Win* study were the first women in their orchestras, some the only women for a long time. Some commented that they no longer feel like pioneers because there are presently many more women in orchestras, but others reminded us that there continue to be glass ceilings in the area of music. Women make up only approximately 15 percent of symphony orchestra members. Female orchestral conductors are rare, although our study did include one, and there are definitely particular instruments that are only rarely played by women—for example, the brass instruments and double bass.

Some of our artists began their careers in other fields until they could afford to work in their beloved arts. Others acknowledged that they could only afford to be engaged in their sculpting, photography or painting because they were financially secured by their spouses.

A slightly larger percentage of both musicians and artists were only children compared to the total group (11 and 15 percent, respectively). There were also more oldest children in both career groups. Musicians tended to come from smaller families. Perhaps their birth order and smaller family size were advantages because of the investment of time and money necessary to develop musical skills.

Although more visual artists identified with their mothers than their fathers, more of these women identified with their fathers compared to the total group. More of the visual artists and musicians also identified with someone other than their parents, namely their music or art teachers.

The musicians were similar to the total group in their developmental milestones, but fewer of the visual artists were very early talkers or readers, and more were somewhat late in their verbal skills. The visual artists seemed to struggle more with their schoolwork despite reported high I.Q. scores. They also reported a greater decline in grades and confidence in middle school. The orchestral women were mainly excellent students, and very few of them experienced that middle school slump. By high school, however, fewer of both groups took advanced math and science classes; instead they were immersed in their specialty areas, practicing for many hours and teaching their skills to younger children who shared their special talent. Both groups spent considerable time alone as well. Despite that, by high school more of the visual artists socialized with other high school students, and more of the orchestral women found their social opportunities within their orchestra and with music-camp comrades.

The orchestral musicians tended to be excellent students and graduated high in their class, while the visual artists tended to do somewhat less well academically. Interestingly, both these groups skipped more grades than was typical. A much higher than usual percentage (93 percent) of orchestral musicians attended public schools at all grade levels. That may be a credit to the public school music programs and the need to have a critical mass of musicians to form bands and orchestras. The visual artists attended public, parochial, or independent schools on average as often as the total group.

Although the artists and musicians often defined themselves by their talents early in life, more women in both these groups were hesitant about recommending their careers to other young women, even though they described them as "challenging," "creative," and "fulfilling"; almost a third of both groups indicated financial disappointment as the reason. In addition, many of the orchestral women cited the too competitive nature of orchestral music as well as how much time their careers take from their families and relationships.

## How Jane Won

Our group of artists and musicians prized their special talents early. Illustrator Mary GrandPré and graphic artist Rodene Brchan both remember their love of art from early on. In adult life, however, both are stressed by economic hard times and talked about a wish to express themselves in art without having to worry about pleasing a customer. Mary's success with the *Harry Potter* books may enable her to have the freedom she seeks; Rodene may have to wait until her children are grown for the time and financial freedom she wishes for.

Photographer Frances Bayless buried her artistic talent, or at least enjoyed it at a very surface level, until she discovered the freedom and the medium in which to communicate her art form. Photography has enabled Fran to express her passions for art, animals, and adventure. Indeed, Fran's story of coming to her art form late in life should inspire women of all ages to continue to explore their talents. Never write yourself off! You may have the right talent at the wrong time, so wait for your opportunity, then take it.

Violinist Pamela Frank's early emotional, intense response to music was so unique that her parents must surely have known she had extraordinary talent. Yet her parents provided her with a balanced childhood instead of focusing single-mindedly on her extraordinary talent. Her total lack of competitive feelings was so untypical for other musicians in our study, yet she emerged a solo violinist in this hugely competitive field. For every generalization, there seems to be extraordinary exceptions, and Pamela is surely an exception, but it may be she felt little competition because she had very few experiences losing in either academics or music.

Flutist Martha Aarons's story is more typical of orchestral musicians. While she no longer feels like a pioneer in her orchestra, she admitted never quite knowing if being a woman has been a disadvantage in her field. She pointed out that thousands of women flutists audition for major symphony orchestras while many fewer men do. Yet within major symphony orchestras, many more of the flute chairs are held by men than women. That same message had been echoed by many of the 140 orchestral women who completed surveys for the *See Jane Win* study. With so many talented musicians, so few available opportunities, and so many male conductors, it seems that orchestral music has a long way to go before there is equality for women.

# ℋARRY POTTER FLEW INTO HER LIFE

## Mary GrandPré

ILLUSTRATOR

*Mary GrandPré's illustrations in children's books may have been familiar to you even before she was chosen to illustrate the famous* Harry Potter *books.* The Vegetables Go to Bed, The House of Wisdom, Pockets, *and* Chin Yu Min and the Ginger Cat *are among them. Mary's dad's storytelling and the holy images in her church contributed to her art. Her struggle to make her contribution should help inspire you with your own struggle. Her success was hard-won, but she persevered.*

Ever since I was a little girl, I've enjoyed drawing. I received my first art set when I was about five and drew cartoon characters because that's what I was most excited by at the time.

My parents and other relatives were always excited about what I drew or painted, but I didn't know if I should believe them or not; after all, they're my parents. I would go to the encyclopedia and look for interesting black-and-white photographs to copy. **If I was punished for something or feeling bad, I can remember soothing myself with drawing.**

My dad had artistic abilities and was creative in other ways as well. He was a carpenter, a storyteller, an inventor of characters, and a very creative thinker. He was an inspiration to me. My father's influence propelled me into the children's book arena because I enjoy the storytelling and fantasy. He was also my first art teacher because he and I would sit at the kitchen table and draw and doodle. He was more personally involved and supportive than anyone else in my family. I'm the youngest of four and, along with my dad, the only introvert. We had that in common and hung out together.

We didn't have art classes in Catholic schools, only basic skills. While I was in Catholic school, the wonderful icons on the holy cards, statues, paintings, and stained-glass windows influenced my artistic sensibilities. They were a constant presence in those early years, and I would be absorbed by them whenever I was in church.

Later in life when I was in art school, I would return to the iconic image, the single figure, the pose, the Renaissance palate, and realize that's probably where it came from. I've never consciously said to myself, "I'll do something like those holy cards," but the images are there for me.

When I was in junior high, **I entered drawings in the church bazaar and sold my first artwork.** I drew those little kids with the huge eyes, which were a popular image in the late sixties. I sold all of them and was written up in the church bulletin. In junior and senior high, **I entered a few painting contests and won first or second prizes.** In ninth grade, I did a mural for the school. Everyone referred to me as "the Artist." **I claimed that identity, nurtured it, and protected it.**

**I didn't have a lot of friends in junior high, but I didn't really care.** In high school I was more socially active, **but I never lost the artist part of me, and I owned it as if it were a badge.** It was my best friend. I knew that part of me best because I had done art so long, and it had been such a comfort.

Public high school was a rude awakening, and I didn't know what to do with all my new freedom. **I put most of it into my artwork, and my art blossomed.** My friends noticed I was good and were encouraging, and that was a new kind of support for me. I was allowed more time in my art classes. It probably wouldn't be done today, but I was allowed to skip some classes and do art instead.

After high school, I didn't really know what I was going to do, so I went to junior college and took basic subjects and art classes. I waited on tables for many years until one of my waitress friends said, "You should really go to the Minneapolis College of Art and Design."

I decided to apply to art college and received a school loan. At age twenty-five, I was an older student at the college. I studied fine arts, graphic design, art history, and illustration. My illustration teacher was a very good artist and **taught his students how to think and communicate an idea in a strikingly creative way.** Because of his classes, I discovered I wanted to be an illustrator. It bothered me that I was older and the younger students were getting art director jobs. I decided that since I've always been an artist, what was the big rush? During my last year in art school, I was still waiting on tables, trying to get the best waitress position so I could put as much time into my portfolio as possible. By this time, I'd been married for five years but didn't have any children. My husband was unemployed for most of our marriage. He wasn't supportive of my going to school, and we had a pretty explosive divorce.

**In college you can be a star a lot more easily than you can in the real world, which was really disheartening.** In school I was one of the best. I was shocked by what it was like in the real world. **I created a whole new portfolio the summer after I left art school. I took it to local publishers and ad agencies and received feedback, and would go back and change the portfolio and do a new piece and go out again.** I landed small jobs with local publishers, a few ad jobs, and was living in Minneapolis in an apartment with a roommate, trying to make it. I was depressed because it was so hard to get started. I would receive letters from national publishers saying, "I love your stuff but can't use you."

**If my work wasn't getting the response I wanted it to get, I would go into my little bedroom studio and do another piece or two and put those in the portfolio. I kept changing the portfolio according to the feedback I was getting. Much of my success has come from my drive to continue, to keep working, practicing, learning new ways of looking at something or new ways to apply chalk to paper. There was a certain experimental part of me that allowed my work to keep evolving.**

**Illustration was competitive, and there weren't many women doing it.** While I was going through those hard times, I thought, "Women draw; they always have," but in art history classes, it was always men, and now, it's still mostly men doing illustration. All the artists we learned about in art school were men. It's not a talent that depends on physical strength or body weight. People took for granted that famous illustrators were going to be men because that's the way it had always been. My medium is pastels, and it has a softer quality to it, and art directors said my work was too feminine. **I didn't know what I was supposed to do with that information. Was I supposed to be less feminine? What's wrong with being feminine?**

I waited on tables for thirteen years, was totally sick of it, and decided to work as an artist full-time. There was barely enough work, **but I arranged for a local representative who took my art**

**around and introduced me to some new art directors.** Finally I was making enough money to pay the rent.

About five years after my divorce, I remarried. He was a designer artist, and we had a lot in common. We formed a business and studio in Minneapolis. During that time I did my first children's book for Random House, called *Chin Yu Min and the Ginger Cat,* and it led to many open doors, to other children's books and publishers, and even some ad work. I was busy, and we were making a good living. **Then I found a representative who was more national.** He pushed my work into the ad agencies in New York, Chicago, and Los Angeles, and I received a lot of exposure. My career was most important to me, as my husband's career was to him. We were a successful business team, but our marriage fell apart, and we divorced about six years ago.

I went through some therapy after my last divorce that opened my eyes to what kind of person I had learned to be growing up in a family where I was the youngest and an introvert. **I was too dependent on validation from others, and as I started making decisions that were good for me, my art changed too. I had more confidence, more faith, and more self-assuredness about who I was and what kind of art I was making. I would approach my canvases with more confidence, which can make the difference between an okay and a great painting. Therapy gave me a major boost.**

Four years ago I decided to be on my own. I was doing more children's books, working for a new publisher, and actually so busy that I decided I should rethink my life, my career, and my time commitments.

Then *Harry Potter* came into my life. I received a call from the art director at Scholastic Books. He said, "I have a story about a boy with magical powers that was originally published in London. We're doing the book, and from what we see of your work, we would like you to do the illustrations. We like your magical quality, and you could bring a lot to the book." I did four or five different concepts for the cover and about fifteen black-and-white little pieces for the inside and sent those off to the art director for his approval. That's the last I thought I'd hear about the whole thing. About nine months later, I received a call about a second *Harry Potter* book. The buzz from the *Harry Potter* frenzy invaded my studio. *Harry Potter* has opened many doors for me, and I've made appearances and presentations at grade schools, art schools, libraries, and bookstores, to the point where I stopped taking calls because I couldn't get any of my other work done! *Harry Potter* is the more popular part of my work, but not necessarily the most important part.

I've started to write stories, and I have some interested publishers. I really need to be writing my own books, illustrating them, and going back to painting from my heart and not so much for someone's problem that needs to be solved, someone's product that needs to be sold, or someone's book that needs to be illustrated. I'm forty-five, and I finally feel like I have found a place where I can start living my dream. It's an exciting time, and it's scary, too, but I feel confident that it will work out.

**I'm at a crossroads again because I've been so busy as an illustrator,** and *Harry Potter* has become such a major part of my life. I have a partner, Tom, who is my best friend and has been for a very long time, a supportive man and an artist who has kids. He's a very stable, constant, levelheaded, giving person, and this is the first relationship I've ever had like that. We both have our own studios in the house. **We have our extended family, and I've found other things in life besides art that excite me. I've learned that we have to keep our arts separate and private.**

Tom's children live with us part-time, every other weekend, and have been here a little over a year. I'm forming some good, but sometimes challenging relationships with them. The youngest boy is twelve, the girl is sixteen, and the nineteen-year-old is not around much. Having kids around is great for me as a children's book writer and illustrator. They are the first ones to hear my ideas for stories, and that's fun because I have built-in critics in our home.

**Having the kids around has also lightened my heart. They have also taken some of the focus off of my artwork and into normal real life. Having Tom and the kids in my life has made it rich and more balanced.**

**My dream is to have enough time in my personal life to enjoy my home with Tom and my friends, and to travel.** I've been working so hard and feverishly the last twenty years that I can now take more time to do whatever is most gratifying for me.

When I think about how busy I have been as a professional illustrator and how much I hate working sometimes, **I think back to how much I used to love to draw as a kid, and how it was a comfort. It should always be like that, but when it becomes a job, art becomes something else. I'm looking for a way to bring that positive feeling back so I can really love drawing again.** I love it now, but it's not as personal as it used to be when I was a kid. I've had to work hard to get here, and now it's going to pay back.

# Emperor Penguins in Antarctica Are a Favorite

## Frances B. Bayless

WILDLIFE PHOTOGRAPHER

*If you see Fran Bayless's photographs, you'll know she is bringing a woman's perspective to her work. She knows the importance of families to all of life. Her photographs show the intimate relationships among penguins, leopards, zebras, tigers, and giraffes. When you read her story, you'll marvel at how Fran, at seventy-one, can take photographs in temperatures of seventy degrees below zero. Her Leica cameras need to be made especially for those temperatures and can't depend on batteries. Fran's personal batteries keep on going and every reader over thirty will be in awe. Fran's story demonstrates that it's never too late to put your passions into practice.*

**I loved to draw as early as kindergarten.** I was always drawing on the sidewalks with chalk. I remember taking charcoal from the fireplace and putting it in my pocket so I could draw on paper. My mother would be very upset with me because of the mess it made, but it never stopped me.

I was a middle child, a girl between two boys, and my oldest brother, always my best friend, Wally, was two and a half years older than I. **I was a tomboy, played baseball with the boys, and listened to the radio show *Jack Armstrong* with Wally and Tom in the afternoon. That was my first introduction to travel and adventure.** Wally and my husband, Tom, were seatmates in school, so I've known my husband ever since I was seven years old. I was a part of their little group.

**I've always enjoyed animals too.** We had dogs and cats, and the kids were responsible for taking care of them. My dogs, Peter Pan and Prince, were a very special part of my life, mine to take care of and to love.

My father was an attorney and my mother was a very social person, so they both led very busy lives. We had a lot of hired help, so my mother was more a director of the staff than a mother. **My parents'** most important expectation for us was that we have good manners and earn good grades. I achieved both.

My fourth-grade teacher, Edith Turner, probably had more impact on my life than anyone. She wore very flamboyant clothing and bright lipstick. She wore a minimum of twenty bracelets on her arms and always draped an old mink scarf around her neck. She was generations ahead of her time for travel, adventure, the love of the earth, and ecology, and she took us on imaginary adventures all over the world. We did a project on Antarctica way back then, and I knew I had to visit there someday.

I was a rather unusual child growing up. I had my own agenda, and when I could use it, I did. When I couldn't, I just melted and let my life go the way my parents wanted it to go. I had rather unusual friends too. We were all pretty much self-contained and never felt swayed by peer pressure. I never had any trouble walking away from anything I didn't feel comfortable about despite peer pressure. I put my heart and soul into what I enjoyed.

Until my junior year, I stayed in public school, where I was part of the Shaker Heights High School swim team, both for competition and synchronized swimming. Then my parents enrolled me in Laurel School, an independent girls' school, in my junior year. I had to catch up because I was way behind in almost every subject. The headmistress, Edna Lake, was another tremendous mentor. She was positive, compassionate, helpful, and understanding. My brother Wally and Tom had gone off to fight in World War II, so I virtually had all of my pins pulled out from under me. She helped me through that difficult period of time. I also had an art teacher who was very supportive. I wanted to go to art school, but my parents wanted me to go to a traditional college. We weren't given choices, but it all worked out in the end.

I'd always been a very quiet, self-contained person. I lost myself in my drawings, but I never showed them to anyone. It was my private endeavor. In many ways, my artwork portrayed my life. Early on, I drew playful pictures of kids climbing trees and playing hopscotch. During my high school and the war years, they were lonesome pictures. When I went to college, my art reflected my more formal art training. Mount Vernon Junior College in Washington, D.C., was an absolutely wonderful growing experience for me because there was so much to experience and see in Washington. I graduated from Mary Washington College, with a B.S. degree. Both were women's colleges. At Mary Washington, I was able to take more art classes along with my academics. Since my parents wanted me to become a good wife and mother, I majored in home economics and dietetics.

Tom returned home from the war, went to the University of Michigan, and we saw each other during the holidays. We had known each other for many years, and Wally and Tom had decided that if they were going to remain best friends (and they did), it would be best if Tom married me. I had been aware of this plan ever since I was twelve years old. We were married two days after I graduated from college. **Fortunately, we were very much in love in addition to being good pals.**

Through the years, Tom and I have gone backpacking and tenting all through Canada and the United States. **We like adventure and exploring.** We wanted to go tenting on our honeymoon, but my mother put her foot down.

After I'd graduated from college, **I really didn't know what I wanted to do with my life, but I knew I didn't want to be a social butterfly like my mother and my mother-in-law.** I had a choice of doing something constructive or playing bridge and socializing, and the latter didn't appeal to me at all. **I felt that if you have a life, you must give of it.** I decided I'd teach school and started in a nursery school in Plymouth Church. Then Laurel School, the high school I'd attended, asked me if I would manage their nursery school, and I was soon promoted to director of the kindergarten. **I taught kindergarten for eighteen years, which was wonderful for my art, too,** because little children are so uninhibited in their artwork.

Our daughters, Margaret and Nancy, attended the same school where I taught. **We had the same hours and vacations. It was the most ideal situation that one could possibly have.** I had both of them in class. Our older daughter called me "Mom," but our younger daughter always called me "Mrs. Bayless." Margaret is now a certified public accountant and CFO of a manufacturing company, and Nancy is an attorney who gave up her practice to be home with her children.

When we camped, we gave our daughters cameras to record the experience. Margaret became a fantastic photographer and artist. She and her father would go off and take pictures, but Nancy preferred to stay with me and collect stones or keep busy in other ways. I was responsible for the children and the cooking; it never occurred to me to pick up a camera.

Tom had heard about Antarctica ever since I was a kid, and when our girls were grown up and had completed their education, he took me and his cameras to Antarctica with a travel group from the University of Michigan.

My husband gave me a little "point and shoot" camera. I shot a couple rolls of film and thought to myself, "This is amazing." I couldn't believe what I was doing with this camera. **It was so exciting to see what I could put on a little piece of film. It changed my life.**

**I was sixty-two when I decided to fulfill my dream of going to art school and majoring in photography.** I enrolled at the Cleveland Institute of Art and started taking photography classes. **Bob Palmer, the head of the photography department, then took me on as a special student. I would go every day from 9:30 to 5:30. He and colleague Nancy McEntee have made me what I am. Art school absolutely fulfills the creative need I have had all these years.**

Tom and I visit Antarctica every year. Last November we took a flying and camping trip, which enabled me to capture the "impossible penguin images," emperor penguins with their chicks on their feet. We camped on the ice, and the warmest our tent ever became was twenty-two degrees below zero Fahrenheit. Most of the images were taken when the temperature was between thirty-five and forty-five below zero. As a Christmas gift from Tom, I flew to the South Pole from our base camp, where it was seventy below zero. Leica Camera sent me with two cameras they had specially prepared for the weather. Since they were manual cameras, I wasn't dependent on batteries or any electronics. In the field, I use all Leica or Hasselblad cameras.

**My husband retired when he was young, and we have been having a marvelous time fulfilling our artistic dreams through the use of still and video cameras. Our art has taken us around**

the world. We also visit South Georgia Island, which is a sub-antarctic island south of the Falklands, almost every winter. We go to Botswana about every other year to photograph the cats, zebras, giraffes, all the predators and the plains animals. We go to India to photograph tigers. In May we're going to Siberia to photograph Kodiak bears, and we'll come home by way of Alaska to spend a week on a little tugboat to photograph grizzly bears.

**What I wish to portray in my images is a personal contact with the animals so others are able to relate to and enjoy the natural activity and beauty of the subjects within their environment. I feel strongly about respecting the animals and the environment.** I never use a flash with the animals and try to be very low-key. **I never try to create a situation for a good picture, and I don't make any preconclusions because that can take away from the spontaneity. I spend hours observing.** When we go to Botswana, where we have our own guide, **we explore without our cameras for a day to become accustomed to the area. If we come across animals, we watch them and try to become part of the scene.** The next day we go back with our cameras. I like the challenge of trying to communicate with a wild animal. Once I made eye contact with a leopard for almost half an hour before I got the photograph. In Antarctica I sit among the penguins, who are very curious. After a short time, **they accept us into their life and activities.** When we visit South Georgia Island, I climb up to the top of the mountain to see a particular albatross that returns every year. **I find it spiritual and a great privilege to see "my" bird year after year.**

**If I am patient and respectful and I try to relate to these animals without disturbing or interfering with them,** I don't feel I'm in danger. If I just plunged in and started snapping my camera, accidents could occur. We have to be especially careful of polar bears. They would have no hesitation in attacking us, as they have been fasting for four months. **We're in their environment, and we must respect that whether or not we get an image. We are the interlopers in their lives.**

Kodak has one of my prints, and Leica is working with me on a portfolio of penguins. I have done images for travel agencies and hospitals, along with several one-person art gallery presentations.

We travel so much that I haven't been home enough to market my work. I will do that when we stop traveling on our unbelievable adventures.

**Beginning with Edith Turner and ending with my husband encouraging me to go to art school, I really have found my niche.** During my young adulthood, I couldn't do or express what I wanted to through art, having other family responsibilities. However, I must have done something right because we have wonderful and talented girls. I waited patiently for my turn after all those years of doing for others. **Now I am free to explore and finally fulfill my artistic endeavors.**

# $\mathcal{U}$SING HER GIFT

### Rodene Brchan
GRAPHIC ARTIST

*Rodene Brchan helps us understand what being an artist is all about. Art truly is her self-definition. The frustrations that come with doing art for a living are somehow very different from those that come with doing art for art's sake, but after she has finished raising her family, Rodene will no doubt arrive at her goals.*

My dad would say, **"If you're given a gift, use it," but he reminded me I would need a strong backbone.** Dad was a handyman and I was his gofer. He was also a perfectionist, and he didn't mince words. I would show him my artwork, and he would say, "Well, it needs to be done a little differently here." **There were times when I would get really mad at him, although I knew it was for the best.**

Dad was also good at math and history. When we went to museums, he would read every piece of information at the museum and tell us about it. He was very intelligent and memorized everything. **I learned so much from him, about how to learn and to memorize, which then helped me through my college art history courses.**

In sixth grade, when I started instrumental music, my dad gave me an old cornet to play. It was a beater, and I was okay with it until I went to school and saw all the other kids take their brand-new, shiny trumpets out of their cases. I looked at my old horn and was so upset, I ran home and told my dad I was never going to play that instrument again. To comfort me and yet make me work hard, he said, "If you play that cornet this year and work hard to sit first chair next year, you can play my trumpet." **I worked so hard until I sat first chair and then proudly played his trumpet. It was a good incentive.** I pursued music in high school and into college, along with art.

**I always drew pictures when I was little, but my sixth-grade art/science teacher discovered my art ability and encouraged**

**me.** Even when I was in high school, he would ask me to come back each year and teach his class for a day.

School was great, but I was sensitive and insecure and needed good close friends so I wouldn't feel left out. My parents were very open, and if I had a problem, I could usually come to them. **My mom was real good about discussing personal things, which helped me many times to get through tough situations.**

My sister and I were only two years apart, total opposites. She was and still is a very immaculate housekeeper, which I never cared about. I never had to do my laundry when living at home because my parents would never let her do just one pair of jeans. I'd always have a pile of clothes sitting on a chair that needed washing, so my sister would launder them so she could wash her one pair of jeans she so desperately needed. My sister has always been a lot like my mom, whereas I am a lot like my dad. Now, as adults, we have become closer, and I truly value our friendship.

Throughout my school years, my room was always a pit. You could barely get through it because I was an animal fanatic. I was constantly raising fish or gerbils and had aquariums all over my room with critters in them. I wanted to be a veterinarian, but when I took biology, we had to dissect frogs, and I wasn't quite prepared for that, so I gave up on veterinary service.

My senior year was great! I satisfied all my academic requirements by junior year, so my senior class schedule consisted of marching band, stage band, and art classes. My art teacher let me do most any creative art I wanted to. She'd say, "How about doing silver casting or something on the loom?" I wove a large rug by collecting dog and cat hair from the local vets, washing and carding it with some wool, and rolling it into thick yarn. It was very different.

I wanted to make rings for all the girls in Job's Daughters Bethel when I became honor queen, but I couldn't silver-cast that many rings. My art teacher instead showed me how to make them out of wood with power tools. **I always loved making things that were different.**

When I went to college, I was so advanced in art that my freshman year was quite boring. Fortunately, the other years were better. I majored in fine arts because I was able to take more studio classes.

**I had one professor I butted heads with, but I learned a lot**

**from him.** I took oil painting, composition, and watercolor from him for almost three years. I remember when he told me my first watercolor was "terrible" and he ripped it up, threw it away, and said, "Start over." I was furious, but the next one was better. He helped me relax and paint more spontaneously. **Over the years, we got along better. I think he knew I had creative possibilities, and he didn't want me to go astray. He came down hard, and at times I felt so inferior, but I learned he just wanted to make me stronger.** I had the same professor for art history classes, and they were the best art history classes I ever took. I learned so much and have retained what I learned to this day. **He expected a lot, and I learned a lot.**

Graphic artists are very structured and more technical than fine artists. I always find myself right on the line between graphic and fine arts, but I chose graphic arts because I needed a steady income. It can be very hard at times doing art and trying to please the customer, but over the years, I have learned not to take rejection of a design personally. When stress is bad, there are times when I look forward to retirement so I can do my own creative art and not have to please anyone but myself.

**Art is so competitive that even when you're working on a project with other artists, you're still competing.** If an artist can find a balanced work environment where competition isn't as important as the final product, only then can everyone learn and grow. I've been a graphic artist, a production manager, a supervisor, and an art director. The management end takes so much time and energy, and I have little time to be creative. Because of this and because I wanted more time for my family, I stepped out of management for a while and went back to being a graphic artist. As a graphic artist, I am able to do more of the hands-on, creative artwork and design, from the beginning of the idea to the finished work.

Over the years, I've grown and feel much more sure of myself and my abilities. I've changed work environments and am now back in a supervisory position. I've received awards for my art, design, and creativity, which helps put a perspective on my career. I feel stronger and have learned how to leave most of my work problems there so I can enjoy my family. I've also learned to live for today and not worry about tomorrow.

When I graduated from college, I seemed to travel a rough road. I started in a retail business with art supplies, which was helpful because I learned more about supplies and their uses. It helped me create my own art studio at home. I married in my senior year of college, but was still somewhat dependent on my parents because I had never lived away from home. Since my sister had done most of the housework, I needed my mom to show me how to cook and use a washer and dryer.

**My parents stayed important in my life, and after I married, it became more of an "adult friendship."** My dad and my husband were good friends. They would go hunting and fishing together. When my father passed away it was, and still is, hard on me, but through my grieving process, I've been able to grow more dependent on my husband, who is a really wonderful man. He's understanding and doesn't let things bother him; and when I fly off the handle, he'll sit and listen to me and try to help by offering suggestions. **My husband is my best friend and knows me better than I know myself at times. My children have grown into young adults, and we enjoy them so much.**

Life is rewarding. **I had a wonderful childhood based on a loving and supportive family. Knowing I had some place to retreat to helped me through the rough times.** There have been times I've thought about going back to school for a different career, but then I remember Dad's words: God gave me a gift, and I should use it.

# THE TRAUMA OF JUNIOR HIGH
## TAUGHT HER RESILIENCE

### Martha Aarons

FLUTIST, CLEVELAND SYMPHONY ORCHESTRA

*Martha Aarons's magnificent flute playing has earned her the honor of second chair in the Cleveland Symphony Orchestra and principal flutist at the Aspen Music Festival. The personal sacrifices she's made to play her beloved instrument were very typical of those reported by many women in orchestral music in our* See Jane Win *study. Perhaps that explains Martha's mother's struggles to encourage her daughter. As concertmistress of the Wellesley Orchestra, her mother probably had no options open for playing in a professional symphony orchestra, because almost no women were admitted in her time.*

My parents were both musical. I went to concerts from an early age and symphonies and operas were played in our home. When I had the measles in second grade and was very sick, my mother put on an opera, *Tosca,* by Puccini. At first, I wrinkled up my face and said, "Ugh." Then I fell absolutely in love with it. I memorized the music and sang all the words in Italian. My father bought a piano reduction of the opera, and I sang while he played. I drew pictures and romanticized the hero in the opera for a couple of years. My dad, a tax lawyer, and ultimately a judge on the tax court in Washington, played piano as a hobby, took a great interest in my music, and gave me important support.

My mother was a full-time homemaker until I was in junior high. Then she went back to library school for a master's in library science and worked part-time. She'd played violin and was concertmistress of the Wellesley Orchestra in college, but she'd pursued music only under pressure. She didn't have the positive feelings about playing that would have enabled her to empathize with me later. She did offer me all the right opportunities and didn't try to discourage me from going into music, but she overidentified with my failures and disappointments and felt them too keenly. When I'd have a success, she didn't revel in it as much as I wanted her to. When I was disappointed, she couldn't give me the "That's okay, just keep going" pep talk I needed. I think it was important that I had two parents to balance out the messages of caution and encouragement.

**My brother, who was twenty months older than me, excelled in all the subjects I was leery of.** I'd come into a math class and the teacher would say, "Are you Charlie Aarons's sister? He's legendary." **I definitely had math phobia and got B's in math. Actually, when I took the SAT, I scored slightly higher on my math test than my verbal test, which was a huge shock. I always avoided the harder sciences and stopped taking math the moment I fulfilled the minimum requirements. I felt overshadowed by my precocious, prodigy brother, but fortunately, I was good in the subjects he wasn't, and that probably reinforced my concentrating on the humanities. I think I would have been good at math if I had tried.**

**I showed a lot of musical aptitude.** When I was a baby, my parents would put music on, and I'd rock back and forth on my hands and knees in time to the music and wiggle my hips. I started taking piano lessons when I was about nine. I took both flute and piano, then dropped piano. **I preferred the more social instrument so I could play with groups, and I was attracted to wind instruments because I heard their solo sounds in the orchestra.**

**Teachers took me under their wings.** I had a fifth-grade teacher who was Italian-American and loved opera. I remember talking about opera with him during recess when other kids were playing. **I felt like an outsider, but he appreciated me.**

In junior high, I was teased a lot because kids were fast in Los Angeles, and I wasn't. In my sixth-grade photographs, you can see the girls already dressed sexily; they hiked up their skirts and had their hair draped over their eyes. They wore stockings, makeup, and shaved their legs. My mother didn't want me to be like that, so she wouldn't let me shave my legs or buy sexy clothes. I was a good student in school, so I had all the ingredients for being teased. They called me "Hairy Legs" and "square." I'd come home every day crying. **My mother was there to comfort me and say, "You'll see. Those kids will turn out to be a mess. You'll be smart, happy,** and successful." I didn't believe her and ended up being pretty disconsolate when I wasn't accepted by the cool group.

There were a few years when I put my flute on the back burner because it was so unfashionable to be interested in classical music. I became a Beatles maniac and listened to rock music. It didn't help me fit in with the crowd, but I found other friends who liked the Beatles.

Toward the end of junior high, I was honing in on my interest in music and orchestras and was finding a very good social niche outside school. It tied in with getting interested in boys, too. I went to music camp every year, was involved and in love with music, and had this incredibly strong desire to succeed, and suddenly I had lots of friends and an active social life.

I was first in competition often, and that compelled me to keep going. If I hadn't been first enough of the time, I probably wouldn't have continued. I had a friend who was also a rival. She always beat me out in the concerto competitions, partly because she'd memorize everything. I was always absolutely terrified and didn't do as well, but when it came to the orchestra, I always got the choice parts over her. I was very comfortable in orchestra and knew the repertoire from an early age, having listened to it incessantly. Our rivalry never interfered with our friendship.

My teacher during high school was the principal flute of the Los Angeles Philharmonic. He had gone to school with many members of the Philadelphia Orchestra. When they came to Los Angeles to perform, he had a party at his house for the flute section of that orchestra and the flute section of the Los Angeles Philharmonic, and I was the only student he invited to meet them. He was grooming me, so I felt pretty special and studied with him throughout high school.

In Los Angeles there was a lot of freelancing. I was called for semiprofessional and community orchestras, and I'd get paid. My summers were exciting times. I'd meet boys and new musicians from other places and fell in love with the whole scenario.

I also did well academically. I was galvanized by some teachers and subjects. I took advanced-placement classes in English and history and loved to read. My parents had always encouraged reading. In my senior year in high school, I qualified to take classes at UCLA, like psychology, cultural geography, sociology, anthropology, and foreign languages. We lived within walking distance of UCLA. **In February, I graduated from high school early and stayed on at UCLA and took more college classes.**

I wanted to go to music school, so I decided on the Cleveland Institute of Music. **Everyone knew the Cleveland Orchestra was fabulous.** When I took my auditions here, I'd heard that school orchestra rehearsing a Mahler symphony and said, "I want to play in that orchestra."

At CIM we worked on our instruments and learned from members of the Cleveland Orchestra. **We went to concerts, ushered, and heard every concert, not just once a week, but sometimes three times a week.** I didn't have to take any academics because I had so many credits from UCLA.

I met a guy at a summer music gathering in Marlborough, Vermont, and we fell in love. He was a senior at Oberlin and a bassoon player. We saw each other throughout our last years in music school and were married after we graduated. We went to Juilliard for graduate school together but neither of us was happy in New York, so we came back to Cleveland and earned master's degrees. **Then it was a question of who was going to get a job first. It's difficult to find placement for two woodwinds in the same orchestra. There are only three or four of each, and the openings don't occur very often, sometimes as seldom as once a generation.** We both found jobs playing principals in a very small orchestra in Fort Wayne, Indiana, not a place we wanted to stay very long. We were each taking auditions. Then my husband got a job in the Houston Symphony, and there was no opening for me. I went to Houston with him and played in the ballet orchestra and was getting some work around town.

We continued going to summer festivals together. **I made deadlines for myself.** I decided that if I didn't get a job within the next few months, I'd take the Graduate Record Examination and go into a different career, perhaps public health. That medical interest was always there, but I had this burning desire to play in an orchestra, and I'd go to my husband's concerts and feel like a backstage groupie. I realized I'd feel more hurt, more pain, in being a peripheral musician than if I went into a totally different field. At that point, I got one of the jobs I was auditioning for, principal flute in the North Carolina Symphony. We tried to keep our marriage together for five years from two different cities. Then there was a job opening with the Utah Symphony for both a principal flute and a principal bassoon. **I auditioned, but they didn't hire me; they later hired a man. There may have been an element of sexism.** The bassoon opening fell through anyway. There was never an opening in my orchestra for him, and there was never an opening in his orchestra for me.

It was getting harder to keep our relationship together. We were discouraged. My husband wanted a family, but **I was so driven about my music, I didn't even think about children, which is maybe too bad. It may have cost me a relationship.** We broke up, and very soon after, my ex-husband remarried and had children.

**Everyone has a problem with competition,** and I have always struggled with auditions. **A lot of people feel that I didn't quite achieve what I deserved because I play second flute.** They say, "I can't believe you're not principal somewhere." I've come very close and was runner-up to getting a major principal job several times. I've had problems with nerves in auditions. It's a question of degree, because I don't think anyone relishes auditions. Some people play their best for auditions, and when they come to the job, they're a little disappointing. There were also two or three times when because of either politics in the committee or maybe gender preference, I didn't get the position despite virtually all the orchestra members on the committee saying I should have gotten it. **No one really knows all the elements that go into those decisions.** It's not like the fifty-meter dash, where it's between the clock and you. It's so easy to say, "I prefer this tone . . . or this style." **In flute, there is a huge women-to-men ratio; yet actual principal positions in the very top orchestras favor men over women, so it's possible** that sexism is involved.

**I've always gotten along really well with my colleagues and have many friends in music.** I'm sure that has something to do with my nature and how my parents raised me. I've never been involved with a man who played the same instrument, and I'm sure that's because the competition element made that unappealing.

With my difficulties in getting what I want, I've always found it an extreme vicarious pleasure to stand by and be party to the success of persons I'm close to. I'm their biggest cheerleader and fan club. Their success doesn't eat me up unless it's at my expense.

I came to Cleveland in 1981 and have been living with the same person since 1987. He's my best friend and a wonderful, inspiring musician.

One year after I joined the Cleveland Symphony Orchestra as the second flute, my former teacher retired as first flute. Some of the key players in the orchestra encouraged me to try out for first flute, which was a sight much higher than I would have set for myself. It was one of the best auditions I ever played, and it was narrowed down to me and another person, who got the spot. That was crushing to me. Nevertheless, I was supportive when the new first flute came in. Normally, when you don't get a job, you don't have to deal with your defeat every day, but here I had to play second to the flutist I lost to. It was emotionally challenging. Those were difficult blows to deal with.

My trauma in junior high motivated me to figure out how to make and keep good friends, and the result of that is that in a highly competitive career, my friends have been my best support. I'd say I'm popular in professional life. People seem to think I'm nice and I'm a good person, and that's always been important to me.

I wish I could be playing principal flute, but it doesn't eat me up. What really made a huge difference was one windfall: the Aspen Music Festival fell into my lap. I was called out of the blue in 1993 and asked if I'd like to play principal flute there. They have several flute players during different parts of the summer because there are three classes of flute students and two professional orchestras. I think this came because I'm well thought of as a person as well as a player. Aspen is very restorative for me.

It doesn't take too much self-talk to realize that I still have this incredibly coveted position and am in a top orchestra. It's a wonderful job, and it's secure. I've built my life here and have a wonderful home and a lot of good things.

# SHE PURSUED HER PASSION WITH A SENSE OF HUMOR

~

## Pamela Frank

NATIONALLY ACCLAIMED SOLO VIOLINIST

*Pamela Frank was born in New York City. She appears with orchestras, in recitals, and with chamber groups. Considering that she has played with almost every orchestra in the United States and Europe, her humility is extraordinary. She is the daughter of the concert pianists Claude Frank and Lilian Kallir. Her formal career began in 1985 when she appeared with the New York String Orchestra at Carnegie Hall. She graduated from the Curtis Institute of Music in Philadelphia in 1989. The Beethoven violin sonatas and the Dvořák Violin Concerto are among her recordings, and she is featured on the soundtrack for the film* Immortal Beloved. *In 1999, Pamela was awarded the Avery Fisher Prize, one of the highest honors given to American musicians.*

*I was in the audience when Pamela was interviewed prior to a concert with the Cleveland Symphony Orchestra and was impressed that her responses to the questions were extremely feminine. I questioned her about that, and her answer is included in her story. If you've heard Pamela play, it would be difficult to agree with the first sentence of her story.*

I was a normal little girl who happened to play the violin, love it, and be pretty good at it. I was an only child but never felt I was missing out because I didn't have siblings. In fact, my parents were fairly juvenile and basically replaced any siblings I would have had. They love life. I thought playing the piano was my parents' hobby—they were really concert pianists—and they just did it for fun. I learned that whatever you do, you ought to do it with total passion as if it were a hobby.

When I was only two, my parents asked me, "Pamela, what is the most important thing in life?" and I responded, "A sense of humor." This was how they lived, and it was passed down to me. There was always laughter in our home. **Later in life, this lesson translated** into the message to take what you do seriously, but don't take yourself too seriously. It grants perspective on life. The bottom line is I feel thrilled to have parents of such integrity. I credit them for my personal success as a human being.

I was demanding of myself and set very high standards, but I remember learning how to make mistakes as a child. I went to my grandparents' home to play violin for the family. If I played something and it didn't go as well as I wanted, I retreated to a back room and wouldn't talk to anyone. I remember my parents saying, "Who do you think you are, Itzhak Perlman? If you were Itzhak Perlman, you would have a right to be disappointed by that performance." The message was to "get a grip."

I'd been given a toy violin when I was three. It was a joke because everyone "knew" I would play piano, but I wasn't interested in piano. Apparently, I said the toy wasn't of high enough quality to learn to play the violin and begged for a couple of years until I got a real violin at age five.

I went to concerts with my parents before I ever started to play the violin. They'd come home and discuss the concert and ask me what I thought. I was encouraged to be an independent thinker and critic; plus, I loved the music. I'd get chills and tears in my eyes—even when I was three or four years old. Granted, crying is a signature of our family. We're all overly emotional people, but **I had visceral reactions to music even then. These images have never left me.**

My first violin teacher, Shirley Givens, made learning to play the violin fun. **There was no pressure to be great or fast or fully formed at an early age. Every step of the way was an adventure.** I couldn't sleep the night before I was to start using the bow. **My parents put no pressure on me, and that's why it was so much fun.** It's remarkable my parents could keep their expectations moderate even though they were in the music business.

**I was a real goody-goody. I'd come home from school, barely say hello, and immediately do my homework. Then I'd practice. I practiced because I wanted to and because I was excited about each step of the learning process.** I enjoyed myself and made progress and balanced it with other activities. **My parents were very into games, and we used to play board games, card games, and word games. I had a few close, loyal friends and**

liked older children rather than children my own age. My being an only child probably contributed to my interest in older friends. I read a lot as a kid and spent a lot of time in my own head, alone, but I wasn't lonely at all.

I had a best friend in my childhood who was very outspoken, verbally confident, and good at sports. I was very shy and not good at sports. She was social and popular, and I wasn't. She influenced me and boosted my confidence and self-worth. Then when I was thirteen, she dumped me. It sounds silly now, **but at the time it was very traumatic for me because she was my only friend. It was a huge ordeal for me and forced me to change my life and not rely completely on one person to the exclusion of all others.**

When my friend dumped me, I was depressed, and I walked to school very slowly and reluctantly. I didn't feel like getting up in the morning. I remember thinking I couldn't go on feeling like this. This episode bothered my parents too. They had meetings with the principal to make everyone aware of my trauma. My mother even called this girl's mother and tried to work things out. Of course, that didn't work. I remember thinking, "Stop it! Stop trying to help! I need to do this alone."

**I was depressed as much as a thirteen-year-old could be, and this was a real turning point for my life. I learned I could change situations if I wanted to, and I was fully responsible for my own happiness.** This experience changed my personality. When I was in high school, I made a complete turnaround and consciously became an extremely social and outgoing person. People who meet me now never believe I was quiet and introverted.

My parents weren't career-oriented, and I still joke that I haven't decided on what I'd like to do when I grow up. **I never made a conscious decision to become a musician. It was a natural evolution, and now, when I wake up in the morning, I can't believe this is my life.** I feel so lucky. **What I love to do the most has become my profession.**

**I was a very good student, loved school, and enjoyed my classes and my homework.** I was always at the top of my class. I went to a bilingual school for French and English, and it was a wonderful place because it bridged my home life with the culture around me in New York City. Both my parents are European; my father's from Nuremberg, Germany, and my mother's from Vienna, Austria, so I learned French and German early. **I didn't compare myself with other people, wasn't competitive, and was happy with myself.** The only unhappiness I felt had to do with my not living up to my own standards and had nothing to do with people around me. **My parents are very secure within themselves, and I picked up on this when I was growing up.** They made me feel like I was the greatest thing since sliced bread and could do no wrong. In my teenage years, my parents almost worshiped me, and I wished I wasn't an only child because I didn't want quite so much attention. **Because of their adoration, I started to believe in myself, and because I believed in myself, I achieved things, and because I achieved things, I believed in myself. It was self-perpetuating.**

I took music lessons from the same teacher all through my childhood, **but I hardly ever entered any competitions. I won a *Seventeen Magazine* competition, a big competition among young musicians, but that was the last competition I entered. My teacher encouraged me to do it to build up my confidence for the "brutal outside world."**

My big extracurricular activity was going to the New York Youth Symphony orchestra every Sunday, and I looked forward to it all week. I was eleven and by far the youngest member of the orchestra. I felt lucky to be with all those "old musicians"—sixteen- and seventeen-year-olds. For a while I sat behind the concertmaster, who years later became my husband. I enrolled in a precollege division at Juilliard and was there all Saturday. On weekends I spent time with my friends who were musicians, but I fought with my parents to do this; they told me I couldn't do both the New York Youth Symphony and Juilliard programs because that would take up the whole weekend for music. They thought I should play and have some fun. I was very upset and had to make a choice. I ended up choosing Juilliard precollege and did other social things on Sundays.

Dating and going out with friends became another source of tension in high school. I was not allowed to go out on weeknights. I had a group of girlfriends with whom I went shopping, to movies, out to dinner, and to parties. If you ask my parents, they would say I had

wild high school days. **I was a true goody-goody trying to rebel
but not succeeding at it.** I partied and had an active social life and
spent time with my music friends on Saturdays. **I went to a private
high school and was a high school student during the week
and a musician on the weekend.**

**I faced a difficult crossroads when I left high school.** My
music teacher at the time taught at both Curtis and Yale, and I enjoyed my academic life so much that I wanted to go to Yale. I did a
lot of soul-searching. I talked to people who helped me understand
that if I was having a hard time balancing my academic work, practicing, and rehearsing in high school, this would only get worse in
college. I realized that if I went to Yale, I'd probably feel like I
wasn't doing anything very well. I decided to go to a conservatory
and chose Curtis. Then, during my first year, I felt I had made a mistake. **I missed the stimulation from people in other fields and
the general pursuit of knowledge, but I learned to find the
stimulation I needed on my own. I took every nonmusic course
offered at Curtis.**

I experienced some real changes at the conservatory. Peers became
primary influences. Because Curtis is tuition-free, they are very selective about the quality of their students, and they attract the best
possible. **I was surrounded by people who were as good as or
better than me, and my awareness of this made me perform at
a much higher level. In fact, I have learned as much from the
people around me while playing** in chamber groups or orchestras
as I've learned in my lessons. **It's very inspiring and exciting to be
around great players of the same age. I felt like I had to rise to
my potential to keep up. For the first time, I experienced real
competition.** The other musicians fostered my intensity. I'm still
my own worst critic, so if I'm not happy with myself, it's bound to
be much worse than if somebody else wasn't happy with me.

There were other very important people who instilled confidence
in me, like a family friend who encouraged me to audition for things
I would not have thought to audition for, and another family friend
with whom I traveled. He took me all over the world, and I played
music with him during my school vacations. **He taught me to have
no fear, and when I was on the stage with him, I felt like I**

could do nothing wrong. I felt like all I was meant to do was pour my heart out and play with all my passion. I became more comfortable, confident, and my playing improved.

I started touring while I was at Curtis. I played chamber music and soloed. I graduated in '89, and by '91 I had an agent who went back to a lot of the places I had been to before and asked if they wanted to get me to perform in a solo capacity. This launched my solo career.

I met my husband when I was fourteen. He was my innocent boyfriend from the New York Youth Symphony. We used to hold hands, and we liked each other. We had brief romantic moments together but eventually had separate lives and didn't stay in touch. He'd gone to Curtis a few years before me, and I asked for his teacher based on his recommendation. Our paths crossed about four years ago, and we rekindled our friendship. **We had special feelings for each other from when we were young. It made me realize that I've built on layers of experience, I've gone through many events in my life, but the core of my life remains the same.** Sometimes we travel together, sometimes we travel separately—it's a nice mix.

**Through my whole life, I have felt like a person, not a girl.** People ask me what it's like to be a female violinist, and my answer is that I feel like I'm a violinist who just happens to be female. **I don't see myself as spectacular and don't think I ever will, but I love playing music and am having this terrific life.** I play about eighty concerts a year, am away about 250 days, and play because it's sheer fun.

# 7

# The Communicators

⌇

$\mathcal{T}$HE women in the media and those in mental health have almost as many differences as similarities, but their emphasis on verbal communication and the fact that these careers are semitraditional bind them together. There have always been some women in the media, but typically they've been producers and executives; the most important radio and television news anchors were men. Currently there are as many women news anchors as men and at least as many women producers, if not more. Even a small percentage of the technical crew are women. Executive producers continue to be mainly men, but more women are making inroads into this field as well. Many more women have become involved in the print media, although everywhere except at women's magazines the positions of editor in chief and publisher continue to be held more frequently by men. There remain glass ceilings, but the media is a career area in which women have made great progress.

The same holds true for the field of mental health. Women have always dominated the field of social work, but few were psychologists. Now there are probably as many women in the practice of psychology as men, if not more, and 67 percent of psychology Ph.D.s are now awarded to women.[1]

---

[1]*USA Today,* November 11, 1999.

## *Results from the* See Jane Win *Study*

These communicating women all described themselves during their childhood as emotional and sensitive more frequently than the women in other careers, although they also saw themselves as "smart," "hardworking," and "independent."

Although all the women in this category had similar I.Q.s, the mental-health professionals did better in school than the women in the media, who seemed to study less than almost any other group and whose grades slumped more in middle and high school. Both groups were strong in English and writing, but the mental-health professionals also indicated a special strength and interest in social studies. Math and science were not strong areas for the women in either group. Fewer of them attended all-girl schools at the elementary, middle, and high school levels. However, although only 10 percent of the women in the media attended women's colleges, 17 percent of the mental-health professionals did (the average for our study was 13 percent).

The women in the media were more typically oldest children, while more of the women in mental health were youngest in birth order. Although they were about equally social in elementary school, the women in the media were more social in high school than the mental-health professionals. Quite a few of the women in both groups indicated that the distraction of boys affected their grades in middle school. Both groups took fewer advanced math and science courses in high school.

Parents of the mental-health professionals tended to be less firm with their daughters as they were growing up, and as girls, they were actually the most rebellious during adolescence compared to other career groups.

Both groups mainly enjoyed their careers but also expressed disappointment over salaries and overcompetitiveness in their fields. Women in the mental-health professions felt that "making a contribution" was the most important reason for recommending their careers; more of the women in the media liked its "creativity." More mental-health professionals were divorced than women in the media (their younger-than-average age may also account for their lower divorce rate), but a greater percentage nonetheless described themselves as very happy in their family life compared to the average for women in the survey. Twice as many women in the media (18 percent) were single compared to our total group; their parents also had a higher divorce rate.

## *How Jane Won*

I feel most personally connected to the communicators because as a psychologist and media person myself, I bridge both groups. You may notice among the television people several NBC representatives; this reflects my correspondent role on NBC's *Today* show. I have had a direct relationship with almost all of the television, radio, and print communicators in this chapter, so it is especially exciting for me to share their stories.

Jane Pauley was the NBC host who first interviewed me on the *Today* show on the topic of why gifted children sometimes underachieve. That interview brought us twenty thousand calls and five thousand letters. I will never forget the excitement of my first national television interview or Jane's support during that first experience. I met Deborah Roberts when she hosted a segment on *20/20* on overindulged children in which I was asked to reverse the overempowerment of two children and give their parents the confidence to take charge. I believe that Deborah and her husband, Al Roker, will be spectacular parents of their little Leila.

I befriended Janice Huff on *Weekend Today* and was incredibly inspired by her story. I found Catherine Callaway and Kathleen Dunn such enthusiastic and knowledgeable interviewers, when I spoke with them about our last book, that I couldn't resist including them in our new book.

I've had the opportunity to admire Janet Schiller's producing skills for seven years on NBC's *Today* show; her story is a fascinating account of how she's fueled her career with the creativity, discipline, and efficiency she learned from ballet. Hers is a story that bridges the career categories of the communicators and the artists and musicians. I also know firsthand that she's a wonderful mother. I worked with Cindy Beckler when she was the producer of parenting segments on CNN. Her low-key approach to achieving success shows young women that you don't have to be a single-minded hard charger to find a place in the media arena.

I also have special relationships with many terrifically talented women in the print media. Jacquelyn Mitchard and I were friends from the days before she wrote her best-seller, *The Deep End of the Ocean.* It was gratifying to turn the tables and interview her now, as she has found life satisfaction once again after the death of her husband. I met Lesley Seymour, editor in chief of *Redbook,* at the Body, Mind, and Soul Retreat in the Colorado mountains I mentioned in my introduction; her inspirational story refreshed all three for us and further encouraged this book.

You all know Florence Henderson, the mom from *The Brady Bunch.* So many times in my clinic, blended families have come in for desperate assistance and told me that they thought joining their families would be as easy as *The Brady Bunch.* Although I had never personally met Florence Henderson before our interview, after one hour of chatting with her, I felt like I had known her all my life and realized why her openness, sensitivity, and warmth have reached out to millions over the years.

My daughter Sara and I have been inspired by all these stories, but the psychologists are, of course, very close to our hearts. I interviewed Frances Culbertson, Ph.D., and Sara interviewed Norine Johnson, Ph.D. Sara and I saw our lives in these women because I had returned to school while Sara was growing up and struggled with how to balance my education, family responsibilities, and the expectation that my spouse's career would always trump my own, an attitude typical of our times. These women took different leadership directions than I, but I resonated with their need to make a difference, their drive to overcome obstacles, and their commitment to family above all while searching for career fulfillment. We look forward to making a presentation on *How Jane Won* at a forthcoming American Psychological Association meeting, where Norine will be presiding. There have been so few women presidents of that organization that her presidency feels like a personal accomplishment for all women.

# Does She Owe Her Career to Mary Tyler Moore or Harry Wilfong?

## Jane Pauley

ANCHOR, NBC NEWS AND *DATELINE*

*Jane Pauley began her career in broadcast journalism in her hometown of Indianapolis in 1972, broadcasting at WISH-TV. Later, she would become the first woman to coanchor a weeknight news program at WMAQ-TV in Chicago. In 1976, Jane began her thirteen-year tenure as coanchor of NBC's* Today. *In 1986, the International Radio and Television Society named Jane Broadcaster of the Year. Jane currently anchors the top-rated, award-winning prime-time newsmagazine* Dateline NBC.

I was, without a doubt, a long shot. Hiring me was not a no-brainer for Lee Giles, the news director at WISH-TV. He says he'd hired someone before without a degree in broadcast journalism or without experience in the field, but I was the first without either! At that, I started as a "temporary, probationary employee for thirty days." **And I did have some catching up to do.** I didn't know a camera lens from an ashtray (didn't make that mistake twice), I'd never seen a TelePrompTer, and I remember being taught how to hold the microphone moments before my first interview ("If the guy being interviewed grabs hold of it, don't let go!"). I certainly had to learn a new vocabulary ("stand-upper," "V/O bridge"), and **I learned from many mistakes** (despite my political science degree, and having come directly from a political campaign, I still managed to blow a man-on-the-street preelection survey by repeatedly getting the actual *date* of Election Day wrong!). Lee might have had some second thoughts about hiring me but, in fact, he only recently told me that at the time his greater concern (which he confided to his general manager) was, "We'll never keep her." And he was right after all: four years later, at twenty-five, I was the cohost of the *Today* show on NBC.

**You could argue that I owe my career to *The Mary Tyler Moore Show*.** As a weekend anchor at WISH-TV in Indianapolis, not only did I try to have my Saturday night show set two hours early so I could watch MTM, I'd all but turn off the police radios in the newsroom. Oprah Winfrey says she'd be sure to put the conditioner in her hair during the preceding *Bob Newhart Show* so she'd be ready for Mary. But the greater significance was that **The Mary Tyler Moore Show and the rest of the CBS Saturday night lineup delivered huge audiences to my eleven o'clock broadcast. That's** the show that got me noticed by NBC's WMAQ-TV (Channel 5) in Chicago. Remember the big "M" on the wall of Mary's studio apartment? I put a big numeral "5" on mine. It was not a coincidence.

Looking back, **the luckiest thing that ever happened to me was *not* making varsity cheerleader in the tenth grade. (A tragedy at the time, I assure you!) You can almost draw a direct line from that event to the WISH-TV newsroom. Why? I joined my school's powerhouse speech and debate team instead.** I don't know what career I would have if it weren't for my high school experience in forensics. **It was the most important extracurricular activity I had in high school or college, and I'd rank it easily as important as any of my academic courses.**

**A major milestone for me was winning first place in extemporaneous speaking at a novice tournament at Ball State University.** My best friend, Judy, took second; I'm sure we were insufferable. **But I had never competed before. I didn't know the feeling of being number one. I really liked it. I kept at it for three years, ultimately becoming a state champion and competing in the national tournament.** I may never have had my byline in a school newspaper, but I became conversant with current events (basic economics, politics, hot-button issues like abortion and gun control, even some foreign affairs).

In those days I had very long Alice-in-Wonderland hair, and I looked really, really young, until I opened my mouth and had this formidable speaking voice. I was a quick study (I heard a kid recently call it a "BS" factor!); **I could absorb information about current events and speak for seven minutes as if I was thoroughly knowledgeable. Not incidentally, I was starting a lifelong habit of reading newspapers and newsmagazines.**

**As a result, I'd have to say that Harry Wilfong, my high school speech coach, was the most influential person in my**

life. He was that "passionate adult" who gets you in his beams and won't let go and says, "What! You got something better to do this Saturday?" We all called him "Uncle Harry," and he was more ambitious than I was; it was at his insistence that I ran for governor of Girls State.

As for my family, **my parents' methods were subtle but powerful. The most consistent, explicitly stated message from my father to his daughters was to "be careful."** This came out of his life experience. His essential nature was optimistic, but heartache and hardship repeatedly taught him that good fortune was fickle and could turn on you. **The other message, also explicitly stated, was "Be a lady." I interpreted this to mean I should always behave in some exemplary way, i.e., "Be a good girl." It was taken for granted we would get good grades.** My sister's certainly exceeded anyone's expectations.

**I knew my father thought we were both smart.** It is his beaming face I recall most vividly in the crowd whenever I was receiving an award. His pride walking me down the aisle and sitting with me onstage as governor of Girls State was palpable. So, he was probably sending mixed messages: "Aim low; don't get hurt" (he thought I should aspire to be a receptionist—I think he appreciated the nice-looking young women who fronted the companies he called on as a salesman), along with "You are very special; aim high."

I'm embarrassed to confess that very recently Hillary Clinton introduced me at a public event as "the daughter of a musician," and for a second I thought she'd made a mistake! Though my mother was an accomplished organist and played at church for many years, I'd only seen her as a "homemaker." She must have aspired for something more for her daughters, because despite the fact that she was also an accomplished seamstress, she signed both of us out of home economics, which was a requirement; she thought we'd learn more in study hall. It was only as an adult that **I saw a letter she had written my sister at college in which she explained that if there was a governing principle to their parenting style, it was to say yes as often as possible. I was struck by how affirming that was.**

All of the above, however, should be considered in the particular context of my birth order. I think my older sister Ann's influence was as great as my parents'. Awed by her academic performance, I avoided the most challenging courses like physics and calculus, though I was probably compensating in extracurricular venues.

During high school, I was a six-time nominee for homecoming queen and a member of the prom queen court (though I never wore a crown) and was often elected to office. I apparently exuded "leadership" qualities, though I don't think "management" qualities were a part of the package.

It never occurred to me that I could leave Indiana for college; it never crossed my young mind. I was so clueless that, by accident, I sent my SATs to a little college in Indiana, Pennsylvania. Everything got straightened out, and I went to Indiana University. Though I loved the place, there was no Harry Wilfong to get after me. My freshman adviser, whom I saw only once, counseled me not to major in radio and television. I chose to major in political science instead, which reinforced my personal interest in current events and enabled me to do a lot of analytical writing. Indirectly it also led me to my career as a broadcast journalist.

**While I never had a newsroom internship, so highly prized by job seekers today, a summer internship at the Indiana Democratic headquarters gave me not only a valuable look at the media at work, but also a "heads up" later on that there was an opening at Channel 8!** Because it was a presidential election year, I was anxious to finish college and completed my degree in January 1972 after three and a half years. The following spring I was Indiana's "John Lindsay for President" campaign coordinator, but by that fall I was working at WISH-TV and the '72 campaign was my first big story.

In addition to some good luck and good timing, **I have come to respect my common sense and good judgment. I think my parents raised a well-grounded daughter. And, in hindsight, I think I have a knack for "getting ready" even before an opportunity presents itself.**

**I think I had particularly good sense when it came to men.** I had a weakness for writers, and the most important figures in my romantic life tended to be engaged in politics or current events or both. **I think it was lucky that I met the only man I ever wanted to marry when I had a career already well established.** But, as

I've said, I also think that good judgment and good timing are my strengths. Writer Anna Quindlen says some of us pick "boyfriends" and others pick "husbands." I picked a "husband." **I think whatever gene it is that says, "Don't squander your DNA on an irresponsible mate," I have it. And I have three wonderful kids to prove it.**

# A Little Girl with a Great, Big Voice

## Florence Henderson

SINGER, MOTHER ON *THE BRADY BUNCH,*
AND NBC TELEVISION HOST

*Florence Henderson was the youngest of ten children in a poor, Irish-Catholic family. Those of us who know her as "Carol Brady" can hardly imagine that the true entrance to her career was through the musical stage. At the age of seventeen, she entered New York's prestigious American Academy of Dramatic Arts, thanks to her earlier debuts on the stage of St. Francis Academy in Owensboro, Kentucky.*

*Florence's career includes Broadway musicals, concert performances, movies, and frequent prime time television appearances. As contributor to NBC's* Today *show, she continues to enter our homes. I had the extraordinary opportunity to meet personally with Florence, and I hope I have communicated to you the openness, sensitivity, and generosity that have fostered her remarkable success.*

My mother said I came out singing, and by the time I was two, she had taught me fifty songs. I don't ever remember not singing. I was a little girl with a great, big voice.

My first teacher, Sister Gemma, a Benedictine nun, had a tremendous influence on me. I still write to her. She found out I could sing at a very early age. One year she had chosen me to play the Blessed Mother in a church pageant at Christmas, and I hadn't yet told my mother about it. I had long, beautiful hair, and my mother cut it and gave me a very tight perm. Sister Gemma saw the short hair and became very upset and angry. I apologized and explained it wasn't my mother's fault. I played the baby Jesus instead and became the star of the pageant. **I learned early from Sister Gemma to take negatives and make positives out of them.**

**My teachers were my motivators, and music was a great part of my life.** The nuns fostered that, and before I knew it, I was in the choir singing four-part Latin masses. I could hardly see over the choir loft. **If there was any event that needed music, I was**

chosen. I've performed for the Democrats, the Republicans, the Moose, the Elks. Everyone encouraged me. **They wouldn't let me smoke in high school because they said, "No, no, no, you are going to be a singer."**

Sister Ruth Marie taught French and English, my best subjects at the school, and she was no bigger than a minute but **was tough, strict, and wonderful.** She gave a lecture on **sincerity being the most important quality you can have in life, and I never forgot that speech. Her message has kept me grounded and natural,** because if I'm sincere, I can't be a phony.

My father was sixty-seven when I was born. **He would say, "We don't have much monetarily, but we can have good character and a great reputation. People can take your money, they can take your material possessions, but they can't take your character, and they can't take your reputation. You give that away."** We would roll our eyes and say, "Oh, here we go again," but we heard and learned his important messages.

**My mother was my first and most important role model. She was strong, a survivor, and a very fair person.** Mom helped on our family farm and was also a domestic worker. We were very poor, so she did everything and anything to help her family of ten children survive.

**My optimism comes from both my parents because they struggled with poverty.** As a child, I didn't realize how difficult it was. I started school with my brothers and sisters when I was three because my mother had to work. I started earning money when I was eight and have always worked. In high school I lived in families' homes to take care of their children. I cooked, cleaned, and did laundry. The job I loved the most was when I was a soda jerk and made fourteen dollars a week. **My mother talked about being independent, and that became my goal.**

My dream was to go to the American Academy of Dramatic Arts in New York City. My best girlfriend in high school, Ruth Helen, was from a very wealthy family. She knew I loved music and wanted to go to New York, where show business was. I had the lead in the high school operetta, and Ruth Helen brought her family to hear me. They said, "If we like her, we'll take her to a talented musician to advise us." The musician said, "This child has a lot of potential, and she deserves a break," so Ruth Helen's parents sponsored me to go to New York and the academy.

**I was terrified when I got to New York because I hadn't ever seen a building over two stories high.** I was just seventeen, but the American Academy was a wonderful place, and I felt like I belonged there. Unfortunately, I had a terrible accent. It was a mixture of a southern drawl and a midwestern twang. People would make fun of me and fall on the floor laughing. A wonderful speech teacher named Aristede DeAngelo said, "I can help you with that accent if you will do as I say. It's one of the hardest accents to lose, almost harder than a foreign accent. **You'll have to practice vowel sounds.**" It was like Eliza Doolittle in *My Fair Lady.* **I worked hard on that accent, and he warned me, "When you go home, people will say, 'You've become stuck up, and you don't talk like us anymore'; but don't fall back, hold fast." Sure enough, I did.**

At the end of my first year, some of my friends from class said, "Why don't you audition for *Wish You Were Here?* We've all been there, and we're not right for it, but maybe you have a chance. Bring a bathing suit." One of the girls loaned me her bathing suit and a piece of music, and I went to the Alvin Theater. It was a cattle call, which meant you didn't have to belong to the union or have an agent. The great Josh Logan was directing the Broadway musical. I had long blond hair and looked like I was fresh off the farm. After I sang, Josh Logan said, "That was very nice. Did you bring a bathing suit?" I had, so they sent me down to the wardrobe room in the basement to change. The bathing suit was too short, so I was pulling on it, and a wonderful old stagehand, Charlie Bauer, found safety pins to bolster me up. I never forgot him for that. I went back onstage, pulling and tugging at the bathing suit. Josh Logan said, "What's the matter with you?" and I explained. He advised me to come back for a second audition, and reminded me as I left, "Next time, bring a bathing suit that fits." **When I came back the second time, I was asked to sing again right away, and Josh Logan asked, "Did you bring a bathing suit that fits?" He remembered about the first time. It worked for me instead of against me. I got the part.**

The academy recommended I not finish school because I'd landed this role and was going to get paid for it. I've never been out of work since.

I did *Wish You Were Here* for a couple of months and then went to an open call for the last national company of *Oklahoma!* They offered me the lead part of Laurey. My family didn't tell me that my father was very ill. We were in New Haven for the opening when I received word that my father had passed away. I wanted to go home for the funeral, but I had no understudy and couldn't leave. **It was very hard for me, and it has taken me years to get over the guilt I felt.**

I met my future husband when he was a casting person for the production team of *Guys and Dolls.* I auditioned for him when I was seventeen. We were married when I was twenty, and ten months later I had our first child. By that time, I was starring on Broadway in *Fanny.* It was overwhelming. To have the chutzpah to pursue a career while trying to raise children was unusual. There was no women's movement yet, no one to say, "Yes, you can do both; go for it." **Most people didn't approve of what I was doing.**

**Most of the time I had pretty good help.** I toured in *The Sound of Music* with two small children and a nanny, and **I learned how to organize my life so I could keep working.** I signed a contract with NBC to host the *Today* show, and I became pregnant shortly after. I was probably the first person to appear pregnant on television. I interviewed guests and sang on the *Today* show, and producers didn't like to use the word "pregnant." When my pregnancy became obvious, they would place me behind potted palms and furniture, and do close-ups of me singing. I went on *The Jack Paar Show* and *The Tonight Show Starring Johnny Carson* pregnant and worked, almost into labor. Actually, I went into labor on *Password* once. Women in those days just didn't do those things, so **I think my experience helped a lot of other women along the way.**

By now I had two small children and my daughter was in Marymount School in New York City. One day I was rehearsing a show for NBC when I had to rush to the school during my break to make a meeting. I was only twenty-four years old, and I remember exactly what I was wearing. The head of the school was a wonderful lady named Reverend Mother Berchmanns. Nuns still wore habits in those days, and she was an austere-looking woman. I was always drawn to her, and I loved the way she moved and the way she treated the children. She took me aside and said, "I see you trying so hard. You have a great talent, and God is with you and the Holy Spirit is with you, and you will always be okay. Don't worry; you're a wonderful mother." **Can you imagine what that meant to me? Here was a woman who'd devoted her whole life to teaching and had the sensitivity to say those words that I needed to hear.** She gave me a little paperweight and inside is the Holy Spirit, and I have never traveled without it all these years. I think of her often.

I had a serious problem with stage fright. It came because I was developing a hearing loss called "otosclerosis," which begins at birth and manifests itself in the teen years. It's so insidious that I didn't even realize until one day I suddenly couldn't hear certain sounds. It was devastating. Otosclerosis is worsened by childbirth. Every time I gave birth, my obstetrician would say, "Florence, you are not hearing." It would be that immediate. I didn't have surgery until after my fourth child, and it was bad by then. I was so fearful that I wouldn't be able to hear the instruments when I sang. I had one surgery that was successful and a second surgery about twenty years ago. Therapy helped me with this problem. **I had to be honest with myself and try to deal with the cause and the problems.**

In 1969, the furthest thing from my mind was a TV series. I was staying at the Beverly Hills Hotel, doing a Dean Martin show, when I received a call from my agent. He wanted me to please come down to Paramount Studios and meet Sherwood Schwartz, Doug Kramer, John Rich, and all these television people I had heard about. I said, "Sure, but I have to get on a plane to Houston because I'm opening there tomorrow at the Shamrock Hotel with my musical act."

I went down and met them, and they said, "We'd love you to take a script home, learn it, and come back and do a scene for us so we can film it and do a screen test." I went to my hotel, learned the scene, came back, and we waited for a break on the *Star Trek* set to do the screen test. I went into the makeup room, and they made me up with far too much makeup for this character named Carol Brady—big false eyelashes, the works! When I got back to the camera, I said, "I would not have put this makeup on for Carol Brady." **I made a joke, they laughed, and I think they remembered that.** I did my scene, they thanked me, and I caught my plane to Houston that night.

The next day when I was getting ready for the opening, I received a call to come back and do a pilot right away. I had to get someone to fill in for me at the Shamrock Hotel, and I promised the booker, "If you let me do this, and if this show is a hit, I'll come back and perform for you for the same amount of money." Of course, the rest is history, and I kept my word to the booker.

I did the pilot, pretty much forgot about it, had no idea it would be successful, and went on with other work. I was doing *Song of Norway* on location in London, Norway, Denmark, and Sweden, and I received a call that the pilot had sold, and they needed me back in Los Angeles. It was really a wild time for me. I had to fly back, and they'd already filmed six episodes without me, so I had to catch up.

We did *The Brady Bunch* for five years, originally on ABC, and I had four small children of my own at the time. I lived in New York and commuted to California. Luckily, the bulk of the show was shot in the summer, so we rented a house in Los Angeles for three seasons, and then we moved there.

I truly enjoyed doing the show; it was like having a second family. We all became very close. We really cared about each other and have remained good friends. It was a great time in my life, and I had no idea that it would last this long and still be so important to people.

**My faith and my family gave me the strength to do all of this. My family had great confidence in me, and we are very close.** My sister Pauline, fifteen years older than I, is like my mother. She has endured hardships in her life, and **her incredible faith and spirit are a model for me. My older brother was my mentor. He was the one who said, "You can do it; you'll make it," and was a tremendous support to me.** After my first child was born, I had postpartum depression, and he came to New York to help me. Four months later, he died at age thirty-seven. **That was a tremendously difficult loss, and it is with me all the time. I have lost many people that I love.** Three of my siblings have died, as well as my parents, two of my best friends, and many other friends. **If you're a sensitive person, death can be very difficult, but if you try to understand it, it really helps you to be compassionate to others who suffer.**

The showbiz community has been wonderfully supportive, and I've always felt privileged to be a part of it. **So much of my identity** is tied up in performing and being in this community. I opened in Los Angeles doing *The King and I* when I was twenty-six years old, and there was a wonderful singer named Lee Venora with an incredible voice who was playing Tuptim. People cautioned me that I'd have problems with her and other female performers who were in competition with me. I had no such problems, and we've usually wound up friends. **I'm very competitive, but I'm extremely generous. If someone has talent, I recognize it because I appreciate all the people who've encouraged me.** I may be able to influence others, so the circle keeps going.

**My children have influenced my life tremendously.** I have two sons and two daughters, two grandsons and one granddaughter. My daughter is an executive with the Television Academy, the Emmys, and the Academy of Television Arts and Science, and my two sons are musicians, but one is also a therapist and works at my present husband's clinic in Los Angeles. My other son just moved to Los Angeles and got a job at NBC there. My youngest daughter is a stay-at-home mom. She loves that role and is good at it. I always say to her, "Lizzie, you are the kind of mother I wish I had had." She worked after her first child was born and then decided she didn't want to do that. **I am so blessed; I have incredibly close relationships with all of my children.**

**My first husband and I were married for many years, and although we're divorced, we're extremely close.** My second husband specializes in hypnosis and is a wonderful man. He's been a big influence on my life because I was helped so much with hypnotherapy for my stage fright and for a fear of flying I had developed. In fact, hypnotherapy worked so well for me that I studied to become a certified hypnotherapist. It is a very powerful tool, and I've worked with several people who were terminally ill. **To be able to help them with hypnotherapy was a great gift to me.**

As for my new NBC television venture, contributing on the *Today* show, I will be forever grateful to Jeff Zucker because of his foresight and confidence in me and his willingness to give me this opportunity. I think he has amazing vision because there are so few people today who will even consider trying to run with an interesting idea, especially if you are past fifty. I feel like I'm still a kid, and the *Today* show is a break, and the next big break is always right around the corner.

# INTEGRATION GAVE HER CONFIDENCE

## Deborah Roberts

CORRESPONDENT, ABC'S *20/20* NEWSMAGAZINE

*Deborah Roberts's courageous reporting from Saudi Arabia and Kuwait during the aftermath of the Persian Gulf War won for her permanent entrée into national news exposure. She has reported for NBC and ABC and now finds her home on ABC's newsmagazine 20/20. She's reported on such issues as refugees in Rwanda and abuse within the Amish community, but I had the opportunity to share with her a 20/20 segment on overindulged children. The amazement with which we watched a three- and six-year-old control their caring parents was a lesson on parenting she and her loving husband, Al Roker, will never forget as they raise their daughter, Leila.*

My mother always encouraged me to try to be the best, and she didn't want me to depend on a man to define myself. She instilled in me this sense of fending for myself and being strong. My parents are not educated people. Neither of them graduated from high school. They were married young and had a life of struggle. I have six sisters and two brothers.

My earliest memories of deciding who I was and what I wanted to do with my life go back to integration in fourth grade. I lived in Georgia and distinctly remember segregation, colored waiting rooms, and a colored school. **Integration was pivotal for me.** When I moved to an integrated school, it was a time of nervousness, but also **a time of wonder and exploration for me.** I met white children for the first time and made friends and **realized that the big scary world wasn't as scary as I thought. It caused me to think about who I was and where I fit in the world, but also assured me that I had the wherewithal to meet people who were different from me and the drive to do well.** I felt confident, and each time I went to a new school I made friends easily and entered new activities. I tried out for cheerleading in seventh grade and was upset because I didn't make it, so I tried again the next year and made it. I was excited to compete and accomplish something with status among my peers. I became a leader in my school. To be a cheerleader, I had to have a certain grade-point average and a standard and rules of moral behavior and not do anything "unbecoming to a cheerleader." I also participated in other activities and clubs, and they emboldened me to feel like I could do well in the world and have greater expectations than many of my peers had in our small town.

Teachers believed in me, and for that reason I felt special and different too. My seventh-grade English teacher was Mrs. Hardy. She wore red nail polish and red lipstick, had graying white hair, her clothes were always right, and she was the prim image of a teacher. Her expectations were very high. We didn't chew gum in her room, we used proper English, and we knew that we had to accomplish high goals. Everyone was terrified of her, but I always wanted to please her. She introduced me to poetry, to speaking grammatically, and to striving to do more. She embodied much more than English. If I read a poem well or punctuated something just right, she would praise me. She was hard but fair, and it meant so much to me to do well in her class. I felt so accomplished, empowered, and strong coming out of her class. She was responsible for my speaking abilities and my yearning to want to be the best. A tough coach makes you feel like you are capable of everything. I was trying to form who I was, and I could have been attracted to the kids who hung out and were the slangy, hip kids or to the ones who strived more and were considered geeks and eggheads. Mrs. Hardy influenced me to make the right choices, and to this day, I remember her.

A librarian I knew, Kathy Tallon, also was an important influence. She used to teach yoga classes. I didn't know anything about yoga, but I remember her opening my mind to the idea of destressing. She also traveled, and she'd come back and regale us with stories. She broadened my horizons and encouraged my wanting to see and learn more about the world.

I knew when I was in high school that I wanted to do something on television, but I wasn't quite sure what it was. I had done a couple of video programs at school and a play. I always had aspirations.

I recall saying, "Well, maybe I want to go to New York City and be an actress." My classmates would look at me strangely and say, "What is your problem? Who do you think you are?" **There were anchorwomen and people of color on television I liked, especially Carol Simpson, and there was Lem Tucker (a man).**

Academically I was successful, but most of all, **I was socially successful. That was important for me because it let me know that I could make my way out in the world, and it wasn't going to be an obstacle for me to be a black woman.**

At the University of Georgia, **I further shaped my ideas of who I was and what I wanted.** Television journalism seemed to satisfy my desire for a career. **I fell into it. It was a good fit, and one thing led to another.** I interned at a station twenty miles from my hometown in Macon, Georgia. The news director, Bill Trible, **let me do reports on the air. I proved to him that I was capable and responsible enough to cover news topics well.** I was only an intern who was just supposed to help the reporters with their tapes and keep track of things. Then suddenly, here I was doing reports, and my family could actually see them at home. They thought I was pretty hot stuff. If I looked at those tapes today, I would be embarrassed, **but it was exciting that the news director believed in me. That had a lot to do with propelling me in this business and making me feel like I could accomplish something.**

I got my first job when I was in college, for the PBS station in Atlanta. From there I got a job in a small television market in Columbus, Georgia, as a green reporter making about $11,000 a year, which was pretty good at the time. I went on from there to other jobs in slightly bigger television markets, until ten years ago, when I came to New York to work for NBC.

Each step along the way **I discovered more about myself as a reporter, and what my capabilities were as a woman in a field dominated by men.** In Tennessee, I did live reporting for the first time and was assigned to cover the legislature. That was a coveted job, and I did the best I could there. I was then pursued by a station in Orlando, Florida, to cover the space program and do anchor work, another step up. It was right after the *Challenger* accident, so eyes were fixated on it. NBC liked my coverage and soon brought me to

New York. I was amazed because that was like jumping a huge step, skipping over a smaller market like Chicago or Detroit. The next thing I knew, I was a correspondent with NBC.

**I did my homework and worked tirelessly. I made myself available any time and every time they wanted me.** A pivotal point came during the Persian Gulf War. I volunteered to cover it, and to my surprise, they sent me. I'd been there less than a year, and here was a chance to prove myself. I remember calling my parents to tell them that I was going to go cover the war. My mother was really upset. My father took over the phone and said, "I think this will be fine. It will be a good experience for you, and we're going to pray for you."

I covered the war for almost two months. It was a proving ground for me. We worked under some really tough conditions. I went into Kuwait after the war was over, and it was devastated. We lived in bombed-out hotels, and we did our reporting the old-fashioned way, driving around and talking to people. The phones weren't working. We wrote our stories in longhand on notepads and fed them back to New York. **I discovered a lot about myself, what I was capable of doing, and how strong I could be under adverse conditions.** When I returned, I was given more high-level assignments because of my experience.

*Dateline NBC* started, and I was one of the original correspondents they talked to. I came aboard and worked there for about three years. Five years ago, Barbara Walters called me and said, "Let's have lunch and talk about adding you to the show." I've been with *20/20* ever since.

I'd met Al Roker by then, and as he says, he'd either won me over or worn me down. Al and I became friends on the *Today* show. He was filling in doing weather; I was filling in on the news set. I was the new kid on the block and had been at NBC only a few months. It was my birthday, and Al came over and said, "I understand it's your birthday. Has anyone offered to take you out to lunch?" I said, "No," and I was feeling sorry for myself because I didn't know anybody. He said, "Well, you know, we should go out to lunch. I can't do it today but maybe tomorrow or in a day or two. Someone should take you out for your birthday." He was a really nice guy. He talked to me about his wife and his daughter, and we became friends. We would send each other E-mails now and again, and he would cheer me on when I did reports. Even after I moved, and we had gone our separate ways, he'd E-mail me. I was in the South and dating people, but when I eventually moved back to New York, he was in the process of separating, and over a period of time, we started to date. I wasn't convinced he was my type, but he was a nice guy. Eventually, it dawned on me that he was this wonderful guy, sweet, kind, loving, warm, and funny, and what was my problem? He was the last guy in the world I thought I would be serious about, and I didn't know that he was my life mate, my soul mate right there in front of my eyes.

The advice I always give all kids, especially young black women, is to **always be your best. It's not just because you think some-one is watching, but be your best, keep yourself sharp, so no one can ever pass you over and say you're not qualified.**

# $\mathscr{A}$ Reporter from the Start

## Catherine Callaway

### CNN REPORTER AND *HEADLINE NEWS* ANCHOR

*Catherine's media exposure took her from radio to local TV and fi-*
*nally to CNN. Her assertive (maybe "gutsy" is a better word) ap-*
*proach to obtaining that job and her family-career balancing act in*
*keeping that job will provide you some tips for your own future.*
*Callaway was hired in 1993 by CNN as an anchor. She joined*
*CNN* Headline News *in 1997 and is currently mainly a week-*
*end anchor but continues to take an occasional reporting opportunity*
*as well.*

**I always wanted to be a reporter.** My mother still has old magazines that I put together as a child. I would cut out pictures from
magazines or draw pictures and then write stories to go along with
them. I called it *Live* magazine after *Life* magazine, which was my favorite. I knew I wanted to see things and meet interesting people.

I always loved stories. Our house was full of books. There were
books in every room of our house! Closets were full of books, even
the attic. There was no need for a nightstand by my mother's bed;
she could just use the stack of books next to it. She loved mysteries,
and **I loved autobiographies.**

**My mother** was a business manager for some of my father's businesses. She **had an incredible ability to balance her full-time job**
**with being a mom.** She never missed a gymnastics meet, ballet
recital, or ball game. Some of her friends were not cognizant she
worked because she was always there with the rest of the moms.

My father had his doctorate in pharmacy. He was on the State
Board of Pharmacy, President of the National Board of Pharmacy,
and very ambitious. He owned several pharmacies, started a business
that serviced nursing homes, even started a bank and was on the
bank board. He was always on the go, and still is. My father would
have been a wonderful general practitioner, but he ended up getting
his pharmacy degree so he could get to work a bit sooner. In fact, he
ended up buying the first drugstore he worked for.

Looking back now I realize I was just like my father in school. **I did not let anything impede my path. I wanted to get out and work.** I was pushed ahead in school as a child and had a late birthday so I was much younger than my classmates. I rushed through college and was a senior at nineteen. **My father is probably the reason I can never focus on just one thing. We are both happier that way. My parents were my best friends, my dad giving me ambition and my mother the ability to balance my life and keep things in perspective.**

Ballet, gymnastics, and horseback riding kept me busy. **Sports were wonderful for me. I learned how much fun it is to compete, to not always win, and not give up. My athletic coaches taught me much more about life than about sports.** In high school my gymnastics coach did not want to put me on the team because she said I was not trying hard enough. She said, **"You can't give halfway; you've got to give everything you have, and you will do wonderfully."** She was right. **I did very well in competitions, but it took hard work.**

**I owned a horse, which was a big responsibility. I had horse shows and cared for my horse every day.** I even took my horse to college with me! Even when I was dating in high school, I had to feed the horses before I went out to see a movie. I would say to my dates, "Come twenty minutes early. We have to swing by to feed Honey." They would say, "What?" I'd respond, "You'll see. Just get here."

**My mother believes sports and the horses kept me out of trouble. She recalls I was a bit too adventurous.** I do remember being so busy going from one practice to another, wanting to experience everything, and not always getting the sleep I needed or desired. Some things have not changed!

Some of my friends started dating. I was thirteen; they were fourteen and fifteen. They were out on a Friday night date; I was at the stables, getting ready for a show the next day, or doing gymnastics. I didn't get to go to my first prom because I was in a state competition at the same time. **I had something that I was passionate about.** By age fifteen or sixteen, I was dating like everyone else, and I went to the prom.

I was a page at the Capitol, an errand person for the legislators.

Once, as I was going up the steps into the Capitol with my mom, there stood this very young, statuesque woman talking into a camera. She really captured my attention. My mother kept saying, "We have to go, Cathy!" The woman was Judy Woodruff. She was working at a local station. She was one of the first female reporters I remember seeing in person. **It had a profound effect on me. It stimulated my belief that I could be a reporter.**

In college I worked at the university radio station as a news anchor and reporter. One of the instructors in the Communications Department, Major Turner, played a tremendous role in my education. He helped me in so many ways. He even assisted in the development of my class schedule. He wanted to make sure I took the best classes and the classes I needed to graduate quickly. I received my bachelor's degree in two and a half years. **Major Turner was also the one who encouraged me to apply at local radio and television stations, "to work any job to get your foot in the door."**

My first job out of college was with a small newspaper. I then went to a small radio station as a news reporter. I got that job by applying at every radio station in the area—I mean every station! I was so young and inexperienced. One of my first assignments was to cover the city council meeting. I approached a council member for an interview and, with no intent to disparage me, he asked, "So what high school paper are you writing for?" I was quite annoyed by that remark.

When I first started my career, I was often the only female reporter on the scene. I also covered many crime scenes, meetings, and events when I was the only female there—period!

I worked in radio for several years, but I knew there were more opportunities in television. I began working at a local TV station at night after I finished my work at the radio station. I was hired as a talk show host and news producer, working a split shift. In the morning I came in to do the live talk show. I was off for several hours in the afternoon but had to be back later in the day to work my job in the newsroom. I eventually became the evening news anchor, but soon left for a bigger market.

I bounced around a few local stations as a reporter/anchor, and I won a number of Associated Press awards. I really wanted to work at CNN in my hometown! I started at the top and called Bob Furnad, the vice president of CNN at the time. Unbelievably, he answered his own phone. I said, "My name is Catherine Callaway, and I want to work for you." He said, "I'm sure you are perfectly charming, but all I really care about is what your résumé tape looks like." I said, "I'll drop it by today," and I did.

Bob liked the tape, but a couple of grueling auditions followed before I was hired for the job I had always dreamed of—a CNN anchor! I knew my life would change, but two months into my new job something happened that really did change my life: I found out I was pregnant. I was quite ill during my pregnancy, getting sick in the garbage can under the news set during live newscasts, trying to hide it from my producers and, of course, the viewers.

**Coming back to work after my daughter was born also proved a challenge.** It was hard to leave her just five and a half weeks after her birth. I was also a lactating mother! One night the supervising producer banged on my office door while I was using the breast pump. He said, "We need you on the set now. We have a chopper down!" Well, I couldn't just jump up and leave in the middle of that! Somehow I got everything together and was on the set in time to do the breaking news.

I was anchoring for CNN *Headline News* after my second child was born—nonstop news, every thirty minutes. It was really a challenge to breastfeed on that schedule. I only had a couple of twenty-minute breaks. I would set everything up during the first break, and during the next break I'd run down the hallway to the lactation room. I had just enough time to get back on the set to do the top stories for the next half hour. I would sometimes pass tour groups as I was running back to the set buttoning my shirt ("Hello, nice to see you . . . have to go!").

I have also had the opportunity to work as a domestic reporter for CNN. **Traveling was difficult, but I wouldn't trade the experiences for anything.** I always tried to make my daughter understand what I was doing. She thought it was exciting. I would leave her little treasure hunts, hiding gifts and giving her clues where they were when I'd call home. She eventually became a bit too excited about the treasure hunts and gifts I would bring home to her. During long periods of time between assignments, she would say, "Mom, isn't it time for you to cover another shuttle launch or something?"

Balancing a career and kids can leave you a bit discombobulated. I have at times changed jobs because of my commitment at home.

I am currently working part-time for both CNN networks. Certainly there are higher profile jobs than mine at CNN, but this schedule works well for me now. I don't know what job I'll be doing in a few years, only that I want to be working in this field.

I know when you're trying to get the job you want, you should not rule out anything. Call everyone you know, visit everyone you know, send out a thousand résumés instead of a hundred. I know my defeats have helped me in some way. I know sacrifices I have made in my career for my family will never be regretted, and I always try to remember how fortunate I am to be working in a profession that I love.

# *H*ER WILDEST DREAMS CAME TRUE

## Janice Huff

METEOROLOGIST, NBC

*In 1995, Janice Huff joined NBC as meteorologist for the weekend editions of* Today in New York *and* News Channel 4. *She is currently a meteorologist for NBC's Saturday edition of* Today. *She is also the weekday meteorologist for* News Channel 4. *Janice's childhood wish to be a meteorologist has been fulfilled many times over. She keeps New York and the nation informed about the weather in a personal way that makes us feel we all know her. Perhaps her childhood love of weather encouraged her to introduce the nationally syndicated* Weather School *program for the Bay Area in 1992. More than five thousand classrooms now participate in the science education program. She is a splendid example of how planning gone awry can sometimes result in even more exciting opportunities.*

I grew up as an only child in a nontraditional household in South Carolina with a single mother, a grandmother, and a grandfather. My mother graduated from high school but didn't go to college. My grandmother didn't go to high school but learned to read and write and worked in the fields or as a domestic. My grandfather never went to school, so he couldn't read or write. **They had high aspirations and big dreams for me.**

My mother used to dream of my becoming a ballerina and performing at Carnegie Hall. I was never interested in ballet, but I loved to dance. I performed in school and church plays. **Being encouraged to do things for an audience is one reason I do what I do today.**

I thought I could read when I was two because **my mother read to me all the time.** The grocery store had little ten-cent books, and I wanted a new one every time I went in. I begged my mother every night, "Read, read, read, please read." I memorized the books. Sometimes she tricked me and skipped a page, but I knew what was on each page. When I was in school plays, I memorized everyone's lines and knew the whole play.

**I was one of the first kids in the Head Start program back in the '60s.** I had a slow beginning, but my grades improved. I was mainly an "A" student all the way through elementary, middle, and high school and was a pretty decent student in college too.

I loved school, and my family always encouraged me. **It was their number one priority that I do well in school. They didn't have to force me. I loved learning, enjoyed taking tests, doing things for a grade, and answering questions in class.**

**When I was five, I knew I'd go to college.** I was very interested in the weather even then. My grandfather and I would sit on the front porch in the summertime and wait for big storms to brew up in the afternoon so we could cool off. **I learned about observing nature and read books about the weather.** I got out the encyclopedia and found that the word "meteorology" meant the study of weather. I went to my twenty-year high school reunion last year, and my physics teacher said, "You're the meteorologist, aren't you? You always said you were going to do that."

Because I was an only child, **I role-played on my own.** I'd gather up the kids in the neighborhood to play school. I was always the teacher. Sometimes the kids felt like playing, but if they didn't, I'd play alone. I'd be both the teacher and the student and switched roles while I played. I'd do the homework and come back into the classroom and check it.

I grew up watching television, but I also read. On those rainy days when I couldn't go out or didn't feel like being around other kids, **I'd get the encyclopedias out and read through them all. Buying those encyclopedias was the best investment my mother ever made** because first I'd pick out the "A" book, then the next day I'd pick out the "B" book. I wouldn't read them from cover to cover, but I'd skim through them. I learned about states and countries and dream about going to these places. Now when I'm in these places, I think, "Wow, I'm really here." When I travel, I like to sit near the window on the plane to see out. I want to see where we're going and pick out the Mississippi River or Cleveland when we fly over. It's almost like being able to go there.

I didn't like my math teacher in fourth grade. He was the first male teacher I had, and he paid more attention to the boys and wasn't encouraging to the girls. I didn't do well because he didn't explain well and didn't warm up enough for me to want to ask him to explain. If I didn't know it, he didn't care. I told my mother, "He won't talk to the girls. He only focuses on the boys," and **she came to school to have a chat with the teacher because she knew I could do better.** After that, it was better, and I got better grades. **Though math was never my favorite subject, I studied it because I loved the weather so much. I didn't let math stand in the way because it was only a part of weather, not the whole thing. I focused because the weather was fascinating.**

I was a Girl Scout for a couple of years and went to a summer camp that was three or four miles from my house and about a mile from the main road. There were about 100 of us, and we brought our sleeping bags. I was so excited to be at camp, hiking and swimming with my friends. About midweek, a car suddenly pulled into the driveway. It was my mother and grandmother, who had decided to surprise me. As a ten-year-old, I didn't want surprises from my mother at camp. I was embarrassed. They stayed the whole afternoon, and everyone loved them. We sang songs, and the counselors talked to them. All the kids said, "Wow, your mom came to see you; that's so cool." I'm thinking, "They're embarrassing me." They missed me, so they came to check on me, and it turned out fine.

"A" students got labeled "brainiac," "Goody Two-shoes," or "She's so smart." The kids didn't want to hang out with brains. They would get jealous because I would make all A's. **I never flaunted it. When I'd get my report card, I wouldn't show it to anyone until I got home because I knew others didn't make the grades I did. I didn't want them to feel bad or get picked on either.**

The schools in South Carolina were segregated until I was in second grade. Integration came in 1968, and I started going to a school that was racially mixed. My grandmother was a domestic, and she took care of white people's children. I was always around them, and it wasn't an issue for me. A white girl and I became very good friends and played together on the playground. After a couple of weeks, she said, "I can't play with you anymore." I asked her, "Why?" She said, "Well, my mom said I can't." That was the first time I was faced with racism—not her racism, but her mother's. We didn't play with each other anymore, and I transferred to a different school because we moved. I told my mother about it, and she explained, and I understood it all; it didn't anger me. I went to a formerly all-white school that gradually changed as people moved out of the neighborhood and integration came. By the time I attended, it was pretty much African-American, including students, teachers, and counselors. The school always had a bad reputation, lots of bad kids in a bad neighborhood. **Despite that, we had lots of good kids there too, and great teachers in the school who cared about us and encouraged us.**

**I was the teacher's pet. I was polite, had good manners, and answered the questions in class. Sometimes I would actually hold back and try not to answer them, wanting people to like me and afraid they wouldn't because I was too smart.**

Much of my involvement in school was scholastic. I was on the student council and in the Honor Society and was the junior class vice president and senior class secretary. I had lots of friends, and many of the kids I graduated from high school with started with me in Head Start, so I've known them all my life.

I was cheerleader for basketball and football and was competitive, but not hard-core competitive. **I knew that in order to be successful, I had to set myself apart from the crowd, but I wanted my competitors to do as well as I. My mother would say to me, "Never be a follower; always be a leader." That would keep me on the right path.** You go through some things when you're a kid, you hang out with the wrong crowd occasionally, and my mom would say, "Now, are those the kind of friends that you want to have? You have to be the leader. They're leading you."

My counselor was actually my cousin. I spent a lot of time in his office going through the manuals for universities and choosing schools. It was a mission for me. **I planned my life,** and my intent was to work for the National Weather Service. The first job I ever had was during the first summer after I graduated from high school, as a student trainee in meteorology for the National Weather Service. I worked directly with real meteorologists who had bachelor's and master's degrees. They were white and black, men and women. I actually had great role models. I was the only trainee, so they all took an interest in me. I learned how to forecast, read forecast models, measure radar, brief pilots, and even became accredited to take weather observations. I passed a required test and worked the last shift alone. One summer, the hydrologist, the man in charge of forecasting floods, left to take another job. In the interim, I took his place. I worked there two or three summers and Christmas vacations too. I was a government employee, GS-5. **I used all the money I earned to pay for school.**

There weren't people that looked like me doing the weather on television. It wasn't anything I ever thought of doing, but in my senior year, the government put a freeze on hiring, so I wasn't able to get another job with the National Weather Service. I thought, "Now what am I going to do?" One of my friends said, "You ought to try TV. Why don't you take some broadcasting courses? You'd be really good at that." I was thinking, "Yeah, okay, sure." I never thought that was *me.* I was in the science part of weather and not interested in performing. I took a broadcasting course that spring semester, graduated in the summer, and got an internship at the CBS affiliate in Tallahassee with the meteorologist on staff there. They were going to hire me to work on the weekends after the internship, but a **station from Chattanooga called me. The freeze on government hiring did me a big favor; thank you, Uncle Sam!** I would have been stuck in some office working shifts for the rest of my life, which wouldn't have been nearly as exciting as television.

I married three years ago. When I met my husband, he was nine and I was thirteen. I was his sweetheart, but he wasn't mine. My husband grew up in New Jersey next door to some of my relatives. I used to visit them in the summer, and my husband and his younger sister and brother were the kids I played with. I visited until I was sixteen, and then I stopped because I had a boyfriend. I didn't see my present husband for twenty years, but I knew what he was doing through my relatives. After I had lived around the country working on television, I came to New York and saw him at my relatives' house. It was like a big reunion. He was all grown up, had gone to college and had his life, and I had my life. He called to invite me to his sister's birthday party. His mom said, "No, you can't invite anybody because I don't want to have to clean up." He volunteered to clean up and brought me. We've been together ever since.

I was working out of San Francisco at the NBC affiliate and coming to New York as a guest meteorologist for *Weekend Today* and

*Sunrise.* NBC would fly me in to fill in on shows. I actually worked on the *Today* show with Bryant Gumbel and Katie Couric. Then my contracts came up for renewal in San Francisco, and at the time, my former boss from St. Louis was the vice president at NBC. He and Bruno Cohen knew my work, so they asked me if I wanted to come to New York to work. So I moved from Chattanooga, Tennessee, to Columbus, Georgia, then to St. Louis, Missouri, to San Francisco, and finally to New York; I love New York.

My mother always gave me great advice: **"Work hard, study hard, and don't give up." I knew where she came from and the opportunities she didn't have and what she wanted for me. My mom, grandmother, and grandfather all wanted me to have a career. The proudest day of my life was the day I graduated from college because it was the proudest day of their lives. I walked the straight and narrow as well as I could because I wanted them to be proud.** I dreamed about my future, but everything that has happened to me is beyond my wildest dreams.

# THE DISCIPLINE OF DANCE STILL DRIVES HER

## Janet Schiller

NATIONAL TELEVISION PRODUCER FOR NBC'S *TODAY*

*NBC producer Janet Schiller has combined the discipline she learned from dance and the creativity and initiative it involves to be an experienced television producer for the* Today *show, the number one national morning show. Whether Janet is called upon to produce a news segment or a parenting segment, it's done with the expertise and efficiency expected in high-level national programming. Whether a call comes at 11:00 P.M. or 7:00 A.M., she copes, working with the flexibility that news programming entails. Janet's story was not an easy one for her to share, but for those extraordinarily talented women who, despite their talent, may not make it in the arts, Janet inspires us to know there are creative alternatives.*

Dance was at the center of my childhood. I started taking dance about once a week at age four. Then it became twice a week, and then more and more. **As I grew into dance, my talent developed, and it became my identity.** By fourteen, I was going into New York City to study at the American Ballet Theater School. **Dance became a serious commitment and a sacrifice. Everyone was excited that I was a dancer, and my school was very realistic** about arrangements. **I was always a good student, so there were no issues about my grades.** I left school at noon, went into the city and danced, and then came home and did my homework. I earned physical education and arts credits through dance.

**I was definitely brought up in a loving household.** My father was a very serious scientist and was after a Nobel Prize when he was younger. He worked constantly at physics. All around the house there were scribblings of formulas that nobody ever understood except him. He believed that we should always apply ourselves. He would say, "Use what you have, and spend every free moment doing something that's going to further you in some way." **We couldn't sit around and be frivolous.** Television was definitely a waste of our minds. We didn't only read stories, we read and acted out plays. Dad gave us the message to challenge ourselves in sports. **We took the challenge to have an active mind and active body seriously, so there was lots of emphasis on learning. I was always very goal-directed.**

My mother was internally motivated too. With three kids, she went back to school, became a chemist, and earned her master's degree. She was disappointed that she didn't finish her doctorate. She had a part-time job, was very politically involved, still making meals for the family, taxiing us around, being a ballet mom, and making things work for me. **Mom was a realist. She made me aware from the start that dancing was very competitive, and encouraged me to be as good as I could be.** She was also careful not to set me up for too high expectations. She made me aware that there were people better than I. I took that as a double message. "Do everything and be as good as you can, but you also are probably not going to be totally great." **It may be easier to go after those dreams if people believe that you're going to be the greatest in the world.**

**I was very competitive and became even more so as dance became more competitive.** I was also competitive with my sister, Laura. As children, we had a tumultuous relationship, and I tried to hold my ground because Laura was so hard on me. She was five years old when I arrived, and she was not interested in having a sibling. I felt rejected by her, and **being good at something she wasn't good at made me feel special.** We had been taking dance classes together at one point, but she stopped dancing. She retreated quickly when it was clear I was the dancer in the family.

I never thought of myself as an excellent student, although my parents tell me I was. I was verbal and expressive, and I skipped kindergarten. I began school in a very poor, inner-city school where we were literally only finger-painting through first grade and doing very little academic work. Then our family moved to a model suburban school system with many bright kids who had already had a very rigorous education. I was a year younger than the kids in my class and didn't have their academic training. I came into the suburban school thinking I was smart, and I was even a little cocky. **It was a rude awakening to find that life was not finger painting. The** move really threw me off, and I had the feeling that I was no longer smart. We had an individualized system of learning math, and we worked in different colors, which were on our cubbies. I remember being embarrassed that I was salmon instead of blue.

My family had high academic expectations. **My parents didn't punish us to do our work, but there was an expectation that we were bright and that we should do well in school. I always talked a lot in class and asked questions.** I remember teachers really liking me when I was very young, but not again until I was older, in junior high.

Every summer, we went to a scientific community, Woods Hole, and that was very formative for me. **I was surrounded by peers who were very motivated.** There was a tremendous amount of pressure for kids to be brilliant in something. I saw myself as different because most of the kids there were establishing themselves academically, going to Harvard and Yale and planning doctorates. My special area was dance, and that took some pressure off me for the academic achievement.

I had many good friends when I was younger, but when I started going to the city for dance, I began seeing myself as separate from other young people my age. I wasn't arrogant about it, but **I felt removed from kids' issues.** I was working my butt off at a career, and I wasn't hanging out at the local ice-cream store. I couldn't identify with other kids my age. **Having a goal grows you up fast.**

I never went through dating and fooling around the way other kids did because I was always tired. Being fifteen and tired is a weird place to be. **I never had to deal with boredom or confusion with what I was going do with my life. I knew. It allowed me to get through those years much better than I would have had I not been a dancer.**

I was always best in my dance class until I started studying in New York, which was a very different scene. **It was definitely a shock that there were so many talented dancers.** I had always had teachers who were wonderfully encouraging and nurturing to me. In New York, getting my teacher to notice me was hard. It was a difficult period in my life, but I was determined. **I had the drive and enough confidence to believe I could do it.** My parents were always supportive, although they were fearful for me. It was hard for them to see their daughter in such a competitive field, where the chances of success are so low.

I became a professional dancer in ballet companies, but they weren't the American Ballet Theater. I danced for the Eglevsky Ballet Company and the Garden State Ballet Company. I studied with a teacher on scholarship who had previously been with the American Ballet Theater School. I was one of five very young students whom she let take classes. She was extremely hard and not very nice to me. I think she saw herself in me.

**I realized that I was going to be a good dancer, but never a great dancer.** I could probably get into a large company and dance in the corps, and maybe once in a while I'd get a solo role, but I saw how miserable most of the professionals around me were and how unglamorous life as a dancer was. My experiences with smaller companies showed me what it was like being on the road constantly. I traveled on buses and trains and would ride ten hours, then get out and rehearse.

I struggled with injury problems. I saw dance as an archaic system. Grown women were called girls and were made to cry by their choreographers. Dancers were forced into remaining childlike. The world was getting far too narrow for me. I decided to try modern dance, because I thought if I could take off my toe shoes and be with mature people, I would fit better. I was getting some professional jobs at modern, but I continued to have problems with injuries. I finally just got tired of the whole thing. To struggle to make the rent, having to figure out where my next paycheck was coming from, and also having to deal with being in pain was too much. **Because ballet had been my entire identity, it was like going through a major divorce. I had to find myself again at twenty-one.**

After I stopped dancing, my mother said she slept well for the first time since I had begun living in New York. I did live in some pretty rough neighborhoods. I had been working incredibly hard; she had good reason to worry. My dad felt extreme disappointment for me, realizing I was giving up my dream.

I had dropped out of high school when I was sixteen, had earned a GED, and hadn't taken math or science for years. After dance, I chose a difficult engineering school because my father taught there and it was tuition-free. When I started, I was given a test to check my skills, and they determined I was definitely far behind other students. I took chemistry, physics, algebra, and one science class after another, and I ended up taking second- and third-year multivariate calculus. **I worked my butt off, and it was painful, but I was determined to get through and do well.** I'd often come to my dad in tears to get his help. I wasn't satisfied to only learn equations. **I was determined to understand the math, much as I had intensely understood every step of my dance.** I was studying management science and statistics and used math to do a variety of analyses. I did incredibly well at it but still felt it wasn't natural to me. **Despite my difficult beginning, I graduated eighth in my class.**

At that point I had several friends who were in television production. It sounded interesting, so I got an internship with NBC. My family wasn't a television-watching family, **but I had always been a good writer, and I had various talents that fit into television production.** First, I worked in logistics and business, but my interests were more in the editorial part. **I gradually worked my way up the ladder to become a producer.**

I go into situations that are incredibly challenging and that I'm not at all confident about, but **I have a very strong drive to succeed. I have a need to prove I can accomplish challenges.** Sometimes the cost is higher than it should be. I push too hard and experience too much pressure. **I try to balance my career and family. I think about where my ambition comes from and what really is important to me.**

**Dance definitely taught me a huge amount of discipline. I had this sense of consequence because if I didn't work out properly, if I didn't rehearse, if I stayed out too late, or if I ate too much, I felt it the next day. When I came out of dance and applied what I learned to other fields, I knew how to work hard. I think dance had negative parts too. There was a lot of reaching for perfection.** I always had a tendency to be a perfectionist, and dance increased those tendencies. It makes everything a more painful ordeal than it has to be. In the end, **maybe I would have arrived at the same place if I'd been more relaxed about it and if I'd opened myself to other possibilities. With perfectionism, the end is what is important and not the process. If I**

allow the process to take me, it takes me to different places, but they can be more interesting. Perfectionism prevents me from taking risks. I haven't been averse to risk, but risks take a lot of energy out of me.

Having spent all those years of dance where good wasn't ever good enough, I do like to be really good at what I do. That makes me very aware of what other people are doing and getting and being given, so I make many comparisons.

I'm trying to come to terms with how my career really fits in my life when I want to spend time with my children, and when I want to give them my good energy. When I come home, I'm exhausted and have given everything to my job. There's not a lot left over for them. I feel the need to push in my work, to be a player, and to get important assignments. I want to be taken seriously, but to get there and to stay there takes so much. It would mean that I'd be at work late at night and on the road, and I know those aren't the things I want in my life with two children. I love my career, but I'm torn by my family's needs as well.

It's particularly hard because career has always been my identity. Everyone always said, "Oh, you're a dancer. Wow!" There is such a special place in this world for dancers and for people who are in the arts. My present job with TV is glamorous. It does define me in many ways. I've always been striving and identified with a career.

I live life seriously. I always have goals. I'm not a laid-back person. I look at my kids, and I see the way my husband deals with them and the way he lets them explore and have time to enjoy themselves. I wish at times that I could be more casual, but after spending a childhood of intense work at successful dance, my drive for excellence remains with me as a heritage.

# Going with the Flow

*Cindy Beckler*

PRODUCER FOR CNN

*When Cindy Beckler produces* Parenting *at CNN, every advice or news segment is meaningful to her, as she combines her commitment to parenting with her commitment to CNN. Cindy has had many different producing opportunities at CNN, but so far,* Parenting *is a favorite because much of what she learns on the job enhances how she raises her own two children. Cindy's story illustrates the option of letting life lead you from one interest to another instead of single-mindedly pursuing one goal.*

My husband, Todd, and I married when we were seniors in college, and we grew up together. We beat the odds. We'll be celebrating our twentieth wedding anniversary.

At the time I graduated, CNN was interviewing students who were earning degrees but had no experience. I interviewed, then received a call from them saying, "Come on down." I called my husband at school and said, "What do you think about moving to Atlanta?" We finished school on a Friday, packed up the U-Haul on Saturday, and moved to Atlanta on Sunday. I started work with CNN the Wednesday after, and I've been here ever since. Todd is an engineer, and it turned out just as well for him as it did for me.

My parents had a very traditional marriage. My father traveled, worked, and my mother stayed at home and took care of the kids. I'm the youngest and the only girl of three. My brothers were ten and eight when I was born, so I was almost like an only child. My dad was an outgoing, vivacious guy who did public speaking, and we often tagged along to his meetings. **He showed me the exciting part of the working world.**

**I learned how to raise a family through my mother.** My mom and I would hang out together often. Dad would come home on weekends, or we'd meet him in Kansas City. She and I were the support system for Dad. **I liked both worlds, and I identified with both of them, so I wanted to be like both when I grew up.**

**The best thing my parents did for me was instill self-esteem. I was told every day that whatever I wanted to do I could eventually do.** They thought that I had ability and was talented and sociable. I've always been more social than academic. School was a fun thing for me; I didn't take it very seriously. **I had a B average, but I thrived on the social part.**

We moved seven times around the Midwest throughout my school years. Moves seemed semitraumatic, but I don't feel they hurt me any. I'm an emotional person, so on the day of the move, I'd cry about missing my friends. I'd be ahead at one school and behind at the next. **I always adjusted and went with the flow.**

In junior high, I had friends and a big slumber-party stage. They were wholesome kids, no drugs or alcohol or anything like that. I remember my first dance and my first kiss. I was probably pretty typical.

We moved again the summer after my sophomore year in high school, and my parents were very concerned about the transition. I started my junior year as the new girl at school and had a boyfriend by the second month and went to homecoming the month after that. That crowd was probably a little more wild, but I survived it. There were more drugs and alcohol there than I had seen before. I'd go to a party and drink a beer, but I never got in trouble, and nothing ever got out of hand.

We always went to church, but we picked a church based on which one had the most dynamic speaker. One week, we'd go to a Congregational church, another time to a Methodist church. We'd decide, "Let's go to the church with the purple doors," and we'd try that one out, or we'd say, "Well, we don't like that; let's go to a different one."

My father always considered himself a cowboy of sorts. When I was a little girl, he would buy me cowgirl outfits, which was his way of trying to stay connected to me. When I was in high school, he bought me a horse for my birthday. I would go horseback riding on the weekends. It was total fun and a way of getting back to nature.

I took a basic curriculum my first year in junior college. After my first year, a friend encouraged me to work at Yellowstone National Park. I finished school on Friday and left the next day for Yellowstone. I absolutely loved it. We had employee cottages, but there was one phone for everybody and no TV. We were in the middle of nowhere, except for kids and science teachers who wanted to be park rangers for the summer. I called my parents every Sunday to keep in touch. At one point, I told them, "I'm having a lot of fun, I want to stay out of school this semester. I'll come home at Christmas and go to school in the spring."

When I went back to junior college, my outlook was much more carefree. I decided to take only courses I wanted to take. I took advertising, psychology, and more English, and it worked out well. I transferred to the University of Nebraska to finish my degree. I started the journalism program in the second semester. I lived in a dormitory, and I wasn't very self-disciplined. I got D's, and my parents blew a cork. They came down on me pretty hard. **I ended up taking all the classes over and brought my grades back up, and I learned from that mistake.**

I met my husband in junior college. He transferred to a school near Lincoln, and we continued to date. **He has a background very similar to mine.** His father was in agribusiness; there are four children in his family instead of three; he grew up in the Midwest; and he is a very honest, hardworking, salt-of-the-earth guy. He was a good match for me, and we connected early on. When we decided to get married, I went around to all my professors and said, "I'm getting married next week, and I'm not going to be in school." They rolled their eyes. To them it seemed like an outrageous thing for a kid to do. **I knew it was right for me. All my parents wanted was that I finish school. I did, and once I got married, my grades went up. I had so much stability, and it was a very healthy thing.**

I was shocked when I came to CNN. I hadn't had much business background, and I wasn't prepared for the wild scene; I was this kid from Nebraska. **There's a lot of help at CNN, and I've had people guide me.** Both my husband and I had crazy hours and weird work schedules, including weekend overnights. We were all over the clock, but **it was nice because we had each other, so I didn't feel neglected or lonely.**

I started as an entry-level cameraperson. Then I was a videotape editor for a couple of years, worked on the assignment desk, and moved on to some special projects. **I've had seven major job changes. I've had all those experiences in the very same** building. That's been good for me because I didn't have to pack up and move to different cities.

I learned that there were many opportunities at CNN, and I had to make choices. When Reagan was going to invade Grenada, CNN wanted to send me down there. They didn't know how long, where, or what. I had no in or out time. It took me a day or two to figure it out, but I decided I might be away for a month or longer, and it was Thanksgiving. I decided that my husband wasn't just a roommate to whom I could say, "Pay the bills; I'll see you later." I knew that it might be unpopular at CNN, but I couldn't do that to him, and I turned it down. They didn't hold it against me. I think they were surprised because at that point most kids were jumping at the chance. I concluded early on that there is more to my life than myself.

I was twenty-eight when I had my son. There were married folks at CNN but very few with children. It was the right time for us. Todd and I had been married long enough and knew that having children was a step we were going to take. I was working on a daily show called *Women Today,* and it was a good environment for me to have a child.

I had a typical maternity leave. After four months, my son became a day-care baby. First, I had a grandma next door, then I had day care I wasn't happy with, then I had a friend. Once my son was three, I found a good place, and later my daughter went there too, and we stayed with the same organization throughout the rest of our child-care needs. I had no guilt until I became a mother, and then I had plenty until I found good day care. I had to explain to my boss that I was only available to work certain hours because that was the time the day care was open. I became more limited in my choices at CNN. Thankfully, I had proven myself, and they gave me shows and programs that were conducive to my family's schedule.

Shows come and go, and I have learned to go with the flow and survive the television scene because none of it lasts too long. The first time we lost a show, it was traumatic because I hadn't been through it before. The show I produce, *Parenting,* went on the air in '95, and we're still here, but in a different form because weekend programming has changed. I've learned how to keep things going and not get upset, because it's TV. If you do your job and prove yourself, you'll land on your feet.

The shootings at Columbine was a rough story for me as a parent because I have a soon-to-be-teenage boy. This year is my son's first year in junior high. School and sports come easily for him. I don't think he'll fall through the cracks, but he knows what went on in Columbine. We talked to him about it, and he said, "Mom, I heard they were going after the jocks." That broke my heart, because my kid is a home-run king. For him not to feel safe is terrible.

After Columbine, **I started a parenting group for mothers of teenage boys in our neighborhood.** We meet once a month and talk. A lot of it is fellowship with other moms so we'll be more pre-pared. I'll start one for mothers of daughters when my daughter goes into junior high too. **It helps to have support.**

I have no dramatic life stories. There's no real reason why I am where I am. I didn't always have a plan; **I went with the flow.** Todd and I came to Atlanta with **the attitude that we were going to make it work. There was no "We're going to give up," or "We're going to quit," or "We're going to move if we don't like it."**

**It's important to marry the right person.** I've witnessed many of my friends who haven't, and it's a terrible struggle. Todd is very supportive. He enjoys my successes as much as I do. **Ours is very much an equal partnership.**

Producing *Parenting* is one of the best positions I have had during my time here at CNN. **It's about things I care about, and it's family-friendly.** I wanted to have a family and to work in TV. I'm happy doing what I'm doing because it's fulfilled both needs.

# THE RIGHT TRAIN CAME ALONG

## Norine G. Johnson, Ph.D.

CLINICAL PSYCHOLOGIST AND PRESIDENT OF THE AMERICAN
PSYCHOLOGICAL ASSOCIATION

*Dr. Norine Johnson runs four psychology businesses. She works with families in an independent practice as a neuropsychologist and consults with schools to educate children with special needs and neurological difficulties. She also helps people start their own businesses and partners a business called Women to Women, which develops products to help women cope with life issues. Her most recent book is* Beyond Appearance: A New Look at Adolescent Girls. *Norine is married and has three children and provides an example of how women whose careers are delayed by parenting often catch up and initiate a set of evolving careers to fit their initial dreams. She is only the eighth woman in 109 years to serve as president of the American Psychological Association.*

**Our family was always concerned about how we used our money** and what would happen if we ran out of it. These concerns preceded the **Depression—they go back to my grandmother, who is the most inspirational person in my life.** When she was twenty-eight, her husband was killed. He was a sheriff in Kentucky, had stopped a feud, and had put a couple of men in jail. Out of revenge, family members of these men ambushed and killed him. My grandmother was left alone—a tiny woman with no education, little money, and four children. **At ninety-six, she told me a story about the turning point in her life.** Six months after her husband's death, she realized she was still setting a place for him at their dining table. She said to herself, "Now, Verna, he's dead. Get on with it." **She picked herself up, moved to Louisville, started nursing school, and earned a degree in nursing. She supported her family capably. Her story of courage and dedication always inspired me.** She led a good life and educated her children. She combined the importance of education and family with fun.

I always wanted to help poor people. One bright, shiny day when

I was ten, my family drove to Indianapolis. We were crossing the White River when I saw large, dark, looming structures that looked scary and threatening to me. I asked my parents what those buildings were, and they explained that they were the "projects" designed for poor people. I said, "I want to help those poor people get out." My parents have told this story repeatedly, and **my desire to empower people with limited resources has been a life goal.**

When I was in high school, I took a course in psychology. I'd like to say it was the content that got me excited about the field, but it wasn't. **It was the young, vivacious, smart, and interesting teacher.** She helped me decide I wanted to become a psychologist. My swim coach had an important influence on me in high school too. I'd get in the water and swim a mile, and he'd say, "Now swim another mile." **He taught me if I wanted to be good, I needed to push myself and persist.**

**My parents taught me the importance of knowledge.** I remember whenever a topic came up at dinner, my brother or I would say, "I don't know where that country is." Rather than telling us, my dad would pull out the encyclopedia. Our dining room table was often covered with books. We'd continue eating, but we'd be looking things up and talking about some new, exciting topic. **My parents taught me that knowledge was something you integrated throughout your life. They emphasized the importance of education for women, a unique perspective at the time.** In fact, my paternal great-grandmother was the fourth woman in Indiana to receive an advanced degree.

I majored in psychology and had wonderful professors who fostered my interest. During college, I decided I wanted to write as well as become a practicing clinical psychologist. I wanted to have the impact on children and adolescents that Anna Freud had in her writing, but I got married instead after one year of graduate school and temporarily abandoned my graduate school ambitions.

During the program, I'd had a hard time getting along with the chair of our psychology department, who had made a special exception to accept me into graduate school and had offered me work-study money. I was taking a clinical psychology class with him during my second semester of school, and I questioned what he was doing. He was taking a Skinnerian maze for running rats and using it on retarded children at the state institution. **I felt the project wasn't ethical and refused to do it, even though it was required.** I did a different study instead—one on self-image in children with hearing deficits. He and I had confrontations in class. My professor was presenting the work as if there was only one way to do things. I knew I had to leave.

My husband got his M.B.A., and we moved every eighteen months. He kept getting promoted, and I was his trailing spouse. We had two children during this time. **I hired a baby-sitter one day a week so I could go up to our attic and write poetry.** It was about three or four years before we moved to a community—Detroit, Michigan—with a graduate program where I could reenter school. I was accepted into the clinical psychology graduate program at Wayne State University and received a scholarship. **My husband wasn't sure about my going back to school, but it was a turning point for me. I made a deal with him that I would continue doing everything I had been doing with the exception of writing thank-you notes after being invited to somebody's house for dinner. I used my grant money to hire child care and studied from ten at night until two in the morning. I loved it. It was invigorating.** I had full days of classes on Tuesdays and Thursdays and spent the other days with my family.

I had my third child while I was in graduate school. In fact, I was in labor during my statistics final exam. I went into labor that morning and asked the professor if I could still take the exam. The professor said, "*No!* Go, go, go to the hospital." I said, "You probably don't understand, but after the baby is born, I'll be preoccupied." I told him I was ready to take the exam, I knew the material, and my husband would stay with me the whole time. I asked him if I could take the exam in the room next door since I was having full contractions. I completed the exam between twelve and one, and our daughter was born at six.

After graduate school, my husband was transferred again, and I started my internship full-time, five days a week, and thrived in it. Afterward, I accepted a staff position and became the first psychologist in the Department of Pediatrics at University Hospital in Cleveland, Ohio. **People began to talk about my work, and I was helping hundreds of children.**

After nine months, my husband was offered a job in Boston. We moved again, and it was painful to leave my wonderful job. **It took me a year to recover from that. I had to find the right schools for the children, make connections, find a place in the community, and recover from the loss.** I met my neighbors, but they were all stay-at-home moms. **I was different and felt like people didn't understand why I wanted to work.** This was a complicated issue for about five years.

When I began to look for work again, I kept asking myself whether or not I was doing the right thing. Then I received some important advice about decision making. **I learned that I should make the best decision for the moment because I couldn't control the future. I learned to think very hard about things before I made a decision, and then to close the door on the decision. I told myself, "I made the best decision I could have made," and I tried not to look back and second-guess myself.**

I took a job as the director of psychology at Franciscan Hospital, a children's hospital in Boston, and immediately saw things I wanted to change. **I held lunch seminars because I'd learned along the way that if you want people to learn something they might not want to learn, it's a good idea to feed them. I invited nursing and medical staff and talked about psychotherapy and cases. Eventually, I began to get referrals from the medical staff and was successful in treating and helping these people.**

I was at Franciscan Hospital for eighteen years. One of my mentors sponsored me for a two-year course for mental-health administrators and planners at Harvard Medical School. I learned about financial planning and how to integrate it into a business plan. **It was an ideal combination. I was raised in a family that acknowledged the importance of money, and later I developed the skills to use money to empower people.**

Over the course of the years, I increased the staff from two to thirty-five people and turned the department around. **It used to be something that cost the hospital money, and I turned it into a moneymaker.** They kept giving us additional resources and increasing the impact that we could have on the hospital.

Ten years ago, I left to go into full-time private practice. I was on my August break, and the phone rang. It was the assistant superintendent in charge of special education for a community in Boston. I had done some consultation in those schools before, and he asked if I had anything to offer to their school to support special education. I just started talking about ways that schools could provide comprehensive services to children with neurological difficulties, attention disorders, seizure disorders, and so forth. I described how schools could provide educational services for children so they wouldn't have to leave their communities or go to residential settings. I talked from the top of my head about a model program and described what schools would have to do to create it. It was an incredible moment. Then I hung up the phone and went about the rest of my vacation, not thinking any more about it.

At the end of September, the superintendent called back and said, "They like it! They want it!" I said, "What?" I had no memory of what I had described. He prompted me a bit, and I started to recall my ideas. Then he said I needed to have a proposal by Monday. I wrote the proposal over the weekend. I put demands in the proposal that would really promote the level of change that I thought the school system would never meet. Then I put a price tag on it. I didn't think they would accept it, but they did. **They invited me to start in two weeks.** I needed a couple of months before I could terminate from my department, but with this, I went into full-time private practice, including training seminars for special-education administrators. I worked very closely with the local schools.

**There's a moral to this story. If you're at the train station and the right train comes by, get on it because another one might not be coming. I believe when an opportunity comes by, and it touches a certain core inside of you, you find yourself relating to it and getting energized. If you feel like your mind is going and your emotions are saying, "Oh, this is really exciting," then that's the train. It's important to pay attention to these cues.** This was my train, and I had to get on it. **It changed the direction of my career.**

**I began to take a leadership position in the field of psychology by joining the Massachusetts Psychological Association. I wanted to change legislation, so I became active, ran for president, and was elected. Then I was elected council representative for Massachusetts to the American Psychological**

Association at the national level. At my first APA council meeting, I didn't agree with the way APA was handling money, so one of my colleagues pushed me up to the microphone. I gave a speech about a magazine we owned, *Psychology Today,* and how we should divest ourselves of that magazine, which was losing us millions of dollars. As a result, I was elected co-chair of the finance committee and was part of a team that guided APA to a financial comfort level with assets over $30 million. Learning how to use money effectively to accomplish goals is something that excites me.

I wanted to take a leadership role in APA not because of my personal ambition but because I wanted to work to empower children and families with limited resources or special needs. Through my work experiences, I've learned that there are only limited things I can do in either private practice or within an institution, and I want to change policy. Every time I hit a barrier when trying to help people, I become more active in organizations whose goal it is to promote change.

When I advise young women about their careers, I tell them passion is important. I believe it's important to do something you feel passionate about because passion will energize you, help you be creative, and carry you through the hard times. It's also important to develop networks of colleagues and friends who will help you get places and meet people you might not otherwise meet. Most of all, I think women today need to know about money. It's very important to know how to use money, get money, and how to empower yourself around issues of money.

Psychology is a wonderful profession. It has so many elements: science, education, public interaction, and practice. I've integrated new parts of the spectrum of psychology at different stages in my life. First, I developed my skills as an administrator and a psychotherapist, then as a consultant, and later, as a policy maker. Now, I've been able to add the component of writer. In the past three years, I've edited two books and written three chapters for other books. It's the train ride I always wanted. I've found my career to be truly gratifying, and I'm passionate about my work.

# *H*ER SOCIAL SKILLS PAVED HER WAY

## Frances Culbertson, Ph.D.

PSYCHOLOGIST AND AMERICAN PSYCHOLOGICAL ASSOCIATION
LIFETIME ACHIEVEMENT AWARD WINNER

*When Dr. Frances Culbertson was recognized by the American Psychological Association for her lifetime achievement in the field of psychology, making her one of a very select group of distinguished persons, I felt a special joy. Fran has been a role model and a mentor to me and an internship supervisor. Early in my work with Fran, we validated my creativity test for children in Taiwan together. Her role in developing the field of school psychology has improved the lives of thousands upon thousands of children. Her international contributions in psychology have been continuous. Mentors have played a crucial role in her life, particularly in helping her smash personal barriers to higher education. What a thrill it is for me to see her efforts deservedly rewarded and to include her story in our book.*

We grew up very poor. My father owned his own store, but it was never successful, and my mother worked at various jobs to sustain the family. She cleaned houses for wealthy people and brought me their hand-me-down clothes.

If my mother needed to go to the grocery store, she would just say, "You stay there," and leave me home alone while she dashed out. I was an obedient child and never left my chair. I can visualize myself when I was two, in my little rocking chair at a desk listening to our old Victrola and playing school with my dolls while my mother ran out. I walked myself to kindergarten at age four, which made me feel important. I had two girlfriends, and we were bright children, did special things and helped other children who were having trouble following rules.

In Boston, wealthy Junior Leaguers came into the poor neighborhoods to help people. My Junior Leaguer was Ms. Ryan, who taught us in fifth grade. On Fridays she wore long flowing dresses for the Junior League formal tea after school. We were awed by her dresses, and we'd try to guess what color she would be wearing. She made our class feel like a family. If we were ill, she sent a card or had one of the children deliver a box of cookies or a book. When she married, she invited our class to her wedding. She sent a limousine for us, and when my mother saw the car stopping at our house, she thought it was the police and someone had done something terrible. **Ms. Ryan sowed the seeds of my international interests. She described exotic tours to Mexico, Canada, France, and other countries. Until then, I didn't think any world existed beyond our neighborhood.**

Public-health nurses came into our poor neighborhood weekly to teach parents how to cook, clean, and keep the family healthy. They were very concerned I would get tuberculosis because I was undernourished. On their advice, I wasn't allowed to play on the school playground, but I went to a portable building where I was given a hot lunch and told to rest on a cot. **During that time, I'd read. The neighborhood librarian and I were good friends and she'd save me special books** and we'd discuss them later. She enhanced my love of reading.

I was a capable, compliant, good little girl and enjoyed being teacher's pet. By sixth grade, I recall, I was doing homework very conscientiously. Other kids always wanted to copy my homework. I gladly gave it to them, but I remember saying, "You don't learn anything if you copy me." I continued that all through high school.

**My all-girl high school was wonderful. Our large high school had many nationalities, but particularly Irish kids. I was elected a class officer,** and it was the Irish students who elected me, I think because I gave them my homework! **I was very sociable, liked people, and had many leadership opportunities that wouldn't have been there if our school had been co-ed.** We were let out a half hour earlier to avoid any contact with the boys. Our schools were very intellectual. We had French, history, literature, symphony, and opera clubs, but no physical education. **The Boston Symphony offered us the opportunity to come and listen to them practice for twenty-five cents on Friday afternoons. We could also go to the opera for the same price. My love of opera started then.** It was like sitting next to heaven. The Italian laborers would come to the discounted seats at the opera, too, and sit with us. At their encouragement, we cheered and booed along with them.

I knew I would have to go to work immediately after high school graduation because my family needed money, so I never even thought about going to college. I was going to be either a secretary, a bookkeeper, or a salesperson. My friends and I went job hunting together. We learned that if you had a Jewish name there was never a job available. My father was a Russian Jew, and when he entered Ellis Island, his name was Ouchitelle. The agent there didn't understand my father, and he said, "I'll give you the name Mitchell." All my job-hunting friends were Jewish. I'd go into the employment agency with my non-Jewish-sounding name to request a job, and they'd give me information about five or six jobs. Then I'd distribute them to my friends. We'd each take one reference and go off to look for the job.

A man from Sunday's Candies called the school saying he wanted a bright person for his candy store, and they recommended me. The owner was Mr. Caplow, a Harvard Business School graduate, and he gave me a series of intelligence, personality, and dexterity tests. He hired me and some Harvard students who were working their way through school as he had. At Christmastime, we worked together until 4:00 A.M. packing boxes. The students would take me to parties on the Harvard campus, where the other students would ask, "What college do you go to?" I dreaded having to tell them that I didn't. I always felt like an outsider, so I told one of the guys, "I don't think I can go to these gatherings anymore. I feel much too uncomfortable among college students." He asked, "Fran, why don't you go to college?" I said, "That's out of the question. I have to give money to my family." One of the guys was a medical student and told me about a lab technician training program at Boston City Hospital, so I decided to try to enter that. I had an uncle who knew the mayor very well, and he said he'd help get me into it. I soon received a letter saying I was welcome to join the training class for lab technicians and began my studies.

My next job was as a lab technician in hematology at the Beth Israel Hospital. Once again, everyone was a college graduate except me. I was there two years when a letter came telling me I had received an Edwards Scholarship for four years to any college of my choice. I was dumbfounded because I had never applied for the scholarship. One of my close friends from the candy store had applied for me.

My parents had sent my brothers to college because they were boys. College had not even been discussed as an option for me. I decided I'd be a biochemist based on my lab tech work, and the best biochemistry school was the University of Michigan. Normally, I wouldn't have qualified, but it was 1944 and the war had created a shortage of students, so I got in.

In my freshman year, I took chemistry despite the fact that I didn't have the required math. It seemed a miracle that I completed chemistry with an A, but somehow I learned the formulas and did the work. My biggest problem was English. I had never written papers in high school. The English professor wondered how I'd gotten into college because I wrote so poorly. I was devastated and told two girls in my dorm my woes. **They said, "That's not going to be a problem, Fran. We'll tutor you."** I think they were impressed that I was four years older, and they didn't want anything to break my bubble. I emerged from English with an A and did so well that I didn't have to take the second-semester course. **Their kindness and dedication is a very precious memory for me.**

In my sophomore year I took experimental psychology and adored it. The professor, who was doing animal research on how rats solve a maze, asked me to be his assistant in class, grading papers and helping people with experimental designs. After doing that for a semester, I changed my major to psychology.

In my senior year I took an industrial psychology course, and the professor asked me what I was planning to do when I got through. By this time, I was seriously involved with John, an economics major. I told the professor I was getting married and was going to get a job because my husband planned to attend graduate school. He said, "Fran, you need to go to graduate school. We'll get you a scholarship or some kind of a job where you'll make more money than anything you can do on your own." He was as good as his word, and after my first year as a graduate student, he suggested I become a teaching fellow. **I was fortunate to always have a mentor who helped me throughout my graduate years.**

I married John in my senior year. He worked on his Ph.D. in

economics, and I went for my Ph.D. in social psychology. After our course work, we passed our preliminary exams and moved to Washington, D.C., where John went to work for the Federal Reserve Board and we attempted to complete our dissertations. I hadn't anticipated getting pregnant, but I did, and we had twins. I was so busy, I couldn't work on my dissertation at all. When the twins were about two, we lived in a housing development where there were seven attached town houses, and our basements opened to a public basement. We set up a little school there so some mothers could have free mornings and the others could supervise the kids while they were playing. **When my friends found out I needed to do my thesis, they evolved a plan where each one took a day when they brought their children to my house and baby-sat for the kids for two and a half hours while I typed away at their house.**

One of John's colleagues, a director at the Federal Reserve Board, and his wife came out to dinner with us. When she found out I had a Ph.D., she was shocked that I wasn't working. I said, "I have kids," and she said, "That's beside the point; you could teach one class." She offered to find me a part-time job at the American University, where she taught. At another party, I met a research psychologist for Children's Hospital in D.C. who wanted me to do research with her on lead poisoning in children. I was on the project briefly; then John decided he wanted to try academia. He received an offer for an academic job at the University of Wisconsin in Madison, and we moved there in 1957.

By this time, we had three children, and I was pregnant with the fourth. We went to all the parties to meet the rest of the faculty. At one of the parties, I met someone who was looking for a researcher at the Central Colony and Training School, a school for severely developmentally delayed children. I suggested I could share the job with a friend who was also an experimental psychologist. We went to work at Central Colony to develop a research lab. I'd been doing that for a year when the state of Wisconsin approached me and offered to pay for my retraining to be a clinical psychologist because they were so desperate for psychologists. I committed to three years of work for the state of Wisconsin.

Once the kids were all in school, I started looking for a job. The nepotism rule at the University of Wisconsin, Madison, prevented me from working there because of John. As was true of so many women of my era, John's job came first and mine was always second.

At a friend's suggestion, I became a school psychologist and loved it. After a year, I was asked to teach at the University of Wisconsin in Whitewater. It meant driving two hours daily, and I didn't think I could do that. John said, "Sure, you can," and he took a week off, and we drove back and forth to Whitewater until I felt comfortable, and I said, "I guess I can," and took the job.

The university was just starting its school psychology program, and I didn't meet the certification requirements, so I had to return to school. I became very active in school psychology and met Dr. Frances Mullen, who was the assistant superintendent of the Chicago public schools and also a member of the International Council of Psychologists. Frances got me involved in the International Council of Psychologists. Eventually I became secretary, and then president.

I was at Whitewater for twenty years. I developed training and international home and job exchanges for the students there. I became very active in school psychology at the American Psychological Association and developed the International Association of School Psychologists.

Although I'm now retired, I continue to arrange programs for international psychologists to come to the American Psychological Association meetings to present their research, which we have done collaboratively. I also continue to do therapy one day a week, but my interest has shifted to hypnotherapy. I'm now developing some hypnosis programs for the elderly. **It seems to me that the people I've met along the way have paved my way to a lifetime of interesting opportunities and engagements, and I feel I've been able to touch so many lives, from very young students to elders.**

# CURIOSITY ABOUT THE WORLD PROPELLED HER ONTO THE AIRWAVES

## Kathleen Dunn

PUBLIC RADIO HOST

*Kathleen Dunn began her lively conversations around the family table and with her grandparents, but now those conversations happen on Wisconsin Public Radio three hours daily; in addition, Kathleen presides over Friday evenings of spirited discussions on Milwaukee Public Television. In the informal way that Kathleen likes to conduct discussions, she successfully involves her Wisconsin listeners. I've had the fun of answering questions on her call-in show, and the questions just keep coming. It looks like Kathleen's passion for social issues led directly to her radio work, but consider the serendipitous role of a car's breakdown and the resulting whopping mechanic's bill in fueling Kathleen's love of radio.*

I grew up in Chicago and then in the northwest Chicago suburbs. **My parents gave me great freedom,** even on my bicycle. I rode it far, exploring neighborhoods and discovering forests. **I've always had a great curiosity about how people live, how they think, and how the world works.**

**My family stimulated my interests.** My grandmother was involved in the women's movement in the 1910s, and I remember sitting on my grandfather's lap in the rocking chair watching *Meet the Press* on Sunday afternoons. My mother was a reporter, wrote a neighborhood news column, and was a court reporter as well. She used to teach us a word a day. I learned from her about ideas and books and reading. My dad engaged me in outdoor adventures, and I appreciated learning that from him. **Our family sat around the kitchen table at dinnertime and talked about news events, politics, the world, and how leaders in the world effected change. I thought about how I could effect change in some way.**

**We traveled everywhere with our parents.** We went to Washington, D.C., Wisconsin, and Gettysburg to see the sights, and to Florida to visit our grandparents. We took family vacations west to various parts of the United States. We visited New York City and went to museums and Broadway shows. My parents even let me go to a Broadway show by myself to see *Oliver!* while they went to a different show. I was so close to the stage that I remember Fagin spitting on me. In our teenage and college years, my brother and I hitchhiked around Europe. **We never feared exploring new ideas, new cultures, new places, and new people.**

I started piano when I was about six, and I still play today. There were times in my life when piano has been a great comfort. We did a lot of playacting. We had a small two-story log cabin in the backyard, and my brother, the neighborhood kids, and I would play Davy Crockett. I was involved in plays in elementary school and junior and senior high.

I loved school except for fifth grade. We moved to a new school, and the class was way ahead of me in mathematics. They were doing fractions, and I had no idea what was going on. **I lost interest in math because I was afraid I couldn't catch up, and it's been a lifelong loss.** I wonder if I would think and act differently if I had a more mathematical sense of the world. Instead, my emphasis has been on language, reading, words, thoughts, and ideas.

**I'd read lots of books,** probably three books a week. **My mother always read to us;** she was an avid reader. We went to the library regularly, and I can't imagine my life without a book or two beside my bed every day. **I day-camped with the Girl Scouts, learning about the forest, the trees, and the natural world, as well as getting a sense of competitiveness by earning badges. I wanted to learn more and put those new badges on my sash.**

In middle school, **I remember alternating between wanting to have a boyfriend and go to parties, and wanting to play baseball and climb trees.** My friend had a baseball that had been signed by famous White Sox players, and she carried it with her as we went from class to class. We'd toss it to each other between classes. **I dressed somewhat differently. I never felt I had to be with the in crowd. I was trying out different roles,** so it might have been a dress one day and blue jeans, a White Sox T-shirt, and a baseball cap the next day. It was part of the performer in me.

**I had wonderful teachers in high school, and the world started opening up.** I had a sociology teacher who wanted us to do a documentary on people who were living in poverty. I used my dad's eight-millimeter movie camera and did a documentary on migrant workers, who lived in horrible conditions a couple of miles from the high school. The film was confiscated, and the police said I couldn't film the workers because it was private property, and **my sense of justice was awakened.** We did an exchange program with inner-city schools in Chicago. **I had a desire to change the world and to have it be more equitable, probably because of the teachers, parents, and grandparents I had.**

**It was important for me to get good grades, but I needed a sense of affirmation from teachers and my family as well.** I was on the debate team, the student council, the dance group, and the speech team. I did poetry readings and won some state competitions for that. I was in every show the high school ever had. **There were early roots of what I do now. I explored conditions that result in some people having it all and some people not, and I wanted to perform or communicate that information in some way. The two threads came together for me,** and I was voted most likely to succeed in my high school class.

The University of Iowa had great English and theater departments and a creative-writing workshop, and it felt comfortable to me. I have a strong sense of midwestern values, so I liked the feel of Iowa City. It was big enough, so we had great entertainment, wonderful speakers, and lots of people to meet. I majored in speech, drama, and English. Those were the Vietnam years, and my whole world was being turned upside down. I left school one semester to campaign for Eugene McCarthy in Nebraska. It was final exam time, and I remember writing, "I'm sorry I won't be able to take these exams; I'm leaving to work for peace in the world." That was very upsetting to my family. I remember vividly the assassinations of John F. Kennedy, Bobby Kennedy, and Martin Luther King Jr. Many of my friends were moving to Canada to dodge the draft. We fought against the war and tried to decide what direction we were going to take in our lives. I simply didn't know what to do about it all. **Life wasn't going along the perfect path I had projected, and I didn't know where I was going.** Those were very difficult years.

After my semester campaigning for McCarthy, I drove with some friends to Washington, D.C., and participated in demonstrations against the war and tried to live an alternate lifestyle. That didn't last long. I decided I needed to go back to school. I graduated in the summer and became a VISTA volunteer. I had been working for WGN Radio and TV in Chicago during my college years, doing script typing. After college, they offered me a job as their first female television reporter. I said, "No, thank you; I have to go to Georgia." I wanted to see if I could make a difference in the poor communities I'd read about there. Everyone told me I was crazy. My family was very upset because they thought I would have this perfect career and wondered how in the world I could give that all up. I took John F. Kennedy's call seriously: "Ask not what your country can do for you; ask what you can do for your country."

I worked in Carrollton, Georgia, for two years with a group of black teenagers, and formed a theater company. We did a production of *A Day of Absence,* which is about what happens in a small southern town when all of the African-Americans leave town. We worked with families who had medical and housing needs. People told me I was stupid to be doing that, but I am forever grateful. Those were a tremendously important couple years of my life. The people I met and their stories haunt me to this day, but **trying to make the world better for people and addressing the injustices of the world has been my lifelong passion.**

I wanted to find an innovative high school in which to teach theater and do wonderful productions. On my way to New York, I decided to drive down to see my brother in school at Duke in North Carolina. The car broke down on the way and I had to borrow five hundred dollars from my mother to get it fixed. Once I got to Duke, I needed a job to pay my mother back because I was out of money. I got a job at an alternative radio station on the campus. We'd do an hour of radio on women's issues, then classical music, then folk music. I did an early-morning show from five to nine, and a half-hour newscast from noon to twelve-thirty. That was my beginning in radio. I love it: I can wear blue jeans; it's my voice and ideas that count. I've been doing radio for twenty-four years.

From Durham I came to Milwaukee and worked for a commercial radio station for eighteen years. I started with a Saturday morning talk show. There were very few women in radio then, and they did mostly cooking, fashion shows, or weather forecasts. I'd come from this alternative station at Durham where half the staff were women, and I never thought it would be difficult being a female in the field. When I grew up in Chicago, there weren't any women in radio. In Milwaukee, audiences said, "We don't like female voices on the air." **I would always have to present ideas to management instead of their coming to me.** I did a nighttime two-hour talk show that was popular, and then they moved me to daytime, and I did a midday program for many years.

I almost got married a couple of times, and it sometimes profoundly disturbed me that I hadn't met the right person, although I wasn't unhappy. I loved my job and felt I was making a contribution to the world. Then I got married at forty-two to a sports columnist, Michael Bauman. I have two stepsons. Michael has joint custody, and the boys spent two weeks a month with us when they were young. When they became teenagers, they came to live with us almost full-time to be closer to their dad. We became a close family. Then, when I was forty-four, we had a child. **Now I have all of the things I ever wanted, and that's humbling. I don't feel any yearning anymore or that things are out of reach. I now feel that I've lived long enough to have some wisdom, and also to have a deep appreciation of the many blessings that I have in my life.**

# MULTITASKING FROM THE START

## Lesley Seymour

EDITOR IN CHIEF, *REDBOOK* MAGAZINE

*Leslie Seymour has taken on a new challenge as editor in chief of* Redbook. *She knows that magazines build relationships. More than that, she will teach you the importance of doing more than what's expected and doing it creatively. She's reinvented the meaning of the word "perseverance."*

I've always been self-motivated. **I was one of those kids who couldn't watch TV without also writing or working on an art project. I was a multitasker from the start.**

My father was a doctor in the navy, very successful. He was always changing his areas of interest. He changed from cardiology to anesthesiology and went back to general practice. **When he got bored with something, he found another intellectual challenge. He taught me early that if I wasn't learning, I needed to find something else to do.** I can remember sitting on my dad's lap while he read his medical journals. For the longest time, I wanted to be a scientist.

My parents divorced when I was ten, and I lived with my mother until I was thirteen. My mother wasn't a terrifically stable person, and when she divorced my father, she became less stable. I can remember cooking for the family, **which may have contributed to my independence.** My sister stayed with my mother, but I went to live with Dad. **The separation was horrible.**

**I was interested in school and liked succeeding. I liked to read, but I wasn't the best reader.** I had to have reading help when I was in sixth grade. While some kids didn't have to study or work hard to get their A's, **I was a worker bee, and it didn't come as easily. I learned to work hard to achieve. I had to constantly come up with creative ways of doing things.** I was never a straight-A student, but I did well academically. **I always worked beyond what was expected.**

I remember girls in fifth grade being boy-crazy, chasing guys and going to their houses. I didn't understand why they were crazed. **First my friends were normal like me, and then they started behaving like they were on another planet.**

I went to private school in sixth grade. **I felt different** because I was painfully skinny, tiny, and underdeveloped. I never could eat enough and was trying to gain weight. **We were all horribly insecure about everything.** My best friend was always dieting because her family was overweight. She tried to get me to go on diets with her. Everyone talked about eating disorders, but I was always drinking Nutrament to develop faster. I was almost a full year behind everyone else because I had a January birthdate and was the youngest in my class. They were in bras and using deodorant, and I was flat as a board, had an undershirt on, and everyone would laugh in gym. I forced my mother to buy me a bra so I didn't look like a retard. That was painful. I had three things working against me. **One was that I was a late bloomer, the other was that I was pushed ahead, and third, I was small.** By seventh grade, I started to mature, and it was better.

I had friends, but the hilarious part is, my best friend was always the tallest girl in the class, and I was the shortest. I think I was attracted to the tallest because they felt as awkward as I did. My dad took me to the doctor and had my bones x-rayed because he was so worried. **I didn't grow until the end of high school.**

**I moved from group to group and was welcomed by different groups.** I never liked cliquishness. **I think it was because we moved around a lot when I was a kid.** My dad changed his job every three years, and we moved from Puerto Rico to Florida, to St. Louis, to New Jersey, and finally to New York.

I went to a girls' boarding school between ages thirteen and eighteen. I hated it because by this time I wanted to meet boys, **but the girls' school taught me not to be afraid to compete.** I would have been one of those girls who was so interested in boys, I would have put my personal interests on the shelf and not done anything that guys didn't like. **Girls' schools made a positive difference in my life. I was very involved in student government there, and in my senior year, I was vice president of the class. I found the vice president job more interesting than that of president because the vice president led a huge creative production, including a full-fledged musical. I preferred the more** interesting, creative position rather than the one with the most status.

My father wanted me to go to Mount Holyoke College to continue the girls' school education, but instead I went to Duke in North Carolina and got totally distracted by the dating. I changed my major from science to English, even though I was very good in science and math. **I tried getting published when I started college and entered every creative-writing contest there was. I never won anything, but I kept trying.**

My stepmother was into fashion. I liked it too and was a ferocious reader of women's magazines. She said, "What about getting an internship at a magazine?" I took her advice and wrote to *Seventeen Magazine* and landed a summer internship. I did all the grunt work, packed bags, and cleaned the beauty closet, and for me, that was like Hollywood. Magazines were where everyone was beautiful and perfect, and girls had dates, and it was fantasyland. I tried out for a teen-to-teen column. I lost to another person and was devastated.

After returning to Duke, I considered joining the school newspaper, but I could see that it was a clique of insider people. **I wanted something more real, so I went to the local newspaper, the *Durham Sun,* and asked them if I could be an intern.** I walked into the Student Union one day and saw students reading my story in the *Sun* about how terrible it was that the Christmas tree was going up in the Northgate Mall the day after Halloween. My article was right next to Carter and Brezhnev shaking hands on the other side of the paper! This, too, seemed like Hollywood to me. I would go up dusty, rickety stairs, and everyone was pounding away on portable typewriters, and there was something so gritty about it that I loved.

After graduation I wanted to put together my interest in writing with the fashion sense I had learned at *Seventeen Magazine.* I pitched a story to *Women's Wear Daily,* a trade publication of the fashion industry, and got the assignment. Then I asked if I could work for them, and they accepted me. They gave me five markets—sweaters, juniors, plus sizes, petites, and everything that no one else wanted—and said, "Here's a list of resources; go cover them." I had never been to Seventh Avenue, and I came back the first week and told my editor that the big news in the teen market was shoal collars. She asked,

"What's a shoal collar?" I said I had no idea. We had someone send a picture of it, and it turned out it was a shawl collar. I hadn't understood their New York accent!

Legendary editor Clay Felker started a paper called the *Tonight Paper,* which was supposed to be a competitor of the *New York Post.* I liked the reality, fast pace, and excitement of the newspaper business. They offered me a livable salary, and I joined. While I was there, Reagan was shot. We were at the heartbeat of what was happening in the world. I was there for a year; then the paper folded, putting 350 journalists out of work. I looked for more newspaper jobs, but newspapers were contracting all across the nation. I was on unemployment for two months, and a couple friends at magazines were pestering me to come there. I thought magazines were too slow, and I wouldn't like them, but I went to *Harper's Bazaar* as a copywriter and liked it. I was there for nine months and wrote as much as I could. Then a friend at *Vogue* called me, and I went there, expecting to stay a year or two. I stayed for nine years. **When I got bored, I knocked on everyone's door.** I got the beauty editor and the feature editor to let me write for them and had five or six articles in an issue.

One day, the editor in chief got one of my articles and called me into her office. Annoyed, she asked, "Who do you think reads this magazine anyway, and how old do you think they are?" I was twenty-two and knew it wasn't my girlfriends, so I answered, "Nancy Reagan?" **I would always sit down at my desk and pretend I was Nancy Reagan as I wrote.** She said, "Do you know that our readers are in their thirties?" I realized I needed to know who my audience was to get ahead.

Another time, my boss knocked at my door and said, "Miss [Grace] Mirabella would like to know if you would like to write the car column?" **I had never learned to drive, but I didn't want to say no to an opportunity.** I said, "Does it matter that I don't drive?" She had this big, flat stare on her face that said, "I don't think that's funny." I said, "Funny, you caught me on the day I'm starting my driving lessons." The second she left my office, I called the local driving school. I learned to drive in the car-unfriendly city of New York and added a car column to the other things I was writing for *Vogue.*

My first press trip was right after I got my driver's license. I received a call from Porsche to test-drive cars in Atlanta. There were only two women on the trip, and they forced me into the driver's seat. I was totally terrified. It was a brand-new $50,000 car. I had never driven anything that was worth more than $10,000, and I asked, "Should I signal here? What do I do?" We got out on the highway, and I was crawling in the right lane at forty-five miles an hour. Volkswagen Bugs were flying by me, and people were hanging their heads out the window to see a bright red Porsche limping down the highway. The manager who was driving with me said, "It would help if you took it up to sixty." I admitted that I had just gotten my driver's license and was terrified. I had this wild, completely loony experience traveling around the world driving new cars. The other girls at *Vogue* wanted to be beauty editors, and I was having a great time driving cars around Europe with the guys.

During the time I was at *Vogue,* I wrote a book for teenagers called *I Wish My Parents Understood* and also wrote for other noncompetitive magazines in a freelance capacity. I was on maternity leave for my first child when the editor in chief asked if I'd like to write the *100 Years of Vogue* anniversary book for them. I said yes and was able to stay out on maternity leave for five months while working on the book. I decided I didn't want to go back, so I asked her if there was any way to do contracting work. **I started my own freelance business and worked for everyone**—*Vanity Fair,* the *New York Times Magazine, Glamour*—**and was able to satisfy my desire to do a little bit of everything. I could also take my kid to the park. It was perfect.** I had no intention of ever going back to a regular job.

Then my son went to nursery school, and I found myself alone in my apartment from nine to five, and it was lonely. He had school and play dates, so when *Glamour* made me an offer to become the beauty director, I took it. Several publishers said to me, "You can really run a magazine," but that's when I started thinking about having my second child. It was a turning point; I was either going to find a job as an editor in chief or start my own consulting business. I was going to give myself six months. Because I had written a book and knew the teen market, *Young Miss* made a lot of sense, and they were shopping for an editor in chief. I went through two months of a grueling interview process and nine interviews. At one point I said to the publisher doing the hiring, "How much does enthusiasm count?" He said, "It counts for a lot." Then I said, "Well, I have the ultimate in enthusiasm." That's what pushed him over the edge. By the time he finally offered me the job, he said, "Well, aren't you excited?" I responded, "I'm so exhausted, I can't be excited," but I was. I guess the moral is, **If you don't have the most experience but are persistent, you can make it happen.**

A year and a half later, Cathie Black, president of Hearst Magazines, called me for my *Redbook* job. This is a fascinating experience in a different way. It's much more of a learning curve, and I've really had to think my way around dozens of roadblocks. I learned in high school as vice president, when we put on those full-fledged musicals together, that **if I can marshal a team and get that team spirit working for me, there is very little we can't do.** In just over a year we've revamped the magazine, garnered many awards, and upped the newsstand sales. That's hard for a magazine that's nearly one hundred years old. **I've always been the mountain mover. When everyone says it can't be done, I'll try to do it. I learned early that 95 percent of my success is tenacity. Many people are more talented than I or can write better, but they give up and bail out. I don't believe in giving up.**

My husband is the complete opposite of me. He works on Wall Street. He never moved as a child, and he had a very tight family. He's very much my rock. He can't understand how I'm so self-motivated. Our interests are different, but **we both value family as number one; we're both interested in being successful; and we both believe that raising our children is something we have to devote ourselves to.** We have totally different temperaments. He is very logical, very analytical, doesn't jump into anything, and I'm jumping all the time. **He has been my greatest supporter and is open to whatever I want to do, which gives me a lot of flexibility. He believes in me more than I believe in myself.**

This is not a life for everyone. My husband and I are always struggling for balance and trying to make sure we're there for everybody. I wish we had more guideposts because it wears us down. We hope we're doing the right thing, and we try to set an example for our kids, and we struggle. It's uncharted territory. **I love what I do, but I also love my family and my kids, so we are constantly balancing.**

# SHE ASPIRED TO BE JO FROM *LITTLE WOMEN*

~

## Jacquelyn Mitchard
#### AUTHOR OF A *NEW YORK TIMES* BEST-SELLER

*Jacquelyn Mitchard's* New York Times *best-seller,* The Deep End of the Ocean, *was the first selection for Oprah Winfrey's Book Club; it was also made into a movie. During her long career as a syndicated columnist and freelance writer, she often interviewed me for pieces on parenting. During one interview, she shared with me the sadness of her husband's death and her struggles with that loss and the simultaneous attempt to write her first novel. So my joy at her success is personal as well as professional. Jacquelyn is now remarried, and she has six children.*

**What I found most inspiring in my life was my mother saying to me when I was twelve, "You can survive anything you can explain."** She had a lot of practice at that. My parents' early life together was tragic because my brother, who was seven years older than I, died from a reaction to a tetanus shot given to him after a horseback-riding accident. They had to overcome something that divides many couples. My mother struggled with her own problems in part because she had talent and vision and not much of a canvas on which to express that. Her canvas was small, but she made the most of it. She didn't think, for example, that her oven had any purpose except as a kiln. She'd bake clay statues in the oven, instead of cooking elaborate meals and making clothes the way other mothers did. Singing, dancing, and mostly reading—those were her passions. She dropped out of high school to marry but was supremely self-educated, having basically set herself a course of great books and read her way through them. Whether they were biology textbooks or French literature, even if she couldn't pronounce what she was learning, she forced her way through them. As a result, she had extraordinary command of a basic knowledge of the world that wouldn't have been typical of a housewife raising a family on the West Side of Chicago after the Second World War.

My mother had a huge personality contained in a rather frail body.

She was physically fearless **and taught me to be fearless. I was made to take risks,** but at that time and in that place there wasn't much opportunity for girls to use their bodies for something other than to hang sweaters on for boys to admire. Girls weren't encouraged to play sports or think of themselves as strong. My mother didn't know how to facilitate my doing that without taking the risk of having me cross over into a girl that wouldn't be accepted socially by other kids. **But she did her best encouraging me to write, act, and dance. I didn't do any of those particularly well; but my mother always told me it was the nerve that counted.**

My mom was definitely the center around which our family revolved. My dad was a shadow figure in my life, and like so many people, his whole life was consumed with making a living. We've grown closer with time. I also have a younger brother, the great joy of my life, the person other than my husband and children whom I love most in the world.

My parents made the mistakes that some parents make, going out to parties on the weekends, drinking too much, and certainly having less challenge going on in their lives than would have made them both more satisfied. They loved each other very much, but beyond that, they were hungry for something else. My dad was a plumber and my mom did the bookkeeping.

**Still, both my parents read to us and to each other, and my mom especially, at an early age, gave me the message implicitly, which I've given to my children explicitly, that if you have a book, no one can imprison your body because you can leave your body behind.**

My mother studied along with me when I did my homework at the kitchen table. I have memories of her pushing me to try harder. **I wanted her to be proud of me.**

**I was a sterling student and a loner. The people who inspired me the most were the writers of the books I read.** Betty Smith, who wrote *A Tree Grows in Brooklyn,* was a primary inspiration to me. Harper Lee and Charlotte Brontë were real people to me and still are. **As I learned about their lives and the enormous courage it took for them to be able to tell stories in their times, I take great courage from them. They were role models for me.**

**Peer pressure didn't bother me. The only thing that bothered**

me about being alone was being lonely. I didn't have any peer pressure because I didn't have any peers. I'd never had a beer. I didn't smoke cigarettes or do anything bad. **Although as a junior and senior I happily participated in social activities, I didn't have an ordinary childhood for my time. I was in student government, the newspaper, and was always a part of things, but I always kept a part of myself back.**

I made the pom squad in high school. Being a pom girl was considered almost a religious experience, to the exclusion of all other pursuits. **I didn't want to quit the school newspaper, so I had my poms ripped off my shoulders after one day of glory because I couldn't do both. My mother supported me in that lonely decision not to surrender the life of the mind for what would certainly have been popularity.**

**As for my writing, I wrote as soon as I could write.** When I was little, after bedtime I would sneak along the edge of the floor until I could get to where the light from the hall would fall on my paper. Then I would write until I fell asleep on the floor. I was a hopeless romantic. **I always wanted to write things that had big drama, and I guess I've continued to do that as a newspaper columnist and a novelist.** Sometimes I feel that I've been rewriting the first poem I ever committed to memory, Alfred Noyes's "The Highwayman," my whole life. **My goal has been to find those things in life worth risking everything for, and to find the courage to be able to do that.** As a teenager, I saw plainly how few risks girls took compared to boys and how risk taking was discouraged for girls. There was this pervasive feeling that a young woman should guard what she had out of fear she'd lose it all.

My mother died of brain cancer when I was almost twenty; it was an extraordinarily dreadful experience for me because it was hard to imagine who I was going to prove things to. It took me about a year to realize that **the person I was going to try to prove things to was inside me.**

**For my whole girlhood and adulthood, when I was lonely, I read and wrote and cried. I think all writers are lonely. I had people who cared; my mom listened. I had best girlfriends, equally lonely and strange souls, who turned out to be successful women.** I was a late bloomer, and **it was hard to be a late**

bloomer when around me everyone was doing things I wasn't ready to experience, but I'm glad I was; memory is short, but life is long. I've continued to be a late bloomer my whole life. I didn't write a novel until I was forty. I didn't have a child until I was thirty. So many of the things that are central experiences to my life have happened in the fullness of time.

I went to the University of Illinois, a big school, and was very homesick and scared. **I carved out a little neighborhood for myself in the English department.** I had a very ordinary college career, distinguished by not much but early recognition for writing. I was a good student, became a high school teacher, and got married. This all happened in a short time period. The marriage was a date that got out of hand. I wanted my mom to see me as a bride, so I married while she was still alive. I thought that would be good, and it turned out to be one of those things. We annulled the marriage because my first husband was a decent kid but we weren't suited as lifelong partners.

I was a high school teacher for one year. At age twenty-two, I had this blinding-lightning-bolt-through-the-head epiphany that if I wasn't careful, **I was going to spend my life teaching kids to do what I was avoiding doing myself.** I left teaching and became a waitress full-time, then became a stringer for a newspaper part-time so I could write. That was twenty-five years ago. I became a full-time reporter, then an editor, then worked for a daily newspaper, and then a bigger daily newspaper. **I would set the gate higher and try to jump the gate.** I finally started writing for magazines, and then became a contributing editor for magazines. **When I started writing novels, as excruciating as it is, I had the firm sense that life knocked on my heart and said, "All right now, you're home. This is what you do. This is what your job is."**

My husband, Dan, and I met because we worked for the same newspaper. I found out about a job and moved to Madison, Wisconsin. It was almost like we didn't know anyone else in town, so we got married. **It turned out to be a long friendship that had a terribly tragic end.**

**When I turned forty, I found out what it meant to lose all. Dan died of colon cancer, a horrible disease, and I was alone with young children to raise. It was the worst thing that could**

happen to a person, but coming to the recognition that I could remake my life out of the ashes of what I expected my life was going to be was not altogether a bad lesson to learn. I don't recommend it. However, if your life feels arid or stifling, I do recommend trying to remake it before tragedy forces you to do so.

A couple of years after my husband died, I took my boys to see the movie of Louisa May Alcott's *Little Women.* In the middle of it, my son turned to me and said, "You're Jo, aren't you?" I said, "Yeah." **All I ever wanted was to be Jo March. I wanted to be that writer girl who had the courage to not have curls and be a decoration for whatever man would put his arm under her elbow. As Eleanor Roosevelt said, "I wanted to have every experience that could possibly fall to the lot of a woman." I wanted to work, I wanted to fall in love and be a mother. I relished that; I always have. I wanted to be a girl without chains around my feet.**

After Dan's death, I didn't think there would ever be a time when I could again say, "I'm happy," or "I've had a good half day," but I'm a happy woman. To me, life is hard and fraught with all kinds of opportunities to feel discouraged. The other night, one of my kids, who has a small role in the play *The Sound of Music,* said, "But you don't know what it's like to try to achieve something and then fail." **I was stunned that he thought I didn't know that, that I didn't approach my work every day fearfully. I'm still lonely with it and feel there is always a great margin for failure. I've had tons of experiences with failure, but I try hard not to let them count. People talk about papering walls with rejection slips. I get rid of mine as fast as I can. I keep saying to myself, "If not this time, then next time, and if not next time, the time after that."**

**If I felt discouraged, I would try to sleep on those discouragements. It's like climbing a mountain. Sometimes all that's available to you is to hold on to the hooks. You can't go back** down, but you have enough hooks to relax, and you can just put your face against the mountain and hold on until you have the strength to proceed. There have been plenty of times in my life when that's all I've been able to do until I gather enough courage to take the next step.

My first book did really well, my second book did not do as well, and there are days when I wonder if I should ever write a third one. Being a writer is one of those businesses where it's not just my product, it's me that is esteemed or rejected every day because I so closely identify with my work. I don't think I have very tough skin. I suffer; as my middle son says, I have really soft feelings, and things hurt me easily. I take things personally. I have to curl up in a little ball and try to comfort myself. I've had to learn to let other people comfort me. I actually have to convince myself to go back and have another whack at it and think, if not this time, if not this man, if not this book, if not this movie, if not this house, trip, church, then the one after.

I've been married now for two years to a wonderful guy. We have a little baby daughter, Maria. My husband is twelve years younger than I am. He had never been married before, but he took the risk and married this huge family. **That's what counts. Taking the risk.**

# Coda

Just as a symphony has a concluding coda, our book with its many voices draws to a close. The successful, fulfilled women in our book have shared with you the themes, passages, movements, and chords that have brought them to where they are in their lives. However, their stories have not concluded. Since their interviews, some who had struggled with fertility had children and some gave birth to planned or unplanned children; others married or have divorced; some were promoted to higher positions, and some left their positions to make different choices. Life stories go on. Perhaps another mark of success is these women's ability to keep enriching and adding to the score with further adventures, thus postponing the coda.

Since Sara, Ilonna, and I began our work, more than five years ago, both Sara and Ilonna have given birth to babies, Sammy and Avi. I've watched Sara grow in her new mothering role, and observed Ilonna's joy in the addition of a third child to her family, joining Miriam and Ben, ages twelve and nine. Sara has been appointed to a new position, and Ilonna has adjusted to a very different opportunity to lead scientific research. I have moved my clinic group to an entirely new setting affiliated with a different hospital. All of us have enjoyed the exhilaration of our successes and struggled with the fears and anxieties of our failures. As a family, we've suffered together and supported each other through some difficult family health issues, but we've also celebrated children's and grandchildren's births and birthdays, and vacationed and played together.

The adventures of fulfilled women's lives are not all happiness. Their lives are indeed like symphonies that involve slow, sad parts; electrifying notes of ecstasy; changing rhythms; varied intense emotions; recurring themes; voices and instruments that enter and leave again; and sometimes, it seems, even an unknown conductor that is indeed in control.

We anticipate that one or more of these women in our book will motivate, strengthen, stimulate, or support you in some small way in your life goals. As you sing or play out your own personal life symphony, we are confident that they will help you strike the best chords, harmonies, and melodies for your own individual fulfillment.

The women in our book who have shared their stories, as well as hundreds of thousands of other men and women, have pried open the doors of opportunity for your fulfillment. As you search for your own personal meaning, it is our fervent hope that you will continue to hold doors open and reach out to other girls and young women who may wish to follow in your pioneering pathways.

# Index

# About the Author

DR. SYLVIA RIMM is director of the Family Achievement Clinic at the Cleveland Clinic and a clinical professor at Case Western Reserve University School of Medicine. She is a contributing correspondent to NBC's *Today* show, Disney's online child psychologist for family.com, host of the national radio show *Family Talk with Sylvia Rimm,* and author of a syndicated newspaper column on parenting. Dr. Rimm received her master's and doctoral degrees in educational psychology from the University of Wisconsin–Madison and is the author of several books, including the bestselling *See Jane Win, Why Bright Kids Get Poor Grades, Raising Preschoolers,* and *How to Parent So Children Will Learn.* A mother of four, she lives in Cleveland with her husband.

DR. SARA RIMM-KAUFMAN is an assistant professor of educational psychology at the University of Virginia and lives in Charlottesville with her husband. They have a son and are expecting their second child soon.

For additional information, see Dr. Sylvia Rimm's website at: www.seejanewin.com.